Eng[d] by Geo. E. Perine

KAMEHAMEHA III.

KING OF THE HAWAIIAN ISLANDS.

Engraved for Dr. Anderson's work, "The Hawaiian Islands"

THE

HAWAIIAN ISLANDS:

THEIR

PROGRESS AND CONDITION

UNDER

MISSIONARY LABORS.

BY

RUFUS ANDERSON, D. D.,

FOREIGN SECRETARY OF THE AMERICAN BOARD OF COMMISSIONERS
FOR FOREIGN MISSIONS.

With Illustrations.

THIRD EDITION.

BOSTON:
GOULD AND LINCOLN,
59 WASHINGTON STREET.
NEW YORK: SHELDON AND COMPANY.
CINCINNATI: GEO. S. BLANCHARD.
1865.

STEREOTYPED AT THE
Boston Stereotype Foundry,
No. 4 Spring Lane.

TO THE

PRUDENTIAL COMMITTEE,

THE

SECRETARIES, AND TREASURER,

OF THE

American Board of Commissioners for Foreign Missions,

THIS VOLUME IS DEDICATED

BY THEIR

COLLEAGUE AND FELLOW-LABORER.

PREFACE.

WHEN the author had prepared the "MEMORIAL VOLUME" of the *Board's First Half Century*, three years ago, the belief was expressed that it was among the closing labors of his somewhat protracted official life. He little thought, then, that it would become his duty to visit the Sandwich (or Hawaiian) Islands, and, as a consequence, to prepare another volume for publication. But "it is not in man that walketh to direct his steps." Fourteen thousand miles are soon traversed in these days of steam; and the Island-visit, — in a fine climate, among beloved missionaries, and in close contact with the native Christians, — though laborious, was a source of constant pleasure. It was an opportunity for "fellowship in the gospel" such as earth seldom affords.

On his return home he was naturally expected to prepare a report of his mission. There was not time, however, before the Annual Meeting of the Board, for drawing up anything like an extended report; and the deficiency was then supplied, as far as it could be, by a verbal statement to the meeting.

Afterwards, on resuming the preparation of his report, he soon found reason to believe, that a suitable memorial of the Lord's work on those Islands required a wider and freer range of statement than was befitting a document of that nature. Referring the matter to the Prudential Committee, he was advised to give himself the latitude of a volume, and was left to take his own course in its preparation.

The work is written throughout with reference to a single object—THAT OF SHOWING WHAT GOD HAS BEEN PLEASED TO DO ON THE HAWAIIAN ISLANDS, THROUGH THE GOSPEL OF HIS SON AND THE LABORS OF HIS MISSIONARY SERVANTS. The author has presented the case just as it appeared to him, after a forty years' correspondence with the missionaries, and after a sojourn of four months upon the Islands, all the while in the most confidential intercourse with those best acquainted with their religious condition. And he has fortified his own statements with such other testimony as seemed necessary to insure to them the confidence of the Christian community.

It was a thing of course that, to one on a mission of this nature, the best side of the Hawaiian people would everywhere be presented. For the most part, the author's intercourse was necessarily with church-members, and with the best portion of them. This was in harmony with one of the grand objects of his visit, which was to ascertain the *nature* and the *extent* of Christianity upon the Islands. With a similar object in view, he could not have had better opportunities, within the same period of time, in London, or even in New York or Philadelphia.

The compression of the materials into a volume of moderate size required double the labor that was expected to be necessary, and also the sacrifice of much that seemed important to the life and spirit of the narrative. For more ample details in the early history of the Islands and of the mission, the reader will need to resort to works frequently referred to in this volume.

The preliminary historical sketch, occupying the first six chapters, is thought to be all that is needful to introduce the reader to the Islands in their present state. The next six chapters, describing the tour, were written with the leading object of the visit constantly in view. They will serve as a further introduction to the seven subsequent chapters, on the social, civil, religious, and ecclesiastical condition and prospects of the people. The chapter on the "Reformed Catholic Mission" has been prepared with care; and that mission will receive, it is hoped, the attention, both in this country and in England, which it demands as an uncourteous and alarming innovation in the working of Protestant missions. What is said of the apprehended dangers on those Islands, will enable God's people more deeply to sympathize with those veteran soldiers of the cross, who have resolved to lay their bones among the trophies of their spiritual contests and victories. The concluding chapters will have a practical value to the increasing number of Christian people who are interested in the development of the missionary enterprise.

It will be seen that the Hawaiian mission is treated as an *experiment;* and should it be thought to have been on a small scale, it will be remembered, that experiments are usually made thus, and that they are not the less satisfactory and decisive on that account. Nor are the results on the Hawaiian Islands wanting in real magnitude. If those Islands contained no huge ancient fortresses, like those of Asiatic paganism, to be overthrown, the mission found there a social demoralization and decay almost beyond a parallel, tending to the speedy destruction of the entire people. Its labors have effected a signal triumph, through the grace of

God; and it now only remains to be seen whether that infant community of Protestant Christians will be able to withstand the onset to be made upon it by the extreme ritualistic portion of the Church of England. If such a conflict is to be, we shall doubtless have the sympathies and prayers, if nothing more, of that large evangelical portion of the English Church which so liberally sustains one of the most honorable and efficient of the great Missionary Societies. It was deemed the author's duty to apprise the churches of the existence and nature of this evil, lest they should not become seasonably aware of the danger.

The adjustments that have been made, regarding the mission as in some important sense a completed work, will be viewed with that forbearance which is due to first and untried measures on a national scale. Should any of them be found ill adapted to the end in view, they may still be useful, leading to the discovery of "a more excellent way." There must surely be some method, in the great process of the world's conversion, for setting nations, converted from heathenism, free from dependence on the older churches of Christendom, when they shall have come sufficiently under gospel influences.

The author thankfully acknowledges his obligations to the Rev. Isaac R. Worcester, editor of the Board's monthly publication, for his valuable criticisms, extended through the volume. The same acknowledgment is due to several members of the Prudential Committee, in respect to some of the more important chapters. He would gladly have delayed the publication longer, in order that the work might be made more deserving of public interest; but that could not be. Prepared amid unceasing interruptions, it is sent forth in obedience to what seemed a positive duty, and with the hope that it will be received by the friends and supporters of missions as a seasonable and truthful memorial of one of the most remarkable among the spiritual revolutions which the Church of Christ has been permitted to record.

MISSIONARY HOUSE, BOSTON, September, 1864.

CONTENTS.

I. PRELIMINARY HISTORY.

CHAPTER I.

THE ISLANDS BEFORE THE ARRIVAL OF MISSIONARIES.

CHAPTER II.

THE ISLANDS AFTER THE ARRIVAL OF MISSIONARIES.

CHAPTER III.

THE ISLANDS TO THE TIME OF THEIR CONVERSION TO CHRISTIANITY.

CHAPTER IV.

THE ISLANDS REGARDED AS CHRISTIANIZED.

CHAPTER V.

MEASURES CONSEQUENT UPON THE CONVERSION OF THE ISLANDS.

CHAPTER VI.

VOYAGE TO THE ISLANDS, AND A WEEK AT THE METROPOLIS.

2

II. TOUR OF THE ISLANDS.

CHAPTER VII.

HAWAII.

CHAPTER VIII.

HAWAII.

CHAPTER IX.

HAWAII.

CHAPTER X.

MAUI.

CHAPTER XI.

OAHU.

CHAPTER XII.

KAUAI.

III. PEOPLE OF THE ISLANDS.

CHAPTER XIII.

THEIR SOCIAL AND CIVIL CONDITION.

CHAPTER XIV.

INDUSTRY AND COMMERCE.

CHAPTER XV.

SCHOOLS AND LITERATURE.

CHAPTER XVI.

DECLINE OF POPULATION.

CHAPTER XVII.

CHARACTER OF THE PROTESTANT CHURCHES.

IV. ECCLESIASTICAL DEVELOPMENT.

CHAPTER XVIII.

ECCLESIASTICAL DEVELOPMENT PREVIOUS TO 1863.

CHAPTER XIX.

THE RELIGIOUS CONVOCATION AND ITS RESULTS.

V. OTHER MISSIONS.

CHAPTER XX.

THE REFORMED CATHOLIC MISSION.

CHAPTER XXI.

ROMAN CATHOLIC MISSION. — THE MORMONS.

VI. THE PRESENT POSITION.

CHAPTER XXII.

APPREHENDED DANGERS.

CHAPTER XXIII.

PRACTICAL LESSONS.

CHAPTER XXIV.

CONCLUSION.

APPENDICES.

List of Illustrations.

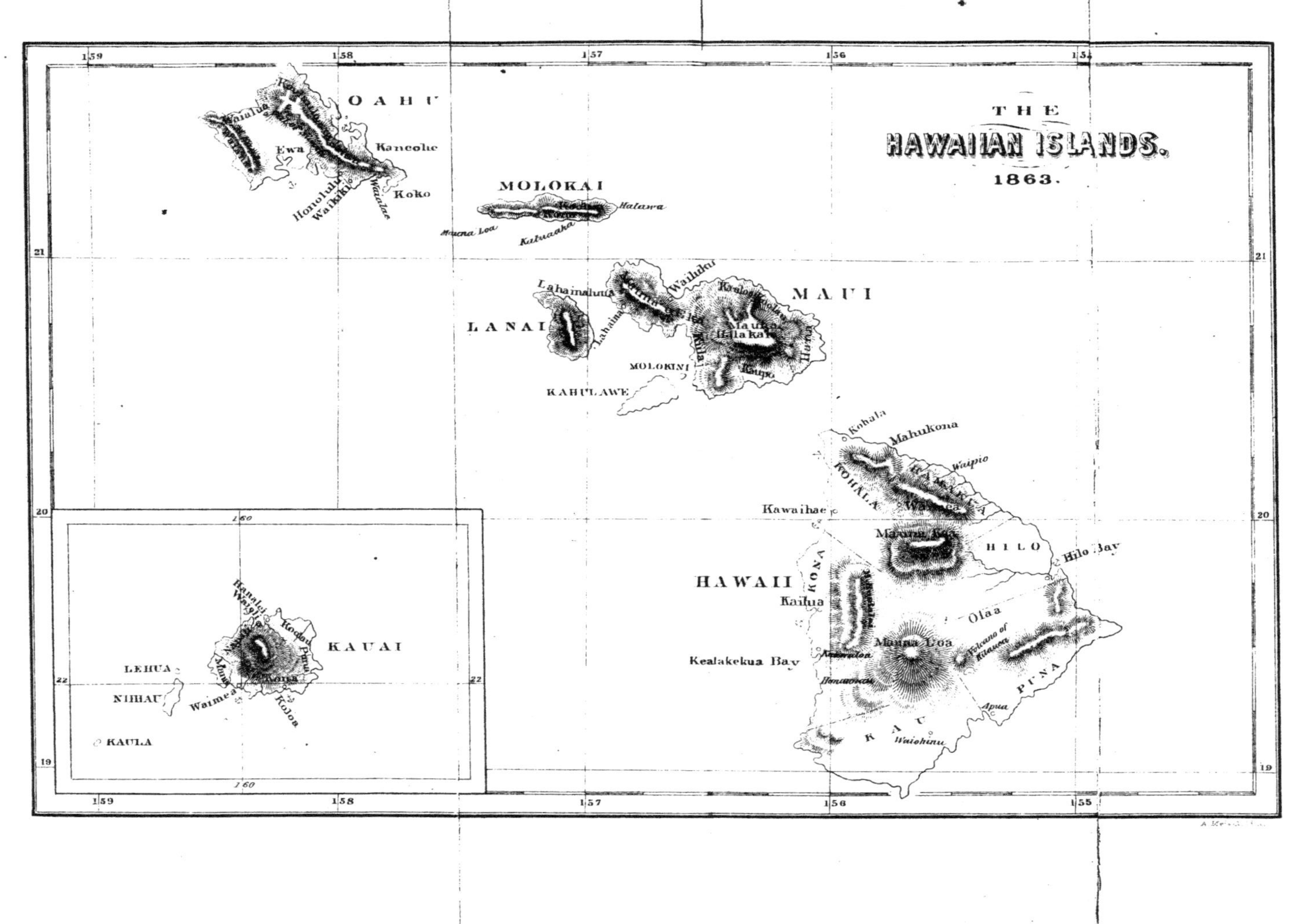

THE
HAWAIIAN ISLANDS.
1863.
OAHU
Waialua
Ewa
Kaneohe
Honolulu
Waikiki
Waialae
Koko
MOLOKAI
Halawa
Mauna Loa
Kaluaaha
MAUI
Lahainaluna
Wailuku
Lahaina
Mauna Hale Kala
Kula
Kaupo
Hana
LANAI
MOLOKINI
KAHULAWE
HAWAII
Kohala
Mahukona
Waipio
KOHALA
Kawaihae
HILO
Hilo Bay
KONA
Kailua
Olaa
Mauna Loa
Volcano of Kilauea
Kealakekua Bay
PUNA
Apua
KAU
Waiohinu
KAUAI
Hanalei
Waioli
Koloa
Waimea
LEHUA
NIIHAU
KAULA
159
158
157
156
155
21
20
19
160
22

I.

PRELIMINARY HISTORY.

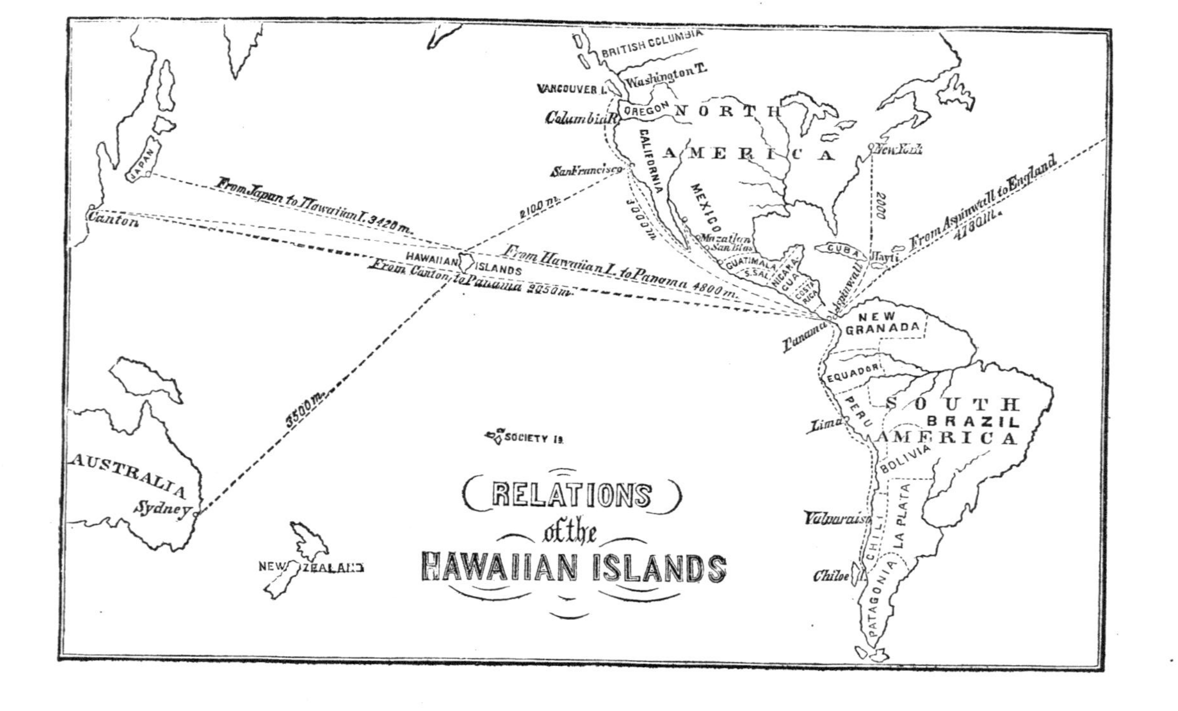

RELATIONS
of the
HAWAIIAN ISLANDS
BRITISH COLUMBIA
Washington T.
VANCOUVER I.
OREGON
Columbia R.
NORTH
AMERICA
CALIFORNIA
San Francisco
MEXICO
Mazatlan
San Blas
GUATIMALA
S. SAL
NICARAGUA
COSTA RICA
CUBA
Hayti
New York
2000
Aspinwall
From Aspinwall to England 4780 m.
Panama
NEW GRANADA
EQUADOR
PERU
Lima
SOUTH AMERICA
BRAZIL
BOLIVIA
LA PLATA
CHILI
Valparaiso
Chiloe
PATAGONIA
JAPAN
Canton
From Japan to Hawaiian I. 3420 m.
2100 m.
3000 m.
HAWAIIAN ISLANDS
From Hawaiian I. to Panama 4800 m.
From Canton to Panama 9250 m.
3500 m.
SOCIETY IS.
AUSTRALIA
Sydney
NEW ZEALAND

PRELIMINARY HISTORY.

CHAPTER I.

THE ISLANDS BEFORE THE ARRIVAL OF MISSIONARIES.

Their Discovery. — Name of the Group. — Names of the Islands. — Importance of their Position. — Superficial Contents. — Origin. — Climate. — Vancouver. — Early Decline of Population. — Prevalence of Infanticide. — Origin of the People. — Population in 1820. — Productions. — Resort of Ships. — Moral Inefficacy of Civilization. — Character of Kamehameha. — His alleged Cession of Hawaii to Great Britain. — Conquest of the Islands. — Division of the Lands. — Government. — Wives and Children. — Death and Obsequies. — Accession of Liholiho. — Destruction of the Tabu and Idols. — Motives to this. — Consequent Civil War.

THE SANDWICH ISLANDS were so named by Captain James Cook, their discoverer, in 1778; but that name is nowhere recognized in the constitution and laws of the Islands. The group is there called the HAWAIIAN ISLANDS, and this is the name used by the inhabitants. The Islands are ten in number, and stretch from the south-east towards the north-west, in the following order: HA-WAI-I, MAU-I, MO-LO-KI-NI, KA-HU-LA-WE, LA-NAI, MO-LO-KAI, O-A-HU, KAU-AI, NI-I-HAU, and

KAU-LA. They are situated between 18° 50′ and 22° 20′ north latitude, and 154° 53′ and 160° 15′ west longitude from Greenwich. Their distance from Panama is 4800 miles; from San Francisco, 2100; from Japan, 3400. They lie midway between the western terminus of the Panama Railroad and China, and nearly on the straight line between the two. Their distance from Australia is but little more than it is from China. The four largest and most important islands are Hawaii, Maui, Oahu, and Kauai.[1] The length, breadth, and superficial contents of the group

[1] The following directions for pronouncing some of the principal names will be helpful to the reader: —

Ha-wai-i,	*pronounced*	*as*	Ha-wye-e.
O-a-hu,	"	"	O-ah-hoo.
Kau-ai,	"	"	Kow-i, or Kow-eye.
Kai-lu-a,	"	"	Ky-loo-ah.
Ke-a-la-ke-ku-a,	"	"	Kay-ah-lah-kay-koo-ah.
Mau-i,	"	"	Mow-e.
Wai-a-ke-a,	"	"	Wye-ah-kay-ah.
Wai-pi-o,	"	"	Wye-pe-o.
Ki-lau-e-a,	"	"	Ke-low-á-ah.
Mau-na-Lo-a,	"	"	Mow-nah-lo-ah.
Mau-na-Ke-a,	"	"	Mow-nah-kay-ah.
Ka-a-wa-lo-a,	"	"	Kah-ah-wah-lo-ah.
Ka-me-ha-me-ha,	"	"	Kah-mé-hah-mé-hah.
Li-ho-li-ho,	"	"	Lee-ho-lee-ho.
Ka-a-hu-ma-nu,	"	"	Kah-ah-hoo-mah-noo.
Ke-o-pu-o-la-ni,	"	"	Kay-o-poo-o-lăh-ne.
Ku-a-ki-ni,	"	"	Koo-ah-ke-ne.
Bo-ki,	"	"	Bo-ke.
Li-li-ha,	"	"	Le-le-hah.

are thus stated by the Rev. William Ellis, in his interesting Narrative of a Tour through Hawaii, performed in 1823 : —

	Length.	Breadth.	Square Miles.
Hawaii,	97	78	4000
Maui,	48	29	600
Kahulawe,	11	8	60
Lanai,	17	9	100
Molokai,	40	7	170
Oahu,	46	23	520
Kauai,	33	28	520
Niihau,	20	7	80
Kaula, Molokini, } little more than barren rocks.			

The group contains six thousand square miles. The circumference of Hawaii is about three hundred miles ; that of Oahu is over one hundred. The whole group had a volcanic origin. Reefs of coral are found on some parts of the coast, though to a much smaller extent than in some of the southern groups. It is by one of these coral reefs that the fine harbor of Honolulu is formed. The trade winds strike the eastern side of the Islands, and there it frequently rains : on the mountains there are rains almost daily ; but on the leeward side they are infrequent. On the rainy side of Hawaii a large number of perennial streams fall into the sea, sometimes forming lofty and beautiful cascades. It is along the windward side of the Islands that disintegration is most advanced, and the soil most abundant and fertile; and it is there that the sugar plantations are now being multiplied. Forests abound in the mountains. The Islands all lie within the range of the trade winds, which blow with great regularity nine months in the year. Where mountains obstruct their course, there are regular land and sea breezes. Occasionally a prolonged gale comes from the south, called a Souther, or "Kona." There was none between February and July, 1863, and they are said to have been of rare occurrence for the few years past. When this wind begins to blow, it drives the miasma arising from the lagoons south-east of Honolulu back upon the land, infesting the town with its unpleasant odor. The natives call it the "sick wind." Much of the weather at all seasons is, however, delightful; the sky cloudless, the atmosphere clear and bracing. Nothing can exceed the soft brilliancy of the moonlight nights. Thunder-storms are rare, and light in their nature. No hurricanes have been known.[1] The general temperature of the Islands approaches near the point regarded by physiologists as most conducive to health and longevity. Mr. Ellis gives the following tabular view of a meteorological journal kept by the missionaries from August, 1821, to July, 1822, — probably at Honolulu; the thermometer being noted at 8 A. M., 3 P. M., and 8 P. M.[2]

[1] Jarvis's History of the Hawaiian Islands, p. 13. [2] Journal, p. 7.

Months.	Greatest Heat.	Least Heat.	Range.	General Range.	Mean Temperature.	General Course of Wind.	General State of the Weather.
August, 1821, . .	88°	74°	14°	75 to 85°	79°	N. E.	Clear; rain but once.
September, . . .	87	74	13	76–84	78	N. E.	Rained on five days.
October, ...	86	73	13	76–83	78	N. E.	Clear; rain but once.
November, . . .	82	71	11	75–80	76	N. E.	Clear; rain but once.
December, ...	80	62	18	70–78	72	N. & N. E.	Clear; rain twice.
January, 1822, .	80	59	21	68–76	70	Variable.	Rain 1 day; 7 others cloudy.
February, ...	77	61	16	68–75	71	N. E.	Rain 4 days; 10 others cloudy.
March, ...	78	66	12	71–75	72	N. E.	Rain 5 days; 8 others cloudy.
April, ...	81	62	19	72–78	73	Variable.	Rain 5 days; 12 others cloudy.
May, ...	81	72	9	75–80	76	N. E.	Rain 4 days; 3 others cloudy.
June, ...	84	71	13	76–81	78	N. E.	Cloudy 6 days.
July, ...	84	74	10	76–83	78	N. E.	Rain 5 days; 7 others cloudy.
Result for the year,	88	59	29	70–83	75	N. E.	Rain on 40 days; generally clear at other times.

By ascending the mountains any desirable degree of temperature may be attained.

The melancholy fate of Captain Cook, who was slain at Kealakekua Bay, on Hawaii, in a tumult of the natives, February, 1779, deterred vessels from touching at the Islands until 1786, when Captains Dixon and Portlock, on a trading voyage to the North-west Coast for furs and sea-otter skins, stopped for refreshments at the Island of Oahu. About the same time La Pérouse visited the Island of Maui. Thenceforward vessels in the fur trade came frequently to the Islands. In opposition to the settled policy of Kamehamcha, a vessel was seized and plundered by the natives on the western shore of Hawaii, and the crew all murdered, except Isaac Davis and John Young, both of whom were taken under the patronage of the king, and afterwards became influential in the nation. Vancouver, being sent by the English government on a voyage of discovery, spent several months of the years 1792, 1793, and 1794 at the Islands, and was treated in the most friendly manner by Kamehameha,[1] then king of the western part of Hawaii, and by the people. Goats, sheep, cattle, which now abound, were first introduced by him from California. Vancouver had accompanied Captain Cook, and now saw painful evidence of depopulation

[1] The name is made up by a reduplication of the word *meha* (lonely, or solitary), with the definite article *Ka* prefixed, which is a part of the name. — *Ellis.*

since the time of his first visit — the effect of the desolating wars which marked the early part of Kamehameha's reign, together with the awful prevalence of infanticide, and the augmented destructiveness of intemperate and licentious habits among the people. According to Mr. Ellis, infanticide must have been among the principal causes. He says, — writing forty years ago, — "It prevails throughout all the Islands, and, with the exception of the higher class of chiefs, is, as far as we could learn, practised by all ranks of the people. However numerous the children among the lower orders, parents seldom rear more than two or three, and many spare only one. All the others are destroyed, sometimes shortly after birth, generally during their first year. The means by which it is accomplished, though numerous, it would be improper to describe. Kuakini, the governor of the island, in a conversation I had with him at Kailua, enumerated many different methods, several of which frequently prove fatal to the mother also. Sometimes they strangle their children, but more frequently bury them alive. It is painful to think of the numbers thus murdered. All the information we have been able to obtain, and the facts that have come to our knowledge in the neighborhood where we resided, afford every reason to believe that, from the prevalence of infanticide, two thirds of the children perished. We have been told by some of the chiefs, on whose word we can depend, that they have known parents to murder three or four infants where they have spared one."

"The principal motive," he continues, "with the greater part of those who practise it, is *idleness;* and the reason most frequently assigned, even by the parents themselves, for the murder of their children, is *the trouble of bringing them up*. In general they are of a changeable disposition, fond of a wandering manner of life, and find their children a restraint, preventing them, in some degree, from following their roving inclinations. Like other savage nations, they are averse to any more labor than is absolutely necessary. Hence they consider their children a burden, and are unwilling to cultivate a little more ground, or undertake the small additional labor necessary to the support of their offspring during the helpless periods of infancy and childhood. In some cases, when the child has been sickly, and the parents have grown tired of nursing and attending it, they have been known, in order to avoid further attendance and care, to bury it at once; and we have been credibly informed that children have been buried alive merely because of the irritation they have manifested. On these occasions, when the child has cried more than the parents, particularly the mother, could patiently bear, instead of clasping the little sufferer to her bosom, and soothing by caresses the pains which, though unable to tell them, it has probably felt, she has, to free herself from this annoyance, stopped its cries by thrusting a piece of tapa into its mouth, and digging a hole in the floor of the house, perhaps within a few yards of her bed and the spot where she took her daily meals, has relentlessly buried, in the untimely grave, her helpless babe."[1]

The most probable supposition in respect to the origin of the islanders is, that they came from the Malay coast. Their features and color are the same with the Malays, and there are said to be many words nearly the same in the languages of the two people. The Hawaiian nation is supposed to have a considerable antiquity. From time immemorial there have been persons appointed by the government to preserve unimpaired the genealogy of their kings, and this genealogy embraces the names of more than seventy.

The population of the Islands, in 1778, was estimated by the discoverer at 400,000. There is reason to regard this estimate as somewhat excessive; but a traveller, forty years after that time, found traces everywhere of deserted villages, and of enclosures, once under cultivation, then lying waste. The mission believed the population to be from 130,000 to 150,000 at the time of their arrival; that of Hawaii being 85,000, according to the estimate of Mr. Ellis and his companions during their tour around that island.

Mr. Ellis is the best authority as to the productions

[1] Ellis's Tour, p. 298.

of the Islands at the commencement of the mission. The only quadrupeds, at the time of the discovery, were a small species of hog with a long head and small, erect ears, the dog, a small lizard, and an animal in size between the mouse and rat. Hogs sometimes ran wild on the mountains; otherwise there were no ferocious animals; and the only poisonous reptile was a small centipede. As early as 1823 there were extensive herds of cattle at large on Hawaii, and on most of the islands were flocks of goats, and a few horses and sheep. These were all brought, originally, from the adjacent continent of America. Horses, cattle, and goats were found to thrive well; but it was necessary to pasture sheep on the hills and mountain sides, it being too warm for them near the shore.

Birds were not often seen near the sea, excepting such as were aquatic, and a species of owl that preyed upon mice; but they were numerous in the mountains. Several kinds were remarkably beautiful, and among them a small paroquet, of a glossy purple, and a species of red, yellow and green woodpecker, with whose feathers the idols were dressed, and the helmets and handsome cloaks of the chiefs were ornamented. The notes of a brown and yellow speckled bird were exceedingly sweet. But the feathered tribes were not generally distinguished for beauty of plumage or richness of song. Wild geese were found in the mountains, and ducks near the lagoons or ponds. Of fish there were several varieties, and the inhabitants procured a tolerable supply. The king and chiefs were owners of artificial ponds, with an entrance from the sea, so constructed that the young fish could enter, but soon became too large to escape. Here excellent mullet were raised, and caught by the hand, the native wading in for that purpose.

The islanders subsisted chiefly on the roots of the *arum esculentum*, which they called *taro*, and which they manufactured into *poi*. This is the taro baked, pounded, mixed with water to the consistency of paste, and allowed to ferment. They also used the sweet potato, which grows to a large size, but is not so sweet as the kind raised in New Jersey. The principal indigenous fruits were the bread-fruit, cocoa-nut, banana, ohelo (a berry), ohia (a juicy red apple of poor flavor), arrowroot, strawberry, and raspberry. Oranges, limes, citrons, grapes, pine-apples, papaw-apples, cucumbers, and watermelons had then been introduced; and beans, onions, pumpkins, and cabbages had been added to the vegetables. Sugar-cane was indigenous, and grew to a large size, though not then much cultivated.[1]

After Vancouver's departure, the vessels which resorted to the Islands were generally traders from the United States in quest of sandal-wood. This was

[1] Ellis's Tour, Eng. ed., p. 8.

conveyed, in large quantities, and as long as it lasted, to China, where much of it was burned as incense in the worship of idols. Afterwards whalers, when they began to frequent the North Pacific, and to pursue the sperm whale along the coast of Japan, found it convenient to refit their ships, and obtain their refreshments, at the Hawaiian Islands.

From the discovery of these Islands to the arrival of the missionaries was a period of forty years; equalling the time which has since elapsed. The number of visitors, on the whole, must have been very great. But, excepting a few suggestions to the king by Vancouver, which speak well for his character, there is no trace of any religious instruction whatever having been imparted by the visitors to the natives. Among all the thousands, not one was a herald of the gospel; and, had the Islands been left to those influences alone, it is probable that nothing more of the nation would now have been remaining than miserable remnants, inhabiting the more secluded districts. Ardent spirits and fire-arms were the chief articles of trade, and the main influence was to foster intemperance and an infamous dissipation, which hurried the unwary people to the grave.

Kamehameha was a remarkable man, with perhaps as good a claim to the title of "great" as an Alexander or a Napoleon. He was wounded by one of the guns fired at the time Captain Cook was killed. Though endowed with physical strength, mental energy, and a majestic carriage, his deportment was mild, and he was frank, cheerful, and generous. "In self-defence, more than from a warlike spirit, he was drawn into a series of battles, first with the chiefs of his own island, and then with the chiefs of the other islands; all of which were victorious, and eventuated in subjecting the whole group of islands to his sovereign control."[1] It was his policy to protect trade; and Young and Davis were taken into his confidence, and rendered him important service. Both rose to be chiefs of rank, and the granddaughter of the former became the wife of Kamehameha IV., and was queen at the time of my visit. The king appreciated the character of Vancouver, and the repeated visits of that eminent navigator exerted a good influence upon him, as well as upon the future history of the Islands. Vancouver refused to purchase supplies by means of arms and ammunition; and it was then that attention was first turned towards sandal-wood as an article of export. He effected a reconciliation between Kamehameha and Kaahumanu, his favorite wife, from whom he had been estranged on account of a suspicion as to her faithfulness. Jarvis says that "tears and a warm embrace ensued; but, before leaving, the queen persuaded the captain to induce her husband to promise, upon her return, to forego beating her." It has been asserted by English writers,

[1] Dibble's History, 1839, p. 58.

even by Mr. Ellis, that Kamehameha, through Vancouver, ceded Hawaii to the British sovereign. Doubtless that officer received some such impression from his interpreter; but the assertion rests on no sufficient evidence. Mr. Dibble, who had great opportunities to learn the truth, and took much pains to draw his facts from native sources, declares that what the king said to Vancouver was this: "Return to Great Britain, and request her king to protect our country." Mr. Dibble's History was published at the Sandwich Islands, in the year 1843, and he makes the following statement in respect to the declaration of Kamehameha: "It was not his intention to surrender wholly, but to obtain protection. And even if it should be maintained that Kamehameha intended to surrender his government to the entire control of Great Britain, the surrender would be a matter of little importance; for *Kamehameha had at that time little to give away*. Kahekili was then king of Maui, Molokai, Lanai, and Oahu; and his brother Kaeo was king of Kauai. The possessions of Kamehameha were on Hawaii alone, and consisted of the districts of Kona, Kohala, and Hamakua, which he had recently confirmed by conquest. He was often at war with the hostile chiefs of the other districts of Hawaii, Hilo, Puna, and Kau, and succeeded in making them tributary; but he did not acquire undisputed possession of those districts until he had subdued the Leeward Islands, a period several years after the visit of Vancouver."[1] Mr. Jarvis, who also wrote and published his History at the Islands, says the natives declared protection from the English sovereign to be the only thing they requested, and that the chiefs who made speeches on the occasion, "as if apprehensive of yielding more than they intended, expressly reserved to themselves the right of sovereignty, and the entire regulation of their domestic concerns."[2] This question, however, except as one of historic truth, has now, probably, no practical importance.

The harbor of Honolulu was discovered in 1794. Two years later the conquest of all the islands, save Kauai, was completed by Kamehameha; and that island submitted to his authority in 1809. The king proceeded on the maxim that all the lands were his, and he apportioned them among his followers according to their rank and deserts; which he did on the feudal tenure of rendering military service and a proportion of the revenues. Heirs were to inherit; though this depended on the will of the sovereign, whose authority was absolute. For a despotism, rising out of anarchy and desolating wars, in the absence of education and of Christianity, the government was remarkable, during the last years of that monarch, for the peace, security, and order that were prevalent. "Kamehameha permitted no crimes

[1] Dibble's History, 1843, p. 48. [2] Jarves's History, p. 89.

except his own, when his interests were not too deeply involved. To consider actions sanctioned by their customs from time immemorial a blot upon his character, would be unjust, however arbitrary they might appear to those whose lot has been placed in a land of freedom. They were merciful in comparison with what the islanders had undergone. No penalty could reach an individual screened by the favor of his chief, and the favorites of Kamehameha enjoyed the exemption common to successful courtiers."[1]

Kaahumanu and Keopuolani, two of the king's wives, have both an honored place in the religious history of the Hawaiian Islands. There will be occasion to speak of them hereafter. The former was his favorite, and bore him a daughter in 1809. But the latter was of higher rank, indeed the highest in the kingdom, and therefore her children were the heirs to the throne. Liholiho, the eldest, was born in 1797, Kauikeaouli in 1814, and Nahienaena, a daughter, about two years later.

Kamehameha I. died at Kailua, Hawaii, on the 8th of May, 1819, at the age of sixty-six, only a few months before a Christian mission embarked at Boston to convey the gospel to him and to his people. Although he had strenuously adhered to the religion of his people, he would not permit human sacrifices

[1] Jarves's History, p. 95.

to be offered, when he was sick, for his recovery, as was customary in such cases; and, in lieu of such victims at his obsequies, three hundred dogs were sacrificed. But there were the customary wailings throughout the Islands. According to usage, the people shaved their heads, burned themselves, knocked out their front teeth, broke through all restraint, and practised all manner of crime, as if it were a virtue. All ages, both sexes gave scope to the vilest passions, in self-torture, robbery, licentiousness, and murder.[1]

Liholiho succeeded to the kingdom, and recognized Kaahumanu as his premier. Indeed, the will of her husband made her a sharer in the government, and she remained so during her life. There soon followed an event which has scarcely a parallel in history, giving an affirmative answer to the inquiry of the prophet, "Hath a nation changed her gods?" The *tabu* system of restrictions and prohibitions was inseparable from the national idolatry. "They extended to sacred days, sacred places, sacred persons, and sacred things; and the least failure to observe them was punished with death. A prohibition, which weighed heavily as any other, was that in regard to eating, and was the first to be violated. A husband could on no occasion eat with his wife, except on penalty of death. Women were prohibited, on the same pen-

[1] Dibble's History, p. 85.

alty, from eating many of the choicest kinds of meat, fruit, and fish. These prohibitions extended to female chiefs as well as to women of low rank. Many of the highest chiefs of the nation were females; and they, especially, felt burdened and uneasy. They did not fear being killed by the priests, for they were chiefs; but the priests, all along, had made them believe that, if they violated any prohibition, they would be destroyed by the gods. This they began to doubt, for they saw foreigners living with impunity without any such observances. Besides, — a fact which shows the power of God to bring good out of evil, — ardent spirits had been introduced among them; and they often, when partially intoxicated, trampled heedlessly on the prohibitions of their idolatrous system, and yet were not destroyed by the gods. The awful dread, therefore, which formerly existed, had in a measure subsided; and, when no longer restrained by fear, the female chiefs were quite ready to throw off the burdens so long imposed upon them. Keopuolani, the mother of the king, first violated the system, by eating with her youngest son. Other chiefs, when they saw no evil follow, were inclined to imitate her example. But the king was slow to yield. At length, however, he gave his assent; and then the work was done. The chiefs, as a body, trampled on all the unpleasant restraints which had been imposed upon them by their system of idolatry. In doing this, they were aware that they threw off all allegiance to their gods, and treated them with open contempt. They saw that they took the stand of open revolt. They immediately gave orders to the people that the *tabu* system should be disregarded, the idols committed to the flames, and the sacred temples demolished."[1]

"The high priest, Hewahewa, having resigned his office, was the first to apply the torch. Without his coöperation the attempt to destroy the old system would have been ineffectual. Numbers of his profession, joining in the enthusiasm, followed his example. Kaumualii having given his sanction, idolatry was forever abolished by law, and the smoke of heathen sanctuaries arose from Hawaii to Kauai. All the islands, uniting in a jubilee at their deliverance, presented the spectacle of a nation without a religion."[2]

But civil war was the immediate consequence. A principal chief rose, with a portion of the people, in rebellion. A battle was fought on the western shore of Hawaii, and the God of battles gave victory on the side of these great innovations. The rebellious chief was killed, and the whole mass of the people then went on, with renewed zeal, destroying the sacred enclosures and idols.

Liholiho seems to have had no higher aim in these remarkable proceedings than to be freed from restraint

[1] Dibble's History, 1839, p. 64. [2] Jarves's History, p. 109.

upon his habits of dissipation; and it is thought that Kaahumanu, the strong-minded dowager queen, favored the changes in order to remove unreasonable disabilities from her sex. No religious motive seems to have had influence with any of them, and the result was to leave the nation so far without any religion as to be really in a less favorable state for self-preservation than it was before. But an unseen Power, though they knew it not, was preparing them for the speedy introduction of a better religion.

CHAPTER II.

THE ISLANDS AFTER THE ARRIVAL OF MISSIONARIES.

Occurrences leading to a Mission. — The Mission. — First Intelligence of the Change at the Islands. — Reception of the Mission. — Establishments at Kailua, at Honolulu, and on Kauai. — Interesting School at Kailua. — Reducing the Language to Writing. — Unfriendly Foreign Influence. — Unexpectedly counteracted. — Arrival of Mr. Ellis. — Further Destruction of Idols. — Notice of several. — School of Chiefs. — The Farmer returns Home. — First Reënforcement. — King's Letter to the Captain. — Keopuolani, the Queen Mother. — Liholiho's Visit to England. — Farewell Address of Kamamalu, his Queen. — Their Sickness and Death in London. — Charge received by Survivors from the English Sovereign. — Character of Liholiho. — The Visit not inauspicious to the Islands. — Christian Influence of Kaahumanu. — Kapiolani's Visit to Kilauea. — Lord Byron's Visit to the Islands. — Great Religious Change in the Government. — Church and State not connected. — Vast Congregation at Kawaihae. — Great Meeting-houses. — Dedication of one at Kailua. — Schools. — Testimony of Mr. John Young. — Origin of the Roman Catholic Mission. — Outrages by Foreign Seamen. — Death of Kalanimoku. — Death and Character of Kaahumanu. — Accession of Kamehameha III. — His Opinion of the Strength of the Christian Institutions. — The several Reënforcements of the Mission. — Summary View.

For ten years, and more, there had been a train of providential occurrences in the United States tending directly to the sending of a mission to the Hawaiian Islands. It will be interesting to glance the eye along this line of events.

While standing on the eastern shore of Kealakekua Bay, opposite to where Cook was killed, my attention was directed to a small ruined *heiau*, or heathen temple, with a cocoa-nut tree rising high above it. I was told it was there that Obookiah was trained by his uncle, a pagan priest, to the practice of idolatry, and that the tree was planted by him. This was more than fifty years ago, for Obookiah was brought to the United States, in the year 1808, by a shipmaster of New Haven. He was an intelligent youth, and learning that a long row of buildings on the public square in New Haven formed a college where young men of America acquired knowledge, he was one day found sitting on the doorsteps of one of those buildings, weeping because the treasures of knowledge were open to others, but were not open to him. Mr. Edwin W. Dwight, who saw him thus, had compassion on him, and became his religious teacher, and the means of his conversion. This antedates the mission to the Islands by more than ten years. Next we find Samuel John Mills writing to Gordon Hall from New Haven, on the 20th of December, 1809, in view of this case, and suggesting a mission to the Sandwich Islands. The institution of the Foreign Mission School at Cornwall, Connecticut, in 1817, by the American Board of Commissioners for Foreign Missions, for the instruction of these and other youths from heathen lands, came next in the order of events. Mr. Dwight, the friend of Obookiah, was its first teacher. Five of the ten earliest pupils were natives of the Hawaiian Islands. Obookiah died while a member of this school, on the 17th of February, 1818, at the age of twenty-six; and the published account of his life and death awakened great interest among the churches in behalf of his people. Then came the offer of a young man named Hiram Bingham, a student in the Andover Seminary, to go as a missionary to those Islands. And he finds a worthy associate in Asa Thurston, a classmate at the Seminary, and a graduate of Yale College, of whom the college traditions speak as one of the most athletic of her sons. These favored men have both been spared to the present time.

The next step brings us to the 15th of October, 1819, to a public meeting in Park-street Church, in Boston, where we find Messrs. Bingham and Thurston, now ordained ministers of the gospel, and their wives; with Thomas Holman, a physician, Samuel Whitney and Samuel Ruggles, teachers, Elisha Loomis, printer, and Daniel Chamberlain, a farmer, and their wives; and Thomas Hopu, William Kanui (Tenooe), and John Honuri (Honoore), three Hawaiian young men from the Cornwall School; about to be organized as a mission to the Sandwich Islands. Dr. Worcester, the first Corresponding Secretary of the Board, was there, and so was Mr. Evarts, its first Treasurer — names once familiar in all our churches, and still affectionately remembered.

A great assembly listened to the eloquent instructions of the Secretary, and gave many tokens of a thrilling interest.[1]

[1] Since the above was written, I have seen the following notice of Tenooe in *The Friend* of February 5, 1864, published monthly at Honolulu, and edited by the Rev. Mr. Damon, the excellent Seamen's Chaplain in that city. Tenooe was in San Francisco when I passed through it on my return from the Islands, and I heard a good report of him from Mr. Rowell. It seems he went back to his native isles, and finished his course there. The Queen's Hospital is at Honolulu.

"Died at Queen's Hospital, January 15, 1864, William Kanui, aged about sixty-six years. The early life of the deceased was so intimately connected with the effort to establish Christianity upon the Sandwich Islands, that it merits more than a passing notice. He was born on the Island of Oahu, about the close of the last century. His father, belonging to the party of a defeated chief, fled with his son to Waimea, Kauai. While there, an American merchant vessel, commanded by Captain Brintnel, touched for supplies. The vessel had previously touched at Kealakekua, and whilst here the master took on board two young men, whose subsequent history was remarkable. They were Obookiah and Thomas Hopu. At Waimea they were joined by William Kanui. These three youths Captain Brintnel took to America. Soon after their arrival, they attracted the attention of the friends of foreign missions, and when the Mission School was opened at Cornwall, Connecticut, they were received as pupils, with another Hawaiian, George Kamaulii, son of the king or governor of Kauai. Obookiah died in America, but the three others came out in the brig Thaddeus, with the first company of missionaries.

"Kanui, or Tenooe, as his name was originally written, early fell under the censure of the church, but was subsequently restored. In 1848, when the gold excitement arose, he went to California, where he remained until about four months ago. He was successful in gold digging, but lost all, or about $6000, by the failure of a mercantile house in San Francisco. During the last few years he has labored in San Francisco, and was connected with the Bethel Church of that

The company embarked at Boston on the 23d of October, 1819, in the brig Thaddeus, Captain Blanchard, expecting a protracted and perilous conflict with pagan rites, human sacrifices, and bloody altars; for, in the then infrequency of communication with those distant regions, no intimation whatever had been received of the wonderful changes that had been occurring at the Islands. The first tidings the missionaries had of them were on reaching the coast of Hawaii, on the 31st of March. Then they heard, with wonder and gratitude, that the idols and altars of superstition had been overthrown throughout the Islands, and the tabu and priesthood abolished. These were great events, and no wonder their hopes were raised. But they found, on reaching Kailua, on the 4th of April, where Liholiho, the son and successor of Kamehameha, then was, that the old religion

city, under the charge of the Rev. Mr. Rowell. Much more might be written respecting his career, but for the present we would merely add, that he departed this life leaving the most substantial and gratifying evidence that he was prepared to die. His views were remarkably clear and satisfactory. Christ was his only hope, and heaven the only desire of his heart. It was peculiarly gratifying to sit by his bedside and hear him recount the 'wonderful ways' in which God had led him. He cherished a most lively sense of gratitude towards all those kind friends in America who provided for his education when a poor heathen stranger in a foreign land. The names of Cornelius, Mills, Beecher, Daggett, Prentice, Griffin, and others, were frequently upon his lips, and often mentioned with a glow of grateful emotion."

Thomas Hopu is understood to have maintained his Christian course to the end of life.

had not been abandoned from any desire for a new one. The king was a polygamist, as were many of the chiefs; and seeing the missionaries each with but one wife, he objected that if he received them he would be allowed but one. He had some apprehensions, moreover, awakened doubtless by foreign residents, lest an American mission might have an injurious effect on his political relations. The missionaries made explanations. The old high priest, Hewahewa, favored them. The king dined with them on board the ship, going with only a *malo*, or narrow girdle around his waist, a green silken scarf thrown over his shoulders, a string of beads around his neck, and a feather wreath on his head. In this scanty attire he was introduced to the first company of white women he ever saw. His mother, Keopuolani, is said to have advised him to allow the missionaries to stay. After twelve days, consent was obtained to their residing on the Islands one year, part of them at Kailua, and the rest at Honolulu. On the 12th of April, 1820, Mr. and Mrs. Thurston, and Dr. and Mrs. Holman, took up their abode at the former place; both families for a time occupying one small thatched hut, which had been assigned them by the king. It was only three feet and a half high at the foot of the rafters, and was without floor, or ceiling, or windows, or furniture, in the midst of a noisy, filthy, heathen village.

The members of the mission destined to Honolulu

arrived there on the 14th of April. The village then contained three or four thousand people, living in wretched huts. Nor were the household accommodations of the missionaries much better there than they were at Kailua. The brig which brought them from Boston was too small and crowded to carry furniture, nor was there a chair to be bought anywhere on the Islands. Mr. Bingham, and Mr. Chamberlain, the farmer, remained at the future capital, while Messrs. Whitney and Ruggles went to reside at Waimea, on Kauai; and Mr. Loomis, the printer, not yet having work in his department, repaired to Kawaihae, on Hawaii, a day's journey to the north of Kailua, to instruct Kalanimoku, one of the most influential of the chiefs, and his wife, with a class of favorite youths whom he wished to have instructed. Confiding in Providence, they thus allowed themselves to be widely dispersed; but no evil befell any of them. At Kailua, Mr. Thurston had for pupils the king, his brother Kauikeaouli (afterwards the well known Kamehameha III.), then only five years old, Kamamalu and Kinau, two of the king's wives, and Kuakini, soon after governor of Hawaii; and among other lads John Ii, since one of the judges of the Supreme Court. It was not long before this whole company removed to Honolulu, and Mr. and Mrs. Thurston deemed it prudent to accompany them, and to remain at that place for a time.

After two years, such progress had been made in

reducing the language to writing, that Mr. Loomis was able to put his printing-press to use. Twelve letters in all — five vowels and seven consonants — expressed every sound in the pure Hawaiian; each letter had but one sound, and every syllable ended with a vowel. This rendered it easy for the natives to read and write; and it is one great reason why so large a portion of the people made such rapid progress in reading and writing.

As soon as the king and chiefs had come to Honolulu, unfriendly foreigners began to stigmatize the missionaries as political emissaries under fair pretences, and advised that they be sent away. So much jealousy was at length awakened among the more credulous chiefs, that the missionaries, not knowing how to allay it, were apprehensive of the consequences. Two things in particular were asserted: first, that the English missionaries at the Society Islands had taken away the lands from the people, reducing them to slavery, and that the Americans, if suffered to proceed, would do the same thing; and secondly, that the presence of American missionaries was offensive to their protector, the king of England, and he might be expected to give proofs of his anger. The latter assertion was of course made by English residents. Both were singularly met, in the ordinary course of divine Providence.

Vancouver, thirty years before, had encouraged Kamehameha I. to expect a vessel to be sent him by the king of Great Britain. It is not known why this promise was so long forgotten. But at last the colonial government of New South Wales was directed to send to the Hawaiian king a small schooner, called the Prince Regent. This vessel was placed under the care of Captain Kent of the Mermaid, and touched at the Society Islands while Messrs. Tyerman and Bennett, two English gentlemen of respectability, were there as a deputation from the London Missionary Society to their missions in those seas. As the captain was to touch at the Marquesas Islands, he offered to take thither two Society Islands chiefs, as missionaries; and finally it was resolved that the gentlemen of the deputation, and also the Rev. William Ellis, a respected English missionary, since well known to the religious world, should accompany them. Contrary to their plans, Captain Kent concluded to visit the Sandwich Islands first; and so they all arrived at Honolulu in the spring of 1822, where they were gladly received by the mission and by the rulers. Immediately the missionary chiefs from the Society Islands held conferences with Liholiho and his chiefs, and described the character, labors, and influence of the missionaries among their own people. The English gentlemen also gave assurance of the favorable disposition of the English monarch; and thus the impositions of the foreigners were thoroughly exposed. These good effects were rendered permanent by the prolonged residence of

5*

Mr. Ellis and of the Taheitians at the Hawaiian Islands, in compliance with a request from the chiefs. And such was the affinity of the Taheitian and Hawaiian languages, that Mr. Ellis was able to preach with facility to the Hawaiians within two months after his arrival.

Mr. Bingham states in his History,[1] that, some time in 1822, Kaahumanu made the tour of Hawaii with a large retinue. She had not then given any attention to the alphabet, nor seriously listened to the gospel; yet she made it an object to search out and destroy the idols, that had been concealed in the "holes of the rocks" and in "caves of the earth." More than a hundred images were then committed to the flames. Among these is said to have been one of Kalaipahoa, the poison-god, which belonged to Kamehameha I. This was a famous idol, of wood, of the middle size, curiously carved; and none was so much dreaded by the people, except the deities supposed to preside over the volcanoes. All who were thought to have died of poison were said to have been slain by this god. The very wood of which the image was made was believed to be poisonous; but this may have been a fiction of the chiefs. Mr. Ellis was unable to procure a sight of this idol, though assured that it existed, — "not indeed in one compact image, as it was divided into several parts on

[1] History, p. 162.

the death of Kamehameha, and distributed among the principal chiefs."[1] Such was the prevailing opinion at that time, but it appears not to have been well founded.

There was a smaller image of the same god, made of a hard, yellow wood, such as was usually employed in making idols. This was allowed to remain at

THE POISON-GOD.

Molokai, the home of Kalaipahoa; the original being always carried about by Kamehameha, and placed, it is said, under his pillow at night. This idol was sent, many years since, to the cabinet at the Missionary House — a small, ugly-looking figure, labelled "The poison-god," with a hole in his back for the

[1] Ellis's Tour, p. 61.

poison. An engraving is here given. Its arms are extended, with spread fingers, its head covered with a sort of woolly hair, its mouth once evidently armed with teeth.

About the same time, one of the national war-gods was received, such as were carried by the priest near

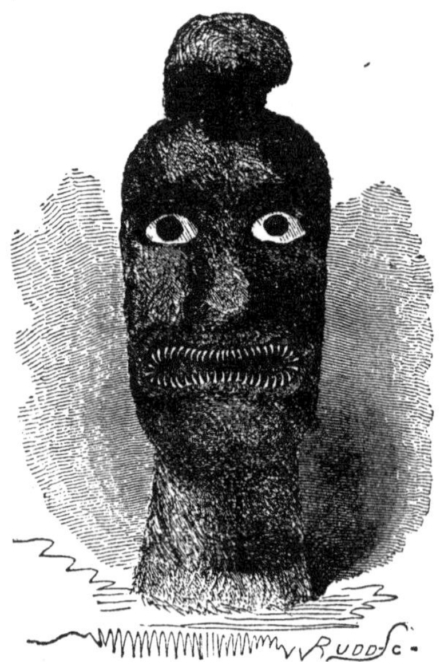

THE WAR-GOD KAILI.

the person of the king in the wars of pagan times. The image is about two feet high, made of wicker-work, and covered with red feathers, with a hideous mouth, and rows of dogs' teeth, the eyes of mother-of-pearl, and a helmet on the head, on which there probably was once a crest of human hair. An engraved likeness is given, but of course without the red feathers.[1]

From some unknown cause, the monuments and relics of idolatry in the sacred depository of the bones of departed kings and princes, called the

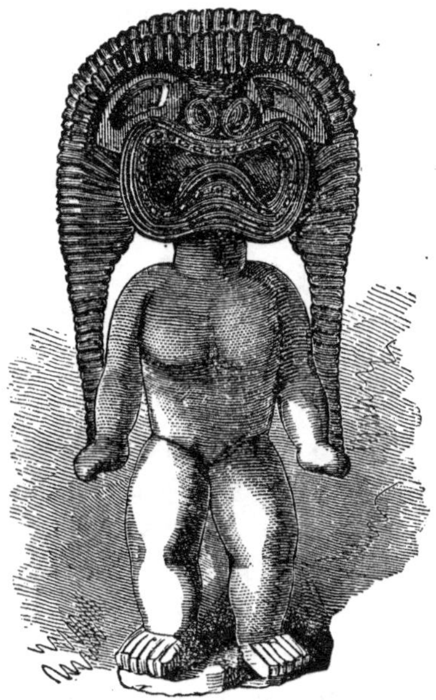

GREAT IDOL AT THE MISSIONARY HOUSE.

"House of Keawe," adjoining Honaunau, on the western shore of Hawaii, were spared amid the general destruction of heiaus and idols in the sum-

[1] Tour through Hawaii, p. 127. These engravings have the merit of strongly resembling the originals in the Missionary cabinet.

mer of 1819; but subsequently the images appear all to have been carried away as curiosities, being on the sea-shore, and easy of access. At the time of Mr. Ellis's visit (1823), twelve frightful representatives of their former deities formed a semicircle, "in grim array, as if perpetual guardians of the 'mighty dead' reposing in the house adjoining." One of the idols from this place, as there is good reason to believe, found its way, many years since, to Boston, and into the Missionary Cabinet. It is six feet and a half high. It is a singular fact that it was found necessary to enclose the idol in a glass case, after it came to the Missionary House, to prevent visitors from chipping off small pieces as mementos. It is represented on the preceding page.

Lono.

The most popular and remarkable of all the idol gods of Hawaii was the one least pretentious in appearance. This was the god "Lono," of which Cook was regarded as an impersonation. How it came to be preserved is not known, and years passed before it could be obtained for the Cabinet. It is simply a pole of hard wood, somewhat more than ten feet long, with a small head at one end; probably made in this form to be carried into battle.

There are some other Hawaiian idols in the Missionary Cabinet, but no intelligent account can be given of them.

In August, Mr. Ellis prepared several hymns in the native language, which gave increased interest to the public worship. The language was found favorable to confessions, petitions, and to poetic ascriptions of praise and adoration.[1]

Kapiolani and her husband Naihe, afterwards so efficient in the introduction of the gospel into southern Hawaii, were now at Honolulu, learning to read and write. At the beginning of the year 1823, twenty-four chiefs, the males and females being about equal in number, were among the pupils. In this year the missionary farmer, finding the time not come for the successful introduction of agricultural industry among the people, returned to the United States. In the spring, the mission received its first reënforcement, consisting of William Richards, Charles Samuel Stewart, and Artemas Bishop, ordained missionaries, Joseph Goodrich and James Ely, licensed preachers, Abraham Blatchley, physician, and their wives, and Levi Chamberlain, superintendent of secular concerns.

The king showed the change there had been in his own views and feelings since the arrival of the first company, by the following note to the captain of the ship, which had brought the new missionaries: —

[1] Bingham's History, p. 163.

"Captain Clasby: Love to you. This is my communication to you. You have done well in bringing hither the new teachers. You shall pay nothing on account of the harbor, — nothing at all. Grateful affection to you.[1]

LIHOLIHO IOLANI."

Keopuolani, the king's mother, being about to remove to Lahaina, on the Island of Maui, and desiring to have missionaries accompany her, Messrs. Richards and Stewart were assigned to that post. As they had not yet learned to speak the Hawaiian language, Taua, a Tahitian teacher, was associated with them, and became a sort of family chaplain to the venerable queen. Of her I shall have occasion to say more when speaking of my visit to Lahaina. She died on the 16th of September, 1823, but not till she had given credible evidence of piety, and received baptism from Mr. Ellis. Daughter of a race of kings, wife of a king, and mother of two kings, she was the first person baptized on the Islands; so that in her the Island-church may be said to have had its first visible existence. In the days of heathenism her person was regarded as peculiarly sacred. There were times when no one might see her; and when she walked abroad at the close of day, — her

[1] Bingham's History, p. 189.

"*E Captain Clasby? Aloha oe. Eia ka'u wahi olelo ia oe. Maikai no oe i kou haawi ana mai i na kumu hou. Aole oe e uku i ka awa, — aole akahi. Aloha ino oe.*"

usual time, — whoever saw her fell prostrate to the earth. She was scarcely more distinguished by her rank than by the amiableness of her temper, and the mildness of her behavior. When drawing towards the close of life, she gave a charge that the customary heathen abominations should not be practised at her death. Her charge was respected, and the decline of those customs may be said to date from that day.

In the autumn of this year the king Liholiho came to the rash conclusion to make a visit to England and the United States. What were his reasons, or whether he had any, was never certainly known. He was impulsive, and probably was led to the measure by a restless desire to see the world. He went in an English whale-ship, the L'Aigle, taking with him his favorite wife, Kamamalu, with Boki and Kekuanaoa. The chiefs desired Mr. Ellis to accompany him, but the captain would not consent. The king and queen were destined never to see their native isles again, and the farewell address of Kamamalu is very striking. Standing on the stone quay, — tall, portly, queen-like, — the daughter of Kamehameha exclaimed, —

"O skies, O plains, O mountains and oceans!
O guardians and people! kind affection for you all!
Farewell to thee, the soil, O country,
For which my father suffered — alas! for thee!"[1]

[1] Bingham's Sandwich Islands, p. 203.

The royal party, though not expected in England, was kindly and hospitably received by the British government. Before there could be an interview with George IV. or his ministers of state, the Hawaiians all sickened with the measles, whereof the king and queen died. The two chiefs recovered, and one of them is still living in a vigorous and venerated old age. I refer to Governor Kekuanaoa, father of the present king. The following is his statement of what was said to them by the English sovereign at Windsor Castle: "This is what we heard of the charge of King George: 'Return to Kauikeaouli, and tell him that I will protect his country. To any evil from abroad I will attend. The evils within the country are not my concern, but the evils from without.'"[1] Liholiho had many of the fine natural qualities of his mother, whom he ever treated with the utmost filial respect and affection. Many of his faults were the result of his position as an expectant of the throne, precluding wholesome restraint, and also of those chosen associates who cared only to minister to his pleasure in wild convivial excesses. His manners were free and dignified. His mind was inquisitive, his memory retentive, and he knew more of the world than could have been expected. He had a thirst for knowledge, and was diligent in his studies. Messrs. Bingham and Ellis were his instructors, and they had known him to sit at his desk the greater

[1] Bingham's History, p. 260.

part of the day. In the later years of his life he was decidedly favorable to the object of the mission, declared his belief in Christianity, attended public worship, and recommended the same to his people. When not under the influence of ardent spirits he was kind; and though not distinguished, like his father, for ardor and strength of character, he was decided and enterprising.[1]

The visit of Liholiho to England, though it seemed inauspicious at the time, was the occasion of a new and strong impulse to the Christian religion over all the Islands. Kaahumanu then became regent, and gave her decided support to the gospel and the schools. The schools took the place, for a time, of the old heathen sports, being attended by people of all ages, though their native teachers were but poorly fitted for their work, and their school-houses were unfurnished and unsightly. Next to Kaahumanu, the most noted of the reformers among the female chiefs was Kapiolani, who held large landed possessions in the neighborhood of Kealakekua Bay. Observing the strong hold which superstition still had upon the minds of the people, she made a journey of a hundred miles, in 1825, to the great crater of Kilauea, the supposed residence of Pele, and there, in ways fitted to impress the native mind, set at nought the power and wrath of the pretended goddess. Her journey, and that of her numerous attendants, was

[1] Ellis's Tour, Eng. ed., p. 425.

performed on foot, horses not having yet come into use. From the volcano she proceeded to Hilo, where she strengthened the hands of the missionaries residing at that place. I shall have occasion to speak of this remarkable woman again, when reporting my visit of a few days at what was once her home on Hawaii.

The limits prescribed for this volume will allow of but a rapid glance at the more important occurrences in the progress of the gospel at the Islands. The visit of Lord Byron, in a British frigate bringing home the remains of the king and queen, is among those occurrences. A council was held by the chiefs of the nation, at which his lordship and the missionaries were present. Even then the national government had begun to assume a Christian character, for the council made a formal acknowledgment of the authority of the Christian religion. Kaahumanu was decided as to the duty of restraining crime, and commended Kapiolani and her husband for their successful efforts to prevent murder, infanticide, theft, Sabbath desecration, drunkenness, and licentiousness. At the suggestion of the governor of Hawaii, the young prince, Kauikeaouli, then nine years old, was placed under the regular instruction of the missionaries, that he might "shun the errors of his deceased brother." In this, and in a general attention to missionary instruction, the islanders were encouraged by the high-minded English nobleman already mentioned.

About the close of 1825, Kaahumanu and nine other principal chiefs, after having been for some months propounded for admission to the church, were received as members in full communion. All these lived and have died in the faith of the gospel; and thus we have the singular fact, that the government of the Islands was in a measure Christianized at that early period, and in advance of the people. But though so many of the chief rulers were brought into the church, and though for a time there may have been a virtual union of church and state, there was never any such formal and acknowledged union. The Hawaiian government never claimed the right to make laws for the church, nor to appoint its officers, nor to control its discipline; nor did the church ever claim the right to control the action of the state. The two were neither identical nor confederate; but the state and the church, being both institutions appointed by God, were of course equally bound to do his will. Each, in its own way, was bound to promote good morals and the general welfare and happiness, and hence there was concurrent action.

At Kawaihae, on the western shore of Hawaii, a congregation, estimated at not less than ten thousand natives, was assembled in the autumn of 1826, to hear the preaching of the gospel; probably the largest assembly for that purpose ever convened on the Islands. Those were the days of great convocations,

6*

and they were generally held near the abodes of the high chiefs. Indeed, the people had long been accustomed to large assemblies.

Great audiences created a necessity for great meeting-houses. These were rude, thatched buildings. Governor Adams built one, this year, at Kailua, large enough to hold nearly five thousand people. It was one hundred and eighty feet long, seventy-eight broad, and covered fourteen thousand square feet. Men drew the timbers for it from the mountain forest, and thousands labored in its erection, and in thatching its broad roof and its capacious sides and ends. When dedicated it was filled with people, presenting a wonderful contrast to the noisy crowd at the outset of the mission in that place, but little more than six years before. The rulers of the nation were present, and the people were addressed by Kaahumanu, Kuakini, Naihe, Kapiolani, and Hoapili Wahine, who declared the determination of the government to follow the precepts of Christianity.

There were then schools in every district of the Islands, numbering four hundred teachers, and twenty-five thousand pupils, who, at that time, were chiefly adults.

The testimony of Mr. John Young, already mentioned, who had been for a long time a naturalized subject, and was the confidential adviser of the first Kamehameha, and grandfather to the queen of Kamehameha IV., is worthy of being quoted entire. It was written at Kawaihaè, on the 27th of November, 1826. He says, —

"Whereas it has been represented by many persons, that the labors of missionaries in these Islands are attended with evil and disadvantage to the people, I hereby most cheerfully give my testimony to the contrary. I am fully convinced that the good which is accomplishing and already effected is not little. The great and radical change already made for the better, in the manners and customs of this people, has far surpassed my most sanguine expectations. During the forty years that I have resided here, I have known thousands of defenceless human beings cruelly massacred in their exterminating wars. I have seen multitudes of my fellow-beings offered in sacrifico to their idol gods. I have seen this large island, once filled with inhabitants, dwindle down to its present numbers through wars and disease, and I am persuaded that nothing but Christianity can preserve them from total extinction. I rejoice that true religion is taking the place of superstition and idolatry, that good morals are superseding the reign of crime, and that a code of Christian laws is about to take the place of tyranny and oppression. These things are what I have long wished for, but have never seen till now. I thank God that in my old age I see them, and humbly trust I feel them too."

In the ship which took Liholiho to England, a Frenchman, named Rives, had secreted himself, and thus secured a passage. On the arrival of the ship in England he went over to France, and attracted some attention there on account of his supposed influence with the Hawaiian king. Falsely representing himself as the owner of extensive plantations at the Islands, he induced several laymen of the Romish faith to go out as laborers on his plantations, and three priests of that persuasion to go as missionaries. They arrived on the 7th of July, 1827. Such was the origin of the Roman Catholic mission to the Sandwich Islands. Their arrival was annoying to the native rulers, who regarded their worship as a return towards their former idolatrous system, and as so far contrary to their laws. It is not my purpose here to enlarge on this mission.

Neither shall I describe the outrages committed at Lahaina and Honolulu by foreign seamen, with a view to break down the laws restraining native females from going on board ships for illicit purposes. I am ashamed to say that a lieutenant in the United States navy was the leading actor at Honolulu, and that he was for a time successful.

These occurrences led the good Kaahumanu to say to her "friends and kindred" in the United States, "I wish you to send hither more teachers to increase the light in the name of Jesus Christ; for great has been the kindness of God towards us, the people of dark hearts." And she received the second reënforcement, arriving in 1828, with unfeigned expressions of joy. About this time, in connection with the young king, she completed a thatched house of worship at Honolulu, like the one at Kailua, and nearly as large.

Kalanimoku, whom the natives called "the Iron Cable" of their country, died in 1827. Anticipating the approach of his dissolution from the progress of dropsy, the old chief sailed from Honolulu for Kailua, where he wished to die. Here, under an unsuccessful operation for his disease, he fainted, and after a few hours expired, on the 8th of February. In him the heathen warrior was seen transformed into the peaceful, joyous Christian. "The world," he said, "is full of sorrow; but in heaven there is no sorrow nor pain — it is good, it is bright, it is happy." His loss was deeply felt by Kaahumanu, for on his counsel she had long relied; it was felt also by the whole nation.[1]

Governor Adams joined the church in 1829, and Kekuanaoa and Kinau, his wife, early in the next year. Kinau was a daughter of Kamehameha I. The good Kaahumanu died in peace, June 5, 1832, at the age of fifty-eight. She possessed great native strength of character, which was enriched and adorned by grace. From being selfish, proud, haughty, and oppressive, she became the humble and kind mother of her people. So great was the change in her, that, on visiting Hawaii, the natives

[1] Bingham's History, p. 306.

called her "the new Kaahumanu." She was a cordial friend of the mission and of the cause of Christ, and was greatly and generally lamented. Kinau was appointed to succeed her as regent, and the young king, assuming his sovereignty in the spring of 1833, made her his premier. She was a wise and good counsellor. When certain irreligious chiefs besought the youthful monarch to oppose the new religion, his reply was, "The kingdom of God is strong."

The names of those originally composing the mission, and also of its first reënforcement, have been mentioned. It is proper that the succeeding reënforcements, and the date of their arrival, should be recorded here.

The second reënforcement arrived March 31, 1828, and consisted of Lorrin Andrews, Jonathan S. Green, Peter J. Gulick, and Ephraim W. Clark, ordained missionaries, Gerrit P. Judd, physician, Stephen Shepard, printer, and their wives; Miss Maria C. Ogden, Miss Delia Stone, Miss Mary Ward, and Miss Maria Patten, assistants and teachers. — The third arrived in 1831, and consisted of Dwight Baldwin, Reuben Tinker, and Shelden Dibble, ordained missionaries, Andrew Johnstone, assistant in secular affairs, and their wives. — The fourth arrived in 1832, and consisted of John S. Emerson, David B. Lyman, Ephraim Spaulding, William P. Alexander, Richard Armstrong, Cochran Forbes, Harvey R. Hitchcock, and Lorenzo Lyons, ordained missionaries, Alonzo Chapin, physician, and their wives, and Edmund H. Rogers, printer. — The fifth, which arrived in 1833, was Benjamin W. Parker and Lowell Smith, ordained missionaries, and their wives, and Lemuel Fuller, printer. — The sixth, which arrived in 1835, was Titus Coan, ordained missionary, Henry Dimond, bookbinder, Edwin O. Hall, printer, and their wives, Miss Lydia Brown and Miss Elizabeth M. Hitchcock. — The seventh, arriving in 1837, consisted of Isaac Bliss, Daniel T. Conde, Mark Ives, and Thomas Lafon, M. D., ordained missionaries; Seth L. Andrews, M. D., physician; Samuel N. Castle, assistant secular superintendent; Edward Bailey, Amos S. Cooke, Edward Johnson, Horton O. Knapp, Edwin Locke, Charles McDonald, Bethuel Munn, William S. Van Duzee, and Abner Wilcox, teachers, and their wives; Miss Marcia M. Smith and Miss Lucia G. Smith, teachers. — The eighth, composed of Elias Bond, Daniel Dole, and John D. Paris, ordained missionaries, William H. Rice, teacher, and their wives, arrived in 1841. — The ninth consisted of George B. Rowell and James W. Smith, M. D., ordained missionaries, and their wives, and arrived September 21, 1842. — The tenth, arriving in 1844, was Timothy Dwight Hunt and Eliphalet Whittlesey and their wives, Claudius B. Andrews, and John F. Pogue, ordained missionaries. — The eleventh, arriving in 1848, was Samuel G. Dwight and Henry Kinney, ordained missionaries, and Mrs. Kinney. — The twelfth, arriving in 1849, was Charles H. Wetmore, M. D., and wife. — The thirteenth, sent in 1854, was William C. Shipman, ordained missionary, and wife.

The last of the clerical missionaries sent to the Islands was as long ago as the year 1854. The whole number since the year 1819 is forty. Several sons of missionaries, educated in this country, have at different times returned to the Islands in the clerical profession. One half of the clerical missionaries went prior to the year 1832, and about half are now in the field. There have also been six physicians, twenty laymen as teachers, printers, etc., and eighty-three females, all but three of them wives of missionaries and assistant missionaries. The term of missionary labor on the Islands, with the clerical members of the mission, averages about twenty-one years. One of them has been there forty-four years; four, thirty-six years; one, thirty-three; four, thirty-two; and two, thirty-one years.

CHAPTER III.

THE ISLANDS TO THE TIME OF THEIR CONVERSION TO CHRISTIANITY.

Testimony of Governor Kekuanaoa as to the Former State of the Islands. — The Government ask for Teachers in secular Matters. — The Signers. — Like Request from the Mission. — Why not complied with. — Aid from Missionaries indispensable to the Government. — Civil Government necessary for the Safety of the Church. — School for young Chiefs. — Testimony of Hon. Robert Crichton Wyllie. — Early Influences of the Holy Spirit. — Increased Vigor in Prosecuting the Mission. — Reason for it. — The Great Awakening, and its Results. — On the Admission of Converts to the Church.

THAT we may the better appreciate the change wrought among this people by the Holy Spirit, I quote the testimony of Governor Kekuanaoa as to their former state. It is from an address delivered by him in the Stone Church at Honolulu, on a day set apart for Thanksgiving in January, 1841, and published in "The Polynesian" newspaper of that time. Of course what we have is a translation.

"In looking," says the governor, "over the years that are past, I see great reason to praise God for his goodness to me, and to all who are here present. I look back to the reign of Kamehamaha I., and around on the present state of things, and I say there is no being so great and good as Jehovah, and there are no laws so good as his.

"I will mention some things which I saw in the reign of Kamehamaha I. There were three laws: the first, *Papa;* the second, *Waioahukini;* the third, *Mamalahoa.* The design of all these laws was the same, which was to deliver all criminals from the operations of justice, by appealing to the favor of the high chiefs. Whoever was protected by these laws might commit what offence he chose, yet he escaped all harm by the favor of the chiefs. We did not at that time see offenders tried by the judges, before witnesses, as we now do. Such a thought was unknown to us. Everything depended on the will of the chief.

"There was also idolatry. We worshipped wooden gods, and feather gods, and all sorts of worthless things. We then thought it was right to do so; but we see our error now, because we have new light. In former days, right and wrong were all alike to us; but now we see there is a difference. There is a right, and there is a wrong. Our idol gods knew nothing; but Jehovah knows all things, and has revealed some things to us. In this we are blessed; and to-day let us be thankful.

"Uncleanness abounded in our times of darkness. Some chief men had ten women; some had more, and some had less. So also those who had property had many women. Neither were the women confined each to one man. The law of marriage was then unknown. Untold evils arose from this source, such as infanticide, quarrels, murder, and such like things. All these evils are not done away, but they have greatly decreased.

"In the reign of Kamehameha I. we were not taught to respect the rights of others. We abused the maimed, the blind, the aged; and the chiefs oppressed the poor without mercy. We did not know then that these things were wrong, for we had no wise teachers; but now it is plain to us that all these things are wicked. It would be well if we had left them off.

"In those ancient times we were greatly given to gambling, drinking, and sports. These were universal, and the chiefs were foremost in them. It was common, also, for the chiefs to seize such property as they coveted, without giving anything in return for it. They took food, pigs, and this thing, and that thing, as they pleased. But in this respect there has been a wonderful change for the better. Property is now secured to all by the laws of the kingdom. We chiefs do not dare now to take property which is not our own. Some chiefs have done so, and they have been called to account. Taxes are now fixed and regular, and we have many good laws, like enlightened countries.

"We are better clad than we used to be. I remember the time when we saw only the *kihei* and the *malo* among the common people. Great, indeed, was the amount of theft in our days of ignorance. It was connected with lying and robbery in every quarter. Laziness was thought to be honorable, and lazy people were the greatest favorites with the chiefs. When a chief died, there were dreadful doings. Teeth were knocked out; uncleanness was seen everywhere, in open day; heads were shaved; food was destroyed, and every sort of abomination committed. Such was the state of things in the days of Kamehameha I. Have we not seen many great and new things since that time?

"I will now speak of Liholiho's reign. He made a law, called *makahonu*, on the death of his father. Great was our rum-drinking, dancing, sporting, singing, stealing, adultery, and night-carousing, at that time. Large houses were filled with women, and whole nights were spent in debauchery. But Liholiho was kind to his chiefs, and to common people, and to foreigners.

"Very good were all these things in my mind in those days. But latterly I have become acquainted with the Word of God and the Law of God, showing a better way than any I knew before. Let us bless the name of Jehovah for all his benefits to us and our nation. Blessed is the man who keeps the law of the Lord."

As many as ten years after a large portion of the influential rulers had become connected with the church, the following letter was addressed, by the young king and the chiefs, to their American patrons. It was dated August 23, 1836, and shows how much greater had been the progress of religion on the Islands, than of civilization.

"Love to you, our obliging friends in America. This is our sentiment as to promoting the order and prosperity of these Hawaiian Islands. Give us additional teachers, like the teachers who dwell in your own country. These are the teachers whom we would specify: a carpenter, tailor, mason, shoemaker, wheelwright, papermaker, type-founder, agriculturists skilled in raising sugar-cane, cotton and silk, and in making sugar; cloth manufacturers, and makers of machinery, to work on a large scale; and a teacher of the chiefs in what pertains to the land according to the practice of enlightened countries; and if there be any other teachers, who would be serviceable in these matters, send such teachers also. Should you assent to our request, and send hither these specified teachers, then we will protect them, and grant facilities for their occupations, and we will back up their works, that they may succeed well.

KAUIKEAOULI,	KAAHUMANU, 2D,	LELEIOHOKU,
NAHIENAENA,	KEKAULUOHI,	KEKUANAOA,
HOAPILI KANE,	PAKI,	KANAINA,
MARIA HOAPILI,	LILIHA,	KEKAUONOHI,
ADAMS KUAKINI,	AIKANAKA,	KEALIIAHONUI."

Of the above named, only Kekuanaoa and Kanaina are living. The king's name stands first on the list; he is also known as Kamehameha III. Kaahumanu 2d is the official name of the premier; she is better known as Kinau, daughter of the first Kamehameha, the wife of Kekuanaoa, and mother of the present royal family. Kekauluohi was also a daughter of the first Kamehameha, and was the one selected by him to become the wife of a son of Pomare, king of Tahiti, in case the mutual agreement, that each should give one of his daughters in marriage to a son of the other, had been found practicable.[1] She subsequently became the wife of Kanaina, and was premier after Kinau, and through the most troublous and critical times of the nation. Commodore Wilkes

[1] Ellis, pp. 44 and 64. Mr. Dibble (p. 230) says she was half-sister of Kinau, but that her father was a high chief named Kaheiheimalie, who died many years ago.

gives a portrait of her in his United States Exploring Expedition to the Pacific, which is here copied.[1]

Nahienaena was the king's only sister, and died early. Adams Kuakini was subsequently governor of Hawaii. His name was a combination of his native name with that of a former president of the United States: foreigners generally called him John Adams. Paki was a high chief residing at Honolulu, who married a descendant of Kalaniopuu, king of Hawaii when the Islands were discovered by Cook. He was remarkable for his stature, of which his coffin, in the royal cemetery, affords evidence. Leleiohoku was a son of Kalanimoku, well known as the prime councillor of Liholiho and Kaahumanu. Kealiiahonui was descended from the kings of Kauai, and was governor of that island in

[1] She was then premier, and this is the description given of her as she appeared at the Commodore's first interview with Kamehameha III., in the year 1840: —

"This lady is upwards of six feet in height; her frame is exceedingly large, and well covered with fat. She was dressed in yellow silk, with enormously large gigot sleeves, and wore on her head a tiara of beautiful yellow feathers, interspersed with a few of a scarlet color. Above the feathers appeared a large tortoise-shell comb, that confined her straight black hair. Her shoulders were covered with a richly embroidered shawl of scarlet crape. She sat in a large armchair, over which was thrown a robe made of the same kind of yellow feathers as decked her tiara. Her feet were encased in white cotton stockings and men's shoes. She was altogether one of the most remarkable looking personages I have ever seen."

Speaking of the feathers in her tiara, he says, "These feathers

KEKAULUOHI.

1845. Kekauonohi, a descendant of a prince of Maui, was one of the wives of Liholiho.

In the same year the missionaries, acting in concert with the government, voted to request the Board to send out a pious carpenter, mason, tailor, and shoemaker, to be connected with the mission. It was not found possible to comply with their request, nor was a compliance deemed of vital importance. In secular life the demand may usually be expected to create the supply. The experience of the Board has painfully shown how much better it is to trust to the operation of that law. Yet it was found, in the process of raising this nation from barbarism, that it was necessary to allow a few of the missionaries, after being released for that purpose from their connection with the Board, to enter the service of the government. In 1838 the king and chiefs, not being able to obtain such a counsellor as they desired from the United States, requested the Rev. William Richards to come into that relation to them. They felt the need of a guide in their new relations to their people and to foreigners, and Mr. Richards had their

are among the most celebrated productions of these Islands, and some idea of their cost may be formed when it is stated, that each bird yields only a few, and that some thousands are required to form a head-dress. The wreath worn by Kekauluohi is valued at $250, and her robe at $2500. The birds (Melithreptes pacifica) are taken by means of bird-lime made from the pisonia, and the catching of them is practised as a trade by the mountaineers. The wearing of these feathers is a symbol of high rank."

entire confidence. To this he was entitled by reason of his excellent common sense and his disinterested zeal for the welfare of the nation. Both the mission and the Prudential Committee approved of his complying with the request. He was afterwards made Minister of Instruction, which office he retained, to the general satisfaction of the people, until his death in 1847. The Rev. Richard Armstrong, D. D., was then released from the mission to take the oversight of the schools, for the support of which the government made an annual appropriation of about $40,000; and in this department, till his sudden and lamented death in 1860, he rendered most important service. Dr. Gerritt P. Judd, a missionary physician, also retired from the mission, that he might give his efficient aid in extricating the government from its financial embarrassments, in which he seems to have been eminently successful. He was the confidential minister of the king through Lord Paulet's strange usurpation of the government, and was serviceable to the nation in many ways.[1]

The mission did right to make these sacrifices; for

[1] It is recorded of Dr. Judd, in Mr. Jarves's History of the Hawaiian Islands, p. 183, that, "fearing the seizure of the national records" by Lord George Paulet, during his forcible occupation of the Islands in 1843, "he withdrew them from the government house, and secretly placed them in the royal tomb. In this abode of death, surrounded by the sovereigns of Hawaii, using the coffin of Kaahumanu for a table, for many weeks he nightly found an unsuspected asylum for his own labors in behalf of the kingdom."

the life of the government was essential to the well-being of the church. Nor can any candid and well-informed observer doubt that, but for the moral support afforded by the mission, the Hawaiian nation would never have surmounted the obstacles in the way of its progress along the path of civilization.

In 1839 Mr. and Mrs. Cooke, missionary teachers, were invited to take charge of a school for the young chiefs, to be supported by the Hawaiian government; and in this school, where other teachers were also employed, the present reigning family received their education, in connection with others of both sexes, belonging to the higher classes. While at Honolulu I met with some native ladies, educated in this school, whose manners and intelligence commanded my respect.

The Hon. Robert Crichton Wyllie, who has been for a long time Minister of Foreign Affairs, in Notes on the Islands printed in 1846 (which he kindly placed at my disposal), takes an enlightened and just view of all these proceedings. "As applied to a people in the circumstances in which the Hawaiians were," he regards the measures bearing on the government, with which the missionaries were more or less directly connected, as deserving the approval of every Christian, philanthropist, and political economist. Certain resolutions adopted by the assembled missionaries in 1838, which will be given substantially in the sequel, expressive of views they entertained concerning their own duties to the rulers, and also of the duties of those rulers to their subjects, he pronounces "worthy to be printed in letters of gold, and hung up in the House of Nobles, as a guide to their legislation."

As early as the year 1825 it was evident that the Holy Spirit had begun, in certain districts, to operate upon the minds of the people at large. As an illustration of this I quote from the journal of Mr. Richards, at Lahaina, on the Island of Maui, where Keopuolani died two years before.

"*April* 19. As I was walking this evening I heard the voice of prayer in six different houses, in the course of a few rods. I think there are now not less than fifty houses in Lahaina where the morning and evening sacrifice is regularly offered to the true God. The number is constantly increasing, and there is now scarcely an hour in the day that I am not interrupted in my regular employment by calls of persons anxious to know what they must do to be saved.

"21. For four days our house has not been empty, except while the door has been fastened. When I wake in the morning I find people waiting at the door to converse on the truths of the Scriptures. Soon Hoapili, wife and train, come and spend the day; and after the door is closed at evening we are interrupted by constant calls, and are not unfrequently awaked at midnight by those who wish to ask questions. Houses for prayer are multiplying in every part of the village, and the interest which is manifested on the concerns of eternity is such as, only six months ago, I did not expect would be seen even for a whole generation.

"23. In the morning several females called, for the purpose of having a female prayer-meeting established. Kaamoku gave me the reasons why they wished to have another meeting. She said that the females were coming to converse with her night and day, and in so great numbers that she could find no rest, and they were all anxious to assemble together, that she might teach them, and they strengthen each other. She said she was acquainted with *thirty-one praying females* in Nahienaena's train. Considering her as a proper person to superintend a religious meeting, I gave my approbation; so that there are now three separate circles of females in Lahaina who meet regularly for prayer, embracing the number of about *sixty* persons. Eleven strangers have called during the day, to converse respecting the truths of Christianity."

The state of the Islands became so interesting about the year 1835 as to lead the Prudential Committee to adopt more efficient measures, in dependence on divine grace, for hastening the close of their proper work; believing that, should it be found possible to complete it in the space of one or two generations, those Islands would be a glorious exemplification and proof of the power of the gospel in missions, for the encouragement of the Church of God in its efforts for the conversion of the world. After having corresponded sufficiently with the mission on the subject, a company of thirty-two persons, male and female, was sent out by the Board, near the close of 1836, including four clergymen and nine lay teachers. Some surprise was expressed, at the time, by patrons of the Board, that so large a reënforcement should be sent to so small a field. It was said in reply, that the smallness of the field was the very reason for sending it; embracing, as it did, an entire people, in one compact group of islands, under one government, all easily accessible, and singularly prepared for the gospel. In no other nation could the Board so well make the experiment of the possibility of an early completion of its work. Events soon showed that this large reënforcement was none too large, and that it was eminently seasonable. The members were cordially welcomed by the king, chiefs, and people; and they had scarcely been distributed over the Islands, and acquired the language, when the wonderful awakening commenced, which resulted in very large accessions to the Christian Church, and the substantial conversion of the Islands to the Christian religion.

The first public indications of its approach were in the general meeting of the missionaries in 1836, and again in the meeting of the following year. The heart of the mission seemed then drawn out in desires and prayers for the conversion, not of the Islands merely, but of the whole world, to Christ; which found expression in a printed Appeal to the Churches of the United States, of singular earnestness and power. Being unfortunately based on the assumption, that the great embarrassment in carrying on the work of missions was rather in the lack of *men* than of *money*, and coming, too, when an unusual number had received an appointment as missionaries, while the country and the treasury of the Board were suffering under one of the severest of our commercial distresses, the address necessarily lost much of its power. It was the joint production of several missionaries, but the substance and spirit of it afterwards appeared in a work entitled "Thoughts on Missions," by Rev. Sheldon Dibble, which has been widely circulated by the American Tract Society, and still has a living voice in the churches. Among the natives the great awakening may be said to have commenced at Waimea, on Hawaii. In the spring of 1838 there was evidence of the presence of the Spirit at nearly all the stations on that island. So there was on Maui, Oahu, and Kauai. It was a work with power, and the power was evidently that of the Holy Spirit. The dull and stupid, the imbecile and ignorant, the vile, grovelling, and wretched, became attentive hearers of the word, and began to think and feel. Even such as had before given no signs of a conscience, became anxious inquirers after the way of life. Whenever, wherever the missionary appointed a meeting, he was sure of a listening audience. However great the crowds, the meetings were generally conducted with ease and pleasure. The Sabbath was extensively observed, and rarely were natives seen intoxicated. Family worship prevailed even to a greater extent than the public profession of religion.

The whole Bible was given to the Hawaiian people in their own language in the year 1839, the last sheet being printed on the 10th day of May; and nothing could have been more seasonable. In 1837 the number of church-members was 1259. In 1842 it was 19,210. In 1843 it was 23,804, then embodied in twenty-three churches. The congregations were immense during this season of extraordinary interest.

> "The congregation at Ewa was obliged to leave their chapel, and meet under a shelter one hundred and sixty-five feet long by seventy-two wide, sitting in a compact mass, in number about four thousand. Of two congregations at Honolulu, one was estimated at two thousand five hundred souls, and the other between three and four thousand. At Wailuku a house ninety-two feet by forty-two was found too strait, and the people commenced building a new house one hundred feet by fifty. At Hilo congregations were sometimes estimated at between five and six thousand. Prayer-meetings were frequently adjourned from the lecture-room to the body of the church." [1]

Reviewing this work after more than a score of years, we can have no doubt that there was a deep and genuine religious awakening. It was first seen in the hearts of the missionaries. A historian from

[1] Dibble's History, p. 349.

among themselves affirms, that "there was among them much searching of heart, deep humiliation, strong feeling for perishing sinners throughout the heathen world, and especially for those at these Islands, and much earnest, importunate, and agonizing prayer."

"Neither can it be doubted," he adds, "that the Holy Spirit was poured down on the churches and congregations throughout the Islands, and at some places very abundantly. Such was the uniform belief and testimony at the time of all the laborers in the field, consisting of more than twenty ordained ministers of the gospel, and nearly the same number of intelligent laymen. And now, in the retrospect, after the lapse of nearly three years, such continues to be their belief and testimony. Among so many witnesses, collected from all parts of the United States, and differing considerably in their training and prejudices, there is of course a variety of views in regard to different aspects of the revival; but no one would dare assert that a work of grace was not experienced. Most pronounce it a powerful work, and some term it wonderful and unprecedented. The revival was the same in character with what had occurred before at particular stations, and the same also with what has been experienced at several places the last two years. It differed only in being more powerful and more general throughout the group. We shall be very much disappointed if at the judgment day it shall not appear that many souls were at that time truly converted." [1]

[1] Dibble's History, p. 351.

From the days of Kaahumanu the great majority of the people would gladly have secured an admission to the church, if permitted so to do. The mere fact, therefore, that great numbers requested to be received into the visible church, in those times of excitement, proves nothing conclusively as to the number of hopeful converts. In the admission of members the practice of the missionaries varied considerably; but most of them took a course between the two extremes. Mr. Dibble closes his account with the following declaration: —

> "It should be kept in mind that hasty and numerous admissions, and extravagant indications of feeling, took place at only a few stations. What great revival was there ever in this world which was not attended with imperfections that were afterwards regretted? With every proper deduction, it must be allowed that a great work was wrought by the Holy Spirit."

CHAPTER IV.

THE ISLANDS REGARDED AS CHRISTIANIZED.

Reasons for adducing Testimony. — THAT OF THE MISSIONARIES, in 1848. — The Witnesses. — Former Nature of the Government. — Contrast of the former and present Character and Condition of the People. — Schools and Education. — Progress in Civilization. — TESTIMONY IN 1860 OF MR. RICHARD H. DANA. — What the Missionaries have done. — What they are. — Schools and Education. — How the Missionaries were regarded by foreign Visitors and Residents. — Struggle between Good and Evil. — Influence of Missionaries on the Government. — How the Nation has been preserved. — Safety of the Traveller. — Prevalent Influence of Religion. — Estimate of the Missionaries.

OUR historical sketch has come down to the year 1848 — nearly a generation after the arrival of the missionaries, and fifteen years prior to my visit to the Islands. As I shall venture to speak confidently on the religious character of the Hawaiian Protestant churches, and as this is a matter of much moment, and one in regard to which there has been conflicting evidence, I shall devote a chapter to testimony as to the condition and character of the Hawaiian people in 1848, after they had received the gospel, and also in 1860, twelve years later.

TESTIMONY OF THE MISSIONARIES.

In tne year 1848, the mission, then numbering twenty-nine clergymen, all of them liberally educated, and twelve intelligent laymen, bore a united testimony as to the contrast that existed between the state of the people at that time, as compared with their state at the commencement of the mission. The reader will not regard this well-considered delineation as too much extended.

"In the year 1820," they say, "there was but one ruler. His word was law, and life and death were at his disposal. The people had no voice in the government; they had no rights that were respected; they could hold no property that might not be seized. A chief or landholder might taboo a field of taro or other food at any time by placing a stick of sugar-cane in one corner, and no one would dare to take anything away without liberty. Every other kind of property was equally liable to seizure; and if a person refused to execute any of the orders of a chief or head man, or neglected to perform any service required at his hands, his house might be burned with all its contents, and he and his family left entirely destitute. The people were ruled with a rod of iron. They were ignorant, degraded, and miserable.

"It is true that idolatry had been abolished; but the hearts of the people were full of idols, and their moral degradation was as great as when they were bowing down to wood and stone. There was gross and shameful wickedness in high places, in low places, in all places. There was no sacred enclosure where Virtue could be found in her unstained vestments. There was no written language. There were no books, or schools, or hymns of praise, or prayers offered to the Christian's God. Nor was there any prophet who could tell how long this night of ignorance and moral death might last. Parents prostituted their daughters, and husbands their wives, for the sake of gain. They went, some willingly, and others by constraint, as sheep to the slaughter, not knowing that it was for their life. Every foreign ship was fully freighted as she passed from island to island, and there was no want of supply when in port. There was no law against this traffic; on the contrary, it was the universal custom of the land. These are some of the traits of character, and some of the customs of the Hawaiian people, in 1820.

"From that period we date the progress of Christian improvement. For the few first years of missionary effort, the effects of their labors were scarcely discernible; but in the lapse of time the onward march of light and truth became more distinctly marked; and now all who are competent judges are ready to exclaim, What hath God wrought! The change is so great, so wonderful, so beyond expectation or example, that it would seem that none could avoid acknowledging the mighty power of God.

"Could the Hawaiians of 1820 be placed side by side with the present inhabitants of the Islands, the contrast in their outward appearance would be very striking. The dress of the natives of that period was very simple, consisting of a *malo* for the male, and a *pa'ū* for the female. The *kihei* was sometimes put on, but not generally; and children of both sexes were entirely naked till they were nine or ten years old. In bathing in the sea, or sporting in the surf, no articles of clothing were ever worn; and females were accustomed to leave their *pa'ū* at their residences, and pass on through the village to the shore, and return in the same manner; and if they were individuals of high rank, they would not unfrequently call at the residence of the missionary to pay their respects, and send a servant to bring the *pa'ŭ*, and put it on in the missionary's presence, and return comparatively clad. Such are a few of the outlines of the appearance of the people in regard to their dress."

"But what is the appearance of the people now? You will not often see a female without one or two garments of foreign manufacture, and most of the people throughout the Islands are decently clothed. In truth many of them go far beyond their means in this respect. Most of the congregations on the Sabbath exhibit an appearance quite civilized; and one would discover no very wide difference between them and an American assembly. You will seldom see a man or a woman in their ancient costume. This universal custom of wearing clothing, so far as they can obtain it, should be regarded as some proof of advancement. The change from nakedness to the use of decent apparel is certainly very important.

"At the period above referred to, none of the relations of domestic and social life were regarded as sacred or binding. A man might have as many wives as he could take care of and feed; and he could turn them all adrift, as best suited his convenience or pleasure. A woman might also have as many husbands as she chose; but she could turn them off and take others at pleasure, or they might leave her, if they so desired. Polygamy was one of the features of that age. The king had five wives; one of them the widow, and two of them the daughters, of his deceased father. Each one had her particular day of service, when she followed her lord with a spit-dish and a fly-brush. It is easy to see that in such a mode of life there could be no such thing as conjugal affection or domestic concord; and there was no such thing as parental authority. Real parental affection, moreover, was rarely seen; and equally rare were filial affection and obedience. No obligation was felt on the part of parents to take care of their children, nor on the part of children to obey their parents; and children were often destroyed, before or after birth, to save the trouble of taking care of them.

"But the Hawaiians of the present day occupy a different position. Indeed, there is scarcely a feature of the generation of 1820 discernible in the one now upon the stage. Then there was no law to regulate society. Now all the natural, social, and domestic relations are respected, and the duties of each are in some measure regulated by good and wholesome statutes; and a neglect to perform the duties attached to these various relations is punishable by fine, imprisonment, or other disabilities. Parents and children, husbands and wives, masters and servants, are recognized in the laws of the nation; and for any delinquency in the performance of their duties they are judicially answerable. No breach of trust or promise, no dereliction of duty, passes unnoticed."

"Of common schools there are 336, with 16,153 pupils; and there are also five schools of a higher order, containing 234 scholars. The elements of a common-school education have become pretty generally diffused throughout the nation. Rarely can a child over ten years of age be found who cannot read more or less fluently, while thousands can answer, with a good degree of correctness, miscellaneous questions in the other branches. Sixteen years ago, schools for children were almost unknown, and very few were then able to read. The change is great. We cannot contemplate it without admiring the agency by which it has been wrought; and we feel determined, by help from the Lord, to press forward this department of our labor, until the blessing of a good education shall be enjoyed by every child."

"In regard to the piety of Hawaiian church-members, we have always told you that there were many of them for whom we have fears that they are not the children of God. Some, we fear, are hypocrites, while others are ignorant and self-deceived. Many of them do not give that unequivocal evidence that they have passed from death unto life which we greatly desire to see. Our field has tares as well as wheat; and some of them, we fear, will grow together until the great harvest-day.

"Indeed, the mass of our church-members are babes in Christ—babes in knowledge, in understanding, in wisdom, in experience, in stability, in strength, in everything. Many of them have grown up amid the thick darkness and abominations of heathenism. Their minds have become darkened by reason of sin, and their consciences seared. Hence it cannot be expected that even when truly converted they will be able to withstand temptation, and develop the perfect symmetry of the strong and full-grown man in Christ. But we have many living epistles known and read of all men — the soldiers of the cross, tried and faithful. These are our joy and crown of rejoicing. Every year increases their number, their experience, their strength, and our confidence in them.

"Every year furnishes additional evidence that a great and glorious work has been wrought among this people. We believe that God has a church here, builded on the foundation of the apostles and prophets, and that the gates of hell shall never prevail against it. Thousands have been redeemed from the bondage of sin and death, and made trophies of the rich and sovereign grace of God. Never have your missionaries had more cheering evidence of genuine piety in the churches than at the present time.

"On the first arrival of the missionaries, the people were a nation of drunkards; and every vice was practised, and every crime was committed, which grows out of such a state of things. In every village the most disgusting licentiousness might be seen, the legitimate and never-failing accompaniment of intemperance. These abominations were not confined to common people; but the kings and the chiefs were the principal actors in the riotous scenes of those days. The eye saw and the ear heard many things which may not be uttered or written. The tongue would falter to speak them, and the paper itself would blush to receive the record.

"Has any change been effected in the habits of the Islanders in this respect? Is every village now, as formerly, filled with intoxicated and licentious revellers? Not at all. There has been a great, nay, a mighty revolution. There has been a transition from brutal intoxication to Christian sobriety. It is a thing of rare occurrence to see a drunken native. The scale is turned. The foreign community are the consumers of intoxicating drinks. There is no nation on the globe that better deserves the appellation of 'temperate,' than the Hawaiian; and they would be more consistently and entirely so, if they were left to manage the subject for themselves, without foreign interference. But, alas! the Hawaiian government has not the liberty to make any article of commerce contraband.

"The king, the government, and the nation itself, adhere to the principles of temperance; and the whole mass might not unaptly be designated as one great temperance society. We regard them as quite a sober people; and we venture to

9

say, that there is as much morality, and as much practical religion, as can be found in any community of equal magnitude which may be selected in any nation under heaven."

"Many more facts might be stated in proof of the progress which the Islanders have made in general improvement. They practise many of the arts and usages of civilized life. They are carpenters, blacksmiths, shoemakers, masons; and in most of the mechanical departments there are respectable workmen. There are those who possess flocks and herds, and hold land in fee simple; there are some who are gaining property; and equal protection is given to all, from the highest to the lowest. Neither the king nor chiefs can take what is not their own, without being amenable to the laws. The people have availed themselves of the inducements held out to them to labor, with the assurance that all the avails of their industry will be secured to them; and many are collecting around them the comforts and conveniences of a civilized people. Their houses are better, and many of them are divided into separate apartments. Some of their residences are furnished with tables, chairs, and many other articles used in Christian lands. But why should we multiply examples in proof of the advanced position which the nation now occupies? Every eye can see it; and the great and commanding facts which go to complete the proof of its advancement are not of difficult discovery. They are distinctly marked on the chart of its progress from downright heathenism to its present civilization." [1]

[1] Missionary Herald, vol. xlv., p. 17.

TESTIMONY OF MR. DANA.

The testimony of RICHARD H. DANA, Esq., a distinguished lawyer, and member of the Episcopal Church, in Boston, though twelve years later, is a significant confirmation of that given by the missionaries. It is contained in a letter written from the Hawaiian Islands, during a visit in the year 1860, and first printed in the New York Tribune. It is explicit, and, coming from an intelligent and candid observer, of a different religious persuasion from the missionaries, deserves a permanent record. Mr. Dana writes as follows: —

"It is no small thing to say of the Missionaries of the American Board, that in less than forty years they have taught this whole people to read and to write, to cipher and to sew. They have given them an alphabet, grammar, and dictionary; preserved their language from extinction; given it a literature, and translated into it the Bible and works of devotion, science and entertainment, etc., etc. They have established schools, reared up native teachers, and so pressed their work that now the proportion of inhabitants who can read and write is greater than in New England; and whereas they found these islanders a nation of half-naked savages, living in the surf and on the sand, eating raw fish, fighting among themselves, tyrannized over by feudal chiefs, and abandoned to sensuality, they now see them decently clothed, recognizing the law of marriage, knowing something of accounts, going to school and public worship with more regularity than the people do at home; and the more elevated of them taking part in conducting the affairs of the constitutional monarchy under which they live, holding seats on the judicial bench and in the legislative chambers, and filling posts in the local magistracies.

"It is often objected against missionaries, that a people must be civilized before it can be Christianized; or at least that the two processes must go on together, and that the mere preacher, with his book under his arm, among a barbarous people, is an unprofitable laborer. But the missionaries to the Sandwich Islands went out in families, and planted themselves in households, carrying with them, and exhibiting to the natives, the customs, manners, comforts, discipline, and order of civilized society. Each house was a centre and source of civilizing influences; and the natives generally yielded to the superiority of our civilization, and copied its ways; for, unlike the Asiatics, they had no civilization of their own, and, unlike the North American Indians, they were capable of civilization. Each missionary was obliged to qualify himself, to some extent, as a physician and surgeon, before leaving home; and each mission-house had its medicine-chest, and was the place of resort by the natives for medicines and medical advice and care. Each missionary was a school-teacher to the natives in their own language; and the women of the missions, who were no less missionaries than their husbands, taught schools for women and children, instructing them not only in books, but in sewing, knitting, and ironing, in singing by note, and in the discipline of children. These mission families, too, were planted as garrisons would have been planted by a military conqueror in places where there were no inducements of trade to carry families; so that no large region, however difficult of access, or undesirable as a residence, is without its head-quarters of religion and civilization. The women of the mission, too, can approach the native women and children in many ways not open to men, — as in their sickness, and by the peculiar sympathies of sex, — and thus exert the tenderest, which are often the most decisive, influences.

"In the course of the two months I have spent upon these Islands, it has been my good fortune to be the guest of many of the mission families, and to become more or less acquainted with nearly all of them. And, besides fidelity in the discharge of their duties to the natives, I can truly say that in point of kindness and hospitality to strangers, of intelligence and general information, of solicitude and painstaking for the liberal education of their children, and of zeal for the acquirement of information of every sort, it would be difficult to find their superiors among the most favored families at home. I have seen in their houses collections of minerals, shells, plants, and flowers, which must be valuable to science; and the missionaries have often preserved the best, sometimes the only, records of the volcanic eruptions, earthquakes, and other phenomena and meteorological observations. Besides having given, as I have said, to the native language an alphabet, grammar, dictionary, and literature, they have done nearly all that has been done to preserve the national traditions, legends, and poetry. But for the missionaries, it is my firm belief that the Hawaiian would never have been a written language; there would have been few or no trustworthy early records, historical or scientific; the traditions would have perished; the native government would have been overborne by foreign influences, and the

9 *

interesting, intelligent, gentle native race would have sunk into insignificance, and perhaps into servitude to the dominant whites."

"The educational system of the Islands is the work of the missionaries and their supporters among the foreign residents, and one formerly of the mission is now Minister of Education. In every district are free schools for natives. In these they are taught reading, writing, singing by note, arithmetic, grammar, and geography, by native teachers. At Lahainaluna is the Normal School for natives, where the best scholars from the district schools are received and carried to an advanced stage of education, and those who desire it are fitted for the duties of teachers. This was originally a mission school, but is now partly a government institution. Several of the missionaries, in small and remote stations, have schools for advanced studies, among which I visited several times that of Mr. Lyman, at Hilo, where there are nearly one hundred native lads; and all the under teachers are natives. These lads had an orchestra of ten or twelve flutes, which made very creditable music. At Honolulu there is a royal school for natives, and another middle school for whites and half-castes; for it has been found expedient generally to separate the races in education. Both these schools are in excellent condition. But the special pride of the missionary efforts for education is the High School or College of Punahou. This was established for the education of the children of the mission families, and has been enlarged to receive the children of other foreign residents, and is now an incorporated college with some seventy scholars. The course of studies goes as far as the end of the Sophomore year in our New England colleges, and is expected soon to go farther. The teachers are young men of the mission families, taught first at this school, with educations finished in the colleges of New England, where they have taken high rank. At Williams College there were at one time five pupils from this school, one of whom was the first scholar, and four of whom were among the first seven scholars of the year; and another of the professors at Punahou was the first scholar of his year at New Haven. I attended several recitations at Punahou in Greek, Latin, and mathematics, and after having said that the teachers were leading scholars in our colleges, and the pupils mostly children of the mission families, I need hardly add that I advised the young men to remain there to the end of the course, as they could not pass the Freshman and Sophomore years more profitably elsewhere, in my judgment. The examinations in Latin and Greek were particularly thorough in etymology and syntax. The Greek was read both by the quantity and by the printed accent, and the teachers were disposed to follow the continental pronunciation of the vowels in the classic languages, if that system should be adopted in the New England colleges. It is upon that system that the native alphabet was constructed by the missionaries. This institution must determine, in a great measure, the character not only of the rising generation of whites, but, as education proceeds downward, and not upward, also that of the natives. It is the chief hope of the people, who have spent their utmost upon it, and are now making an appeal for aid in the United States — an appeal that ought not to be unsuccessful."

"Among the traders, shipmasters, and travellers who have

visited these Islands, some have made disparaging statements respecting the missionaries; and a good deal of imperfect information is carried home by persons who have visited only the half-Europeanized ports, where the worst view of the condition of the natives is presented. I visited among all classes — the foreign merchants, traders, and shipmasters, foreign and native officials, and with the natives, from the king and several of the chiefs to the humblest poor, whom I saw without constraint in a tour I made alone over Hawaii, throwing myself upon their hospitality in their huts. I sought information from all, foreign and native, friendly and unfriendly; and the conclusion to which I came is, that the best men, and those who are best acquainted with the history of things here, hold in high esteem the labors and conduct of the missionaries. The mere seekers of pleasure, power, or gain, do not like their influence; and those persons who sympathized with that officer of the American navy who compelled the authorities to allow women to go off to his ship by opening his ports and threatening to bombard the town, naturally are hostile to the missions. I do not mean, of course, that there is always unanimity among the best people, or perhaps among the missionaries themselves, on all questions; *e. g.*, as to the toleration of Catholics, and on some minor points of social and police regulation. But on the great question of their moral influence, the truth is that there has always been, and must ever be, in these Islands, a peculiar struggle between the influences for good and the influences for evil. They are places of visit for the ships of all nations, and for the temporary residence of mostly unmarried traders; and at the height of the whaling season the number of transient seamen in the port of Honolulu equals half the population of the town. The temptations arising from such a state of things, too much aided by the inherent weakness of the native character, are met by the ceaseless efforts of the best people, native and foreign, in the use of moral means and by legislative coercion. It is a close struggle, and, in the large seaports, often discouraging and of doubtful issue; but it is a struggle of duty, and has never yet been relaxed. Doubtless the missionaries have largely influenced the legislation of the kingdom, and its police system; it is fortunate that they have done so. Influence of some kind was the law of the native development. Had not the missionaries and their friends among the foreign merchants and professional men been in the ascendant, these Islands would have presented only the usual history of a handful of foreigners exacting everything from a people who denied their right to anything. As it is, in no place in the world that I have visited are the rules which control vice and regulate amusements so strict, yet so reasonable, and so fairly enforced. The government and the best citizens stand as a good genius between the natives and the besieging army. As to the interior, it is well known that a man may travel alone, with money, through the wildest spots, unarmed. Having just come from the mountains of California, I was prepared with the usual and necessary belt and its appendages of that region, but was told that those defences were unheard of in Hawaii. I found no hut without its Bible and hymn-book in the native tongue, and the practice of family prayer and grace before meat, though it be over no more than a calabash of poi and a few dried fish, and whether at home or on journeys, is as common as in New England a century ago.

"It may be asked whether there is no offset, no deduction to be made from this high estimate of the American missionaries. As to their fidelity and industry in the worst of times, and their success up to the point they have now reached, I think of none. As to the prospects for their system in the future, and the direction the native mind may take in its further progress, there are some considerations worthy of attention."

Then follow suggestions on the probable effect of certain modifications in the Protestant worship of the Island churches, should such modifications be made. Relating as they do to the future, they need not be quoted here.

CHAPTER V.

MEASURES CONSEQUENT UPON THE CONVERSION OF THE ISLANDS.

True Idea of a Mission. — Its Application to the Hawaiian Islands. — New Measures adopted. — These partly successful. — Difficulties encountered. — The great Difficulty. — Light from an unexpected Quarter. — New Problem. — The Resort for its Solution.

Missionary Societies have been slow to act on the idea of working their missions professedly with a view to an early completion. A mission should obviously be planned and prosecuted with the expectation of completing it, through the grace of the almighty Saviour, within a time compatible with the measure of faith and patience in the churches supporting it. The great awakening at the Sandwich Islands, and the surprising changes consequent thereupon, had the effect to bring this idea home to the Prudential Committee. But this was still more effectually done by means of a subsequent unexpected development in the mission itself — a simultaneous outburst of parental solicitude in the missionaries, which, for a time, threatened seriously to diminish the working force of the mission. The climate of those Islands is favorable to an increase of population. The number of children now living in fifty-three mission families is two hundred and thirty-five, or more than four for each family; and as many as fifty-eight grandchildren are recollected as belonging to those families. About the year 1847, when the great awakening had in a considerable degree subsided, and the thousands of hopeful converts had been gathered into the churches, there began to be a strong disposition in those families to go to the fatherland to make provision for the older children. The case, as it came before the Prudential Committee, was new in their experience, no such homeward tendency of missionary families having occurred elsewhere. The fact awakened solicitude among the missionaries themselves; and at their general meeting in May, 1848, they passed a resolution, urging upon the Board to go as far as possible in removing obstacles to their permanent residence on the Islands. Before an intimation of this action of theirs was received, the Committee had taken a step in that direction, perhaps somewhat farther than the missionaries, as a body, were then fully prepared for. They adopted the conclusion, that the Islands had been virtually Christianized; that the nature of the work had therefore changed essentially; and that what was needed, thenceforward, was pastors, rather than missionaries. It was also assumed (though this proved to be an error), that in case the missionaries should be released from their connection with the Board, and become pastors, they would act wisely to look for at least a part of their support from the native churches.

It was clearly seen, also, that there was a striking peculiarity in the location of the mission. Not only was there a genial clime, but the Islands were centrally situated as regards the great trading world, being at the junction of several of the future great highways of commerce, while the government of the Islands was wholly favorable to the mission. It would seem, therefore, that at least a portion of the children of the mission might reasonably be expected to make their permanent home on their native Islands.

With this expectation (which events now seem likely to realize), the Prudential Committee, in July of 1848, entered upon a series of measures with the avowed purpose of putting it in the power of the missionaries to remain there, with their families. They encouraged them to take a conditional release from their connection with the Board, and become Hawaiian citizens. They provided for the transfer of the greater part of the property held by the Board, consisting of houses, lands, herds, etc., to the missionaries, with the understanding that they would remain at the Islands. The lands were originally received from the rulers of the Islands; and the government, which was favorable to this measure, to make the transfer more sure, gave the missionaries a right to their lands in fee-simple. It was understood, moreover, that the missionaries would have the same liberty in the acquisition and investment of property, that popular sentiment gives to pastors in the United States.

Some fear was expressed at the time, both at home and also at the Islands, that this great change in the circumstances of the mission would operate unfavorably upon the spiritual condition of the missionaries. But I was assured, by those best competent to know, that the mission gained in spirituality after this change was made in its relations to property and to the Islands. The missionaries of course felt it to be their duty to husband the property thus given them, and some availed themselves, to a moderate extent, of the privilege conferred by the government of purchasing land at a low rate. In my tour through the Islands, the brethren everywhere made me acquainted with their temporal affairs, and I was glad to find so many of them in circumstances favorable to their comfort, and to the settlement of their children there. In point of fact, the great body of the missionaries are still there on the ground, with their families; and in sufficient numbers, I trust, to be the salt, and light, and safety of the nation. I believe they all now agree, that some such measures as those adopted in the year 1848 were needful, to the end that the Protestant Christian community on those Islands might hope to become independent, at some time, of foreign aid.

The difficulties experienced in working out these

changes were really very great. Not only was there the want of precedents to guide the executive of the Board, but the early experience and training of the missionaries themselves at the Islands had not been favorable to a feeling of self-reliance and independence in pecuniary matters. The missionaries had at first received their support on the principle of *common stock*, each one drawing from a depository what articles he deemed needful. This at length was so far modified, that a limit was put to the value of what each might draw in a given time; but the goods were to be furnished at cost. Meanwhile a market had grown up at Honolulu, and a change to salaries paid in money was thus rendered possible, leaving the missionary to make his purchases where he pleased. Simple as the whole case may seem, the actual working of it out, in all its details, required the correspondence of near a dozen years. The effort of some of the brethren to live on salaries derived wholly from native churches diminished the feeling of dependence on the churches at home. But the looking to native churches for any part of the support had also the effect to retard the institution of a native ministry.

In respect to the matter last named, so vital to the great end in view, there was considerable diversity in the practice of the missionaries, and still more in their opinions. The Islands were divided into about a score of missionary districts. Excepting Honolulu, each of these districts was under the care of one missionary. The metropolitan district had two missionaries and two churches; but the other districts had each only one church. On Maui and Oahu several small communities or churches were set off for native pastors; but those churches and pastors were regarded as under the ecclesiastical direction of the missionaries in their respective districts. The desirableness, even the ultimate necessity, of these purely native formations, was conceded by all; but it is not known that, up to the year 1863, any one missionary regarded the time as fully come when native churches and pastors should be set free from direct missionary intervention and control. The Island of Maui approached, perhaps, nearest to this result; but even there the native pastor held a subordinate relation to the missionary. The native pastorate has been, indeed, for many years, the great missionary problem of the Islands. The tendency in the minds of the brethren was doubtless in the right direction; and it should not surprise us if a portion of the older missionaries, after their long experience of duplicity and instability in the native character, were slow to invest natives with the responsibilities of the sacred office.

Happily, in the year 1853, God in his providence led to the sending of several Hawaiian preachers as missionaries, alone, to the Marquesas Islands — to have only an annual visit from a missionary of another race. Whatever may be the final result of the mission on those Islands, its reflex influence on the Hawaiian Islands has been eminently good. It has shown that the native ministry need much less of constant personal oversight than had been supposed. If the promised grace of Christ has upheld them among the cannibal Marquesans, — as it has marvellously, — why might not the same gracious and adequate support be expected on their native Isles? However, the correspondence on the subject of constituting a native pastorate on the Hawaiian Islands came to no satisfactory result. The testimony was conflicting, and some of it was very adverse, as though the natives were thoroughly demoralized by licentious ideas and habits, and were everywhere and always unreliable.

This subject will come up again in a more hopeful aspect, as we proceed. But it should be stated here, that while the Prudential Committee were by no means convinced that proper materials for pastors could not be found among so many thousands, who had been called by the Holy Spirit into the churches, they were greatly perplexed by seeing so little prospect of effective measures at the Islands for inducting native preachers into the pastoral office. At the same time it was known that all except four of the missionaries were past the age of fifty, and a portion of them considerably beyond that age; while there really was not a call for new missionaries, since additional missionaries would only occupy more of the ground, and leave still less for native pastors.

This state of things, resulting partly from the progress of events since 1848, brought up a new problem for solution, very different from the one then resolved; namely, *what ought to be done to supply the place of the missionaries, as they are successively called to their rest, and, at the same time, to enable the Board to withdraw gradually from the Islands?*

It was the apparent impossibility of solving this problem by means of correspondence alone, at least within a safe period, that induced the Prudential Committee, with the hope of doing it by means of a few months of unreserved fraternal conference with the brethren at the Islands, to send out their Foreign Secretary, in the year 1863, for such a conference.

CHAPTER VI.

VOYAGE TO THE ISLANDS, AND A WEEK AT THE METROPOLIS.

Question of Duty. — Companions of the Voyage. — Railroad across the Isthmus. — A magnificent Coast. — From San Francisco to the Islands. — Honolulu. — Introduction to the Queen. — The Officers of Government. — Governor Kekuanaoa. — Favorable Impression of social Life in the Capital. — Introduction to the Native Christian Community.

THE reason for my visiting the Islands was stated at the close of the last chapter. The resolution of the Prudential Committee, making it my duty to go, was passed December 16, 1862. I then wanted scarcely four years of threescore and ten; and I knew well the laborious nature of the service proposed, having thrice visited the missions of the Board in Western Asia, and once those in India. More than a dozen ocean transits, and nearly as many of inland seas, had not reconciled me to sea-life, and I had no passion for foreign travel. The first thought of so long a tour, though in a new and interesting direction, was not pleasant. But while I had found such visits laborious, my intercourse with missionaries and their families on the ground had always been a source of high enjoyment. Nowhere had I had a sweeter experience of Christian fellowship. And the anticipated renewal of such an experience on the Hawaiian Islands, along with a conviction, which sprang up, that I was called of God to this service, soon led to a cheerful preparation for departure, and in a few days I was ready to go. My wife consented to accompany me, — going of course at private expense; and we took our youngest daughter with us, having regard in so doing to the benefit of her health.

We left Boston on the 9th of January, 1863, and on the 12th of the same month embarked in the steamer Ocean Queen, at New York, going by way of Aspinwall and the Isthmus, and arrived at San Francisco February 7. The railroad passage across the Isthmus occupied three hours. The road lies between the 9th and 10th degrees of north latitude, and is about forty-eight miles long, terminating at Aspinwall on the east and Panama on the west, with a maximum grade of sixty feet. The summit grade is two hundred and sixty-three feet above the mean tide of the Atlantic Ocean. The road was completed in January, 1855. Considering the climate, the morasses that were to be explored and filled, the distance of the field from those undertaking the work, the mortality among the laborers, the number of bridges, etc., the work must be regarded as a wonderful result of human genius and enterprise. The first native wood employed for the ties on the road soon perished, and was replaced with ties of lignum vitæ brought from Carthagena. The telegraphic posts suffered in the same manner as the original ties of the road, and it was necessary to manufacture posts which the worms would not attack; and they are now a composition of pounded stone or gravel and cement, cast in a mould, and apparently durable as rock. The number of water-ways on the route is said to be one hundred and seventy, the greater part of them, however, requiring only short culverts and bridges; but the iron bridge across the Chagres, at Barbacoas, is six hundred and twenty feet long, with six spans of a hundred feet each. The cost of the road up to 1859 was eight millions of dollars. Its gross earnings in its first seven years, during only four of which was the road in use throughout its entire extent, were $8,146,605, and its clear gains $5,971,728.[1] The profits must be much greater now, but I have not the means of stating what they are. I know we paid twenty-five dollars each for railroad passage, and ten cents for every pound of baggage we had over fifty pounds, and it was very carefully weighed.

The steamer Constitution, one of the largest and finest American vessels, awaited us on the other side, and we went pleasantly, in thirteen or fourteen days, over the three thousand miles from Panama to San Francisco, almost always in sight of the mighty

[1] Otis's Hist. of Panama Railroad, pp. 36, 41, 46.

range of mountains forming the eastern barrier of the Pacific Ocean. On the Pacific side there was a marked superiority in the arrangements on board for the health and comfort of the passengers. Being anxious to proceed, since the general meeting of the missionaries in June would restrict the time for our island surveys, I induced Captain Cresey, of the Boston clipper ship Archer, bound to China, to land us at Honolulu, where we arrived on the 27th of February, a little more than six weeks from the time of our embarkation at New York.

The week following was spent in active, fatiguing, but interesting social intercourse. The population of Honolulu and its suburbs has risen to ten or twelve thousand, and its garden-like, city-like appearance surprised me. Missionaries are living who well remember when there was only one wooden house in the place, the rest being grass or thatched huts, and when there were only footpaths instead of streets, and scarcely tree or shrub in town, not to speak of the naked, barbarous inhabitants. Now there is the reverse of all this. The gardens are the result of water brought down the Nuuanu Valley. This valley, running up between cloud-capped mountains, is itself a prominent and interesting feature in the landscape. The most conspicuous edifice in Honolulu — a landmark for seamen — is the large Stone Church, with massive walls of coral blocks, and a tower and town-clock. It is here the first native congregation and

Stone Church at Honolulu.

church worship God. The edifice proving too large, a part has been shut off by a partition; but it will now seat twenty-five hundred in the simple Hawaiian dress.

Our first week in the metropolis brought us into agreeable contact with much good foreign society, and some native. The king was absent, having left for his country-seat at Kailua, with the English bishop, just before our arrival. We were glad to wait on the amiable and accomplished queen, at her invitation, and were gratified with the interview. Those who have traced the progress of these Islands in social life will be pleased to see how an event of this kind was noted in The Polynesian, under the head of "Court News."

"Dr. Anderson, Mrs. Anderson, and Miss Anderson were very graciously received by Her Majesty the Queen, in her private apartments in the Palace, yesterday, at 11 o'clock forenoon. To mark how much she welcomed these philanthropic visitors to this kingdom, it pleased Her Majesty to send her carriage to convey them to and from the Palace. The reception being a friendly one, without etiquette, only her Royal Highness Princess Victoria, the Chancellor of the Kingdom and his lady, and the Minister of Foreign Affairs, were present."

Mr. Wyllie, long Minister of Foreign Affairs, called immediately on our arrival, and invited us to dine with him, in company with other guests. In early life, while in South America, he had known Mr. Hill, the brother of my wife, and for many years Treasurer of the American Board, who was then American Consul at Santiago and Valparaiso. Chief Justice Allen (the worthy Chancellor of the Kingdom), with his accomplished lady, soon after did the same. Nothing could exceed the cordiality and friendliness of our intercourse with the officers of government, down to the close of our visit. The Secretary expressed regret at his table that His Majesty was then absent; for he felt assured, under the circumstances, that it would have afforded him pleasure to have met us. In responding, I expressed the hope of meeting the king after making the tour of Hawaii, and stated that the Board appreciated the aid which the government had rendered to the missionary enterprise; and, furthermore, that what the Board now expected from the government was, that it would act impartially towards the different denominations of Christians.

Among the native gentlemen of rank who obliged us with personal attentions, I am happy to name Kekuanaoa, the father of the king and governor of Oahu. He and Kanaina, whose acquaintance we made at a later period, are now almost the only survivors of the old chiefs. The name of the former appears very early in the history of the mission. He is a member of the first church at Honolulu, and takes an interest in its prosperity. Tall, erect, well developed, he is one of nature's noblemen. In his call upon us he was accompanied by Kanoa, governor of Kauai, who is also a church-member. I afterwards had much acquaintance with the latter on his own island. I might mention several Hawaiian ladies of rank who contributed materially to our pleasure at the capital, but am restrained by the apprehension of trespassing upon private life. It would illustrate the progress of society at Honolulu, were I to go minutely into the history of our sojourn in that city; but it would be taking liberties that perhaps are not allowable to travellers. Our reception by the large native congregations worshipping in the first and second churches, on the two Sabbaths following our arrival, at each of which I made a short address, was but an earnest of what we afterwards experienced from the masses of the people throughout the Islands.

II.

TOUR OF THE ISLANDS.

TOUR OF THE ISLANDS.

CHAPTER VII.

HAWAII.

The Propeller Kilauéa. — Approach to Hawaii. — The King and Queen. — First Landing. — The Northern Coast. — Magnificent Scenery of Hilo. — Welcome Reception. — The Memorable Past. — A Christian Congregation. — Visit to the great Volcano. — A Baptism. — Religion in Rural Districts. — The Hilo Station. — Boarding Schools. — District of Kau. — Missionary Station at Waiohinu. — Interesting Services at the Church. — Historical Review. — The Children instead of the Fathers.

A PROPELLER sails every ten days from Honolulu, touches at Lahaina and other places on Maui, and makes the circuit of Hawaii. But for this, and a smaller steamer every few days to the Island of Káuai, our observations would have been comparatively limited in the three months devoted to travel. The Kilauéa (our propeller was named after the great volcano) sailed March 9th for Hilo. An arrangement was made by Mr. Castle by which we were at liberty, without increase of expense, to leave or rejoin the steamer at any point. And we have much reason to speak well both of the vessel and its obliging officers.

Our approach to Hawaii was on Wednesday morning, March 11th, off Kawaihae, when we had a grand profile view of the island. Mauna Kea, the more northerly of the two great volcanic mountains, rose before us 13,950 feet, and Mauna Loa, farther south, to the height of 13,760. This last-named mountain, however, was pronounced "unfinished" by a missionary brother, because it still continues to send forth vast streams of lava. It was partially concealed by Mauna Hualalai, not far from 10,000 feet high. Those lofty masses break the trade winds, and make a smooth and tranquil sea along the western shore; and this, probably, is the reason why that portion of the island, in former times, was so much resorted to by chiefs and people.

OUTLINE VIEW OF HAWAII FROM THE EASTWARD.

I was at first somewhat disappointed in these mountains, in consequence of their extremely gradual ascent. This is illustrated by the annexed cut, derived from Professor Dana's Geology of the Hawaiian Islands. The two tallest mountains seem less elevated than they really are, because of their dome-like appearance, and the very gradual inclination from their base to their summit. That of Mauna Loa is estimated to be only 6° 30′. With so great a horizontal thickness in the mountain to its very summit, we see how the crater, which opens at the top, is able to sustain the amazing pressure of a column of molten lava of more than thirteen thousand feet.[1]

The queen was a passenger, with her suite, going to the king at Kailua; and, just before reaching that place, he came on board from his barge. The meeting between them was affecting, the queen not having visited their country-seat since the death of the young prince, their only child. In 1850, while the king was quite a young man, he visited Boston with Dr. Judd, in company with his brother (the present king), and both of them were at my house. He recognized the acquaintance formed at that time, and expressed the hope of seeing us on our return to Honolulu. I observed the queen call his attention to a beautifully bound copy of the "Memorial Volume," which I had sent to the palace, and which she had brought with her. The good old governor of Oahu, father of the king, was also on board, and I could not but admire his physical development. I was sorry to see such an appearance of ill health in the king. In the morning of his life, thirteen years before, I thought I had never beheld a more perfect specimen of the human form. In the last month of

[1] Geology of United States Exploring Expedition, p. 159.

my sojourn on the Islands I was present, by invitation, at his public reception of Mr. McBride, our new American Minister Resident, and was pleased to observe a degree of royal dignity and propriety in his majesty which the crowned heads of Europe could hardly excel. His death occurred on the 30th of November following, before he had reached the age of thirty.

After landing the royal family we proceeded to Kealakekua Bay, and took in wood from the very spot where Captain Cook was killed. Mr. Paris has his residence two miles above, with a grand sea prospect, and one of the best of climates. Oranges flourish in that region, and excellent coffee, and a variety of delicious fruits and flowers. Having been apprised of our coming, Mr. Paris was down with horses, and we accompanied him up the steep road along the face of the precipice. We could stay only to dine. Retracing our way along the coast, we next morning rounded Kohala point, and met the north-east trades, and an uncomfortable sea, which lasted until we reached Hilo. Kohala was a beautiful region as beheld from the ship, and the more so to us because we could see, amid its verdure, the dwelling of our brother Bond, and the Christian church erected by his people. Then came a singular succession of mountain ranges and ravines, with lofty cascades falling into the sea. Next the lovely vale of Waipio revealed its white church, — one of perhaps a dozen erected under the superintendence of Mr. Lyons, — with a waterfall behind, descending from the top of a mountain. Two or three more such buildings came into view along the high lands as we proceeded. In a clear day the entrance into the harbor of Hilo reveals one of the magnificent scenes of the world, having Mauna Loa in front, sometimes with banks of snow along its crest, and Mauna Kea on the right, towards the west, looking down upon one of the greenest landscapes that ever rose from the sea-shore; for it is long since volcanic eruptions have swept over that surface, and being the windward side of the island, it is watered abundantly. The harbor of Hilo is formed by a coral reef, at the entrance of the bay, extending a couple of miles from an island on the south-eastern side, which is connected with the shore by a number of rocks. There is good anchorage within, and the reef destroys the dangerous force of the waves, though it does not prevent a heavy surf rolling upon the beach at the bottom of the bay. The entrance to the harbor is along the bold western shore, where the water is deep, and the passage free from rocks.

We reached Hilo late in the evening, and were borne in the dark through the high surf on the shoulders of friendly natives. Though more or less wet, we forgot all in the welcome of our reception by the family of Mr. Coan, where we made our home, and by all our brethren and sisters in that favored place.

Mr. Coan, not having received my letter in time, was then absent on one of his missionary tours; but word was sent to him, which brought him home on Saturday. It was with peculiar feelings of interest that I visited Hilo. In the wonderful outpouring of the Spirit during the three years following 1838, more than eight thousand were added to the church from the districts of Hilo and Puna, then containing a population of about fourteen thousand. Mr. Coan deemed it proper to admit five thousand in one year, and as many as seventeen hundred in one day, — after personal inquiry, as he informed me, into the case of each individual, extending through some time previous. The extraordinary method by which he was able to baptize so large a number of persons at one time, even by the simple process of sprinkling, will be remembered by many. He assures me that the number then admitted have held on their Christian course as well as the rest. The old grass-covered meeting-house, large enough to hold the average congregation of four thousand, when people came in from all the surrounding region, has given place to a beautiful framed edifice, painted white, having a tower and well-toned bell, and capable of seating perhaps seven hundred persons. I learned that there are now twenty-three meeting-houses in the districts of Hilo and Puna, many of them framed buildings, and some of stone. The church includes all the Protestant professors of religion in these two districts, which, after the lapse of twenty-five years, number four thousand and five hundred. The decrease has been only in proportion to that of the population. The male and female church-members are nearly equal in number.

On the Sabbath following our arrival, the church bell sent forth the hallowed sounds to which I had been accustomed in my native land, and a suitably dressed congregation assembled, of whom, thirty years before, very few would have had any decent clothing, or any feeling on the subject. And that congregation listened, in the forenoon of that day, and also of the next Sabbath, with marked attention, to a statement, interpreted by Mr. Coan, of what I had seen during my visits to our missions in the Eastern World, accompanied by such practical suggestions as occurred to me. On the second Sabbath, fifty or sixty of the "leading men," — *lunas* perhaps they would be called — remained after the service, and repeated among themselves (as the pastor informed me) nearly all my facts; showing that they had in a good measure remembered and appreciated them. There was something significant, moreover, in the warm greeting and shaking of hands, which followed our meeting, not only with myself, but with my wife and daughter. And then their *aloha* — their expressive word of greeting! There could be no mistaking the facts, nor their significance.

Hilo, notwithstanding the beauty of its scenery,

used to be regarded with disfavor, as a place of residence, on account of the excessive rains. During our visit they sometimes poured down in torrents. But the intervals were bright and cheering, and there is said to be a season of the year when the rains are intermitted, of which season the residents speak in terms of warm admiration. Such is the productiveness of the soil in consequence of this abundant moisture, that foreigners are appropriating large tracts in Hilo to the culture of the sugar-cane.

We started for Kilauéa, the great volcano, on Tuesday, March 17th, under the guidance of Mr. Coan, within whose missionary district the volcano is situated. Our company, which was all on horseback, consisted of three ladies and four gentlemen. We were two days on the way, both in going and returning, and it rained nearly all that time. The first four miles was over a bad road, in an open country, with more or less of the *pandanus* and *kukui* trees; then through a forest of *ohias*, with their trunks nearly concealed by the climbing vines. Then came gigantic ferns, and an extensive tract covered with the *ti* trees, their bright green leaves overtopping the ferns. These abound in saccharine matter, and our horses were eager to pluck them by the way. Elsewhere I found natives eating the root of the *ti* plant, as a part of their daily food. They bake it under ground, as they do the taro, when it is softened, and abounds in sweet, nourishing juice.

Nothing but a faithful execution of the temperance law prevents the abundant manufacture of an intoxicating drink from this plant.

We were thankful for a pleasant day at the volcano, as well as for a comfortable grass house during the two nights we were there. The crater is four thousand feet above the level of the sea, yet the ascent was scarcely perceptible. The party of Commodore Wilkes, when here some years since, visited another active crater at the top of this mountain, at an elevation some ten thousand feet higher. Of course the two craters could have no connection; or, if they have one, it must be at a vast depth. The crater at Kilauea has a diameter of three miles, and the only practicable descent appeared to be in front of the house. It is fatiguing, but not dangerous — a walk of half a mile. You then stand on the great black ledge, or floor of the crater, and have a walk of two miles to the burning lake. The surface is broken, irregular, and indescribable. We passed a miniature range of mountains, enough to show how the mighty ranges along the eastern shore of this ocean may have resulted from similar agencies. Jets of scalding steam were seen all over the field, and so they were on the upper surface around the house. The burning lake was at that time about fifty feet below the black ledge, but is said to rise and fall. A few days later we heard that the molten mass was near the brim. A mighty power operates beneath; for every now and then the lava swelled into an immense dome, while elsewhere it tossed itself up in jets of sixty or eighty feet. The heat and gases allow of approach only on the windward side. The scene was most impressive. We saw one of God's wonderful works. The Hawaiians, in their heathen state, recognized a godlike power here, to which they gave the name of Pele, and when they came it was with offerings and prayers. In a book belonging to the house where we lodged, we recorded our impressions — "GREAT AND MARVELLOUS ARE THY WORKS, LORD GOD ALMIGHTY!"

Kanoa met us here — a native foreign missionary, then on a visit home from Micronesia. He was making the tour of his native isle, with his wife and child, giving the people an account of his mission. He is an interesting man, and preceded me just one week in my circuit of the island. I was glad afterwards to know that he had nearly as large audiences as my own. He himself travelled on foot. At the joint request of Mr. Coan and the parents, I baptized Kanoa's infant daughter at the volcano, by the name of Harieta Kaui.

This visit afforded me an opportunity for seeing something of religious life as it exists in rural districts and grass houses. The first night we stopped in a wild region. There being but one room in the native house, the family cheerfully vacated it for us, going to a hut near by, after spreading their best mats on the floor for our convenience. At the proper time they came in to prayers, as did the men who

NATIVE GRASS HOUSE.

carried our luggage. The master of the house then produced his Hawaiian Bible, in the royal octavo form, and, at the request of Mr. Coan, made one of the prayers. At the volcano house our natives always joined us at family prayers, and more than one of them led in the devotions. There is only a small native population on this route, the people preferring to live along the sea-shore.

The station at Hilo was commenced by Messrs. Ruggles and Goodrich, in 1824; and the subsequent laborers were Messrs. Coan, Dibble, Lyman, Wilcox, Green, and Wetmore. Mr. Coan has been the chief laborer, and commenced his residence in

1836, and only he, Mr. Lyman, and Dr. Wetmore have made Hilo their place of permanent abode.

The Boarding School for boys, under the care of Mr. Lyman, has been in operation twenty-seven years, having been commenced in 1836. Its average number of pupils is fifty-four, and the whole number from the beginning is six hundred. It has furnished a goodly number of schoolmasters for the island, and its graduates are found scattered over the group. It was founded, and has been mainly supported, by the American Board; which also contributed $2000, some years since, towards erecting the present excellent building, in place of one destroyed by fire. The government advanced $4000, and foreign and native friends on the island $2500. The institution has a charter, and the missionaries on the Island of Hawaii are the trustees. Mr. Lyman derives his support from the Board, and his associate, Mr. Alexander, from a government grant.[1]

In the year 1839 Mrs. Coan opened a boarding school with twenty girls, which was in great measure

[1] "Through the kindness of Mr. Lyman I was present at an examination of the scholars. Sacred geography and arithmetic were the two branches most dwelt upon. The exercises in mental arithmetic would have done credit to our own country, for they were quite as proficient in them as could possibly have been expected. I was much pleased with the arrangements of the dormitory, eating-rooms, hospital, and with the appearance of the 'farm,' or the few acres they had under cultivation." — *U. S. Exploring Expedition*, vol. iv. p. 211.

self-supporting.[1] It was continued nearly ten years, with much success, until increased family cares obliged its founder to discontinue it.

The district of Kau lies on the south-east side of Hawaii, and Waiohinu, the station, is forty miles from the volcano, on the opposite side from Hilo. On Tuesday, 24th of March, we took steamer, and I landed at the port a few miles from Waiohinu, with my daughter; while my wife, not being equal to the severe land journey from thence to Kona, went on to Kaawaloa by water.

My third Sabbath on Hawaii was spent in Kau. Rev. O. H. Gulick, son of a missionary, resides at this place. Here I was more interested than I expected to be. The population of the district scarcely exceeds four thousand, and the Roman Catholics have obtained more hold than we could wish, owing to past adverse circumstances. The stone church holds six or seven hundred people, and was full on the Sabbath. Scarcely less than two hundred horses stood fastened to lava stones in the adjoining fields. Near the close of one of the meetings an aged deacon addressed me thus: "Sir, had you come to these Islands when you began to correspond with the missionaries, you would have found us naked; but now we are clothed from head to foot." It was

[1] Missionary Herald, 1840, p. 251.

even so; and I began to think, in view of what I had already seen, that the burden of proof rests with those who presume to deny to these people the Christian name.

The stated ministrations of the gospel were commenced here by Mr. Paris in 1842, and the subsequent laborers were Mr. Kinney and Mr. Shipman, who are both now deceased. When I expressed my admiration of the roads, I was told they were mainly owing to the enterprise of these departed brethren. A valuable two-story house, built by Mr. Paris and owned by the Board, stands on the hill-side, with a small stream of water running down from above, and an extended view of land and sea. Waiohinu seemed to me an eligible place for a boarding-school for the education of female teachers and the wives of native ministers. Though retired, it is accessible by steam.

Mr. Kinney died in California, nine years ago, whither he had gone for health. Mr. Shipman took his place, and finished his career at the close of 1861. Mr. Gulick succeeded him in the fall of 1862. Intemperance, an easily besetting sin of the people, made sad inroads upon the church while it was without pastoral care; though the people kept up their public worship, and their usual collections for the institutions of the gospel. Mr. Shipman possessed a rare executive talent, and was regarded by foreign residents as a model missionary. I was told it was his own impression, as he drew near the close of life, that he had given an undue proportion of time and strength to merely civilizing influences, and the material prosperity of his people. This may account in part for their spiritual weakness when the supporting hand of their pastor had been withdrawn. How slow we are to learn that civilization is a blessing to a barbarous people only as it is permeated by the spirit and power of the gospel! Under the new pastor the church resumed its discipline, and the disorders ceased.

A younger brother of Mr. Gulick was at this time at Waiohinu, and the two being missionary sons, their observations were from a somewhat different point of view from those of the fathers. The pastor's wife is a daughter of Mr. Clark, of Honolulu; and the wife and family of Dr. L. H. Gulick, of the Micronesia Mission, who was then in the United States, were also there. Mr. Lyman, another missionary son, came twenty miles from his ranch towards the volcano. Thus I found myself in a choice company of the second generation. Sabbath evening I baptized three children — a child of Dr. Gulick, an adopted (native) child of the pastor, and the son of a native preacher. Cherished be the memory of Kau, — its roads, and scenes, and Christian people!

CHAPTER VIII.

HAWAII.

Fatiguing Ride. — Vast Lava Deposits. — Family Scene. — Enter Kona. — Pleasant Sojourn. — Kealakekua Bay. — Home of Kapiolani and Naihe. — Their Christian Labors. — Results. — Their Farewell to Mr. Stewart. — Their Death. — The Station. — City of Refuge. — Last Battle for the Idols. — Fiery Cataract. — Home of Obookiah. — Christian Congregation. — Monthly Concert Contribution. — Scenes on the Way to Kailua. — Lands owned by Foreigners. — The first Station. — Interesting Anniversary and Sabbath. — The People coming to Church. — Female Equestrians. — Meeting the Lunas. — Church Edifice and Congregation. — Horses tied in the Fields. — Interesting Celebration of the Lord's Supper.

A HORSEBACK ride of sixty miles from Waiohinu to South Kona, in a day and a half, is no pleasure excursion. At least I found it not so, though the young lady with me professed to enjoy it. Mr. O. H. Gulick was our companion and guide. Nearly a dozen miles were across those rough clinker fields called *a-a*, on which the broken lava is piled ten or fifteen feet above the smooth, hard *pahoihoi*. But for a narrow horse-path made by the government, our way would have been impracticable. The scenes were novel and interesting. Whence came these masses of scoria over so many thousand acres? The geologist should pass that way. The clinkers were often very large, and lay in every conceivable position, looking as if they had been forced up, and broken, and tumbled about by some mighty agency underneath.[1] After crossing the *a-a*, we travelled a

[1] Since writing the above, I found that a highly intelligent geologist had been in that neighborhood, if not actually that way. I refer to Prof. James D. Dana, who visited the Hawaiian Islands in 1840, as the geologist of Commodore Wilkes's Exploring Expedition. The following is his account of the clinker fields: —

"The solid lava fields (the *pahoihoi* of the natives) and the clinker regions are generally associated together. In several instances we passed abruptly from the former to the latter, and then returned to the smooth lavas again. There is no doubt that the whole was one single region of eruption, and these different results arose from different phases in the volcanic action of one and the same period. The clinker fields are usually twenty or thirty feet the highest, and the passage from one to the other is by a steep ascent.

"Clinker fields are a common feature over the whole surface of Mount Loa. They evidently proceed from a temporary cessation (either complete or partial), and a subsequent flow of a stream of lava. The surface cools and hardens as soon as the stream slackens; afterwards there is another heaving of the lava, and an onward move, owing to a succeeding ejection or the removing of an obstacle, and the motion breaks up the hardened crust, piling the masses together either in slabs or huge angular fragments, according to the thickness to which the crust had cooled. It is probable that these clinker regions are sometimes over a fissure of ejection, and arise in these cases from a second outbreak after the previous flow has partially cooled. We thus account for their forming a narrow district crossing a field of pahoihoi. If the motion of a lava stream be quite slow, the cooling of the front of it may cause its cessation, thus damming it up, and holding it back till the pressure from gradual accumulation behind sweeps away the barrier. It then flows on again, carrying on its sur-

score of miles over the *pahoihoi*, hard as adamant, sometimes smooth as glass, along the slope of the mountain, where the molten mass had been indurated in every form of its downward rush towards the sea. It was a wearisome road the first twenty or thirty miles, with scarcely an inhabitant. For the last twenty miles of our journey it was otherwise. We were then in Kona, still travelling high above the sea. Here was more depth of soil; the hill-sides were often beautifully covered with the dense, wide-spreading foliage of the *kukui*, or candlenut tree; and there were breadfruit, banana, and coffee-trees. But we found a scarcity of water, even to quench our thirst, owing to the porosity of the ground. If showers fall, they are immediately absorbed by the cavernous rocks.

The owner of the native grass house where we lodged at night was absent; but the family received us kindly, spread their best mats, gave us a fine large

face masses of the hardened crust, — some, it may be, to sink and melt again, but the larger portion to remain as a field of clinkers. The breaking up of the ice of some streams in spring exemplifies imperfectly this subject, especially those instances in which the crust of lava is thin, and *slabs* are formed. But to obtain a just conception of the magnitude of the effect, the mind must bring before it a stream, not of the limited extent of most rivers, but one of five or ten miles in breadth; besides, in place of smooth and clear ice, there should be substituted shaggy heaps of black scoria, and a depth or thickness of many yards, in place of a few inches." — *Dana's Geology in U. S. Exploring Expedition*, p. 162.

tapa for bed-covering, and lighted a double row of candlenuts. As the evening advanced the neighbors came in, and took their seats on the floor around the room, the family Bible was produced, and, besides a prayer in English, we had two from native brethren resident in the place. As yet the population resides chiefly down near the sea, but is gradually ascending to the more arable regions. Our mountain road was comparatively of recent origin. After entering Kona we could see villages, and one or two stone churches, on the sea-shore, far below us. Mr. Paris met us with fresh horses, ten miles from our journey's end; and about midday, March 31st, father and daughter had a glad welcome from the wife and mother who had preceded us; all the more joyful to her for the letters we brought from loved ones at home. The wife of our host assured us that "all Paris" rejoiced in our arrival.

The steamer being delayed at Honolulu a week for repairs, we enjoyed the hospitality of this family till the 11th of April. In this time we saw much of the region around, and of the people. As has been already intimated, Mr. Paris's house is upon high ground, with a broad view of the sea. Mauna Loa has long forborne to send its lava streams that way, and there is a good depth of soil, with plenty of woodland. Here was the favorite abode of Kapiolani, and her husband Naihe. They owned these lands, and upon them, near where we had our lodgings, she built a stone dwelling-house, which is still standing. When first seen by missionaries, Kapiolani was sitting upon a rock, oiling her person. She was then dark-minded, superstitious, and intemperate. A few years later, this descendant of ancient kings, neatly dressed, serious, dignified in her deportment, a devout and resolute Christian, delighted to receive the messengers of her Lord and Saviour in her well-furnished house, and to discuss with them her plans for improving the character and condition of her people. She united with Kaahumanu in removing the bones of her father, and more than a score of other deified kings and princes of the Hawaiian race, from their sacred deposit, — it may be the "House of Keawe" at Honaunau, — placing them out of the way, in one of the caves high in the precipice at the head of the bay where she resided.

The early introduction of the gospel among the people of this region was through the zeal of Kapiolani and Naihe. At Kaawaloa, beneath a cocoanut grove, where the natives could launch their canoes for fishing, or plunge into the surf for sport, was the residence of these exemplary chiefs. They there built a thatched house of worship, where they and some of their head men read, sung, proclaimed what they knew of the gospel, and urged the people to accept it. They did the same, also, in neighboring villages. Though Kailua was fifteen miles distant, they frequently sent a canoe to that place on Saturday

VIEW OF KEALAKEKUA BAY.

for a missionary, and back with him on Monday. Next they built a house near their own dwelling, and invited Mr. Ely to come and reside there. He came in 1824.

In their heathen state the natives were universally addicted to stealing; but it is recorded that, in less than four years from this time, valuable goods were left in an open shed, unguarded at night and by day, without apprehension or loss. Failure of health sent Mr. Ely from the Islands in 1828, and Mr. Ruggles took his place. His health being impaired, the two good-natured chiefs removed up near where Mr. Paris's house now stands, taking the missionary with them, but leaving the main body of the people on the shore.

The Rev. Charles S. Stewart visited Kaawaloa in 1829, as chaplain of the United States ship of war Vincennes, and speaks of his intercourse with Kapiolani and her husband in strong terms of admiration. He thus describes the final parting, at midnight: —

"The paddlers of the canoe had been aroused from their slumbers; other servants had lighted numerous brilliant torches of the candlenut, tied together in leaves, to accompany us to the water; and I was about giving my parting salutation, when not only Naihe, but Kapiolani also, said, 'No, not here, not here, but at the shore;' and, throwing a mantle around her, attended by her husband, she accompanied us to the surf, where, after many a warm grasp of the hand and a tearful blessing, she remained standing on a point of rock, in bold relief amid the glare of torchlight around her, exclaiming, again and again, as we shoved off, 'Love to you, Mr. Stewart! love to Mrs. Stewart! love to the captain, and love to the king!' while her handkerchief was waved in repetition of the expression, long after her voice was lost in the dashing of the waters, and till her figure was blended, in the distance, with the group by which she was surrounded."

It was gratifying, at the meeting of the American Board at Rochester, in 1863, to see with what freshness and interest Dr. Stewart retained his impressions of that time.

Kapiolani died in 1841, but I did not learn the place of her burial. Naihe preceded her by ten years. They were unlike, but both are believed to have entered upon the "rest," which "remaineth for the people of God." I had long been an admirer of Kapiolani, and had great delight in treading upon ground once familiar to her steps. "Blessed are the dead which die in the Lord."

The other laborers in this district, until the year 1852, were Messrs. Forbes, Van Duzee, Ives, and Pogue; and these were followed by Mr. Paris. Mr. Forbes removed the station down upon the south side of Kealakekua Bay, as being more convenient for the people. The meeting-house stands there now; but the site for the dwelling of the missionary was not so happily chosen. We could realize, as we crossed the broad waste of *a-a*, between it and the shore, that there was heat enough in that dreary expanse of lava to spoil the best sea-breeze that ever passed over it. We were then on our way, with Mr. Paris, to Honaunau, — the celebrated "city of refuge" in times of heathenism, — five or six miles beyond the bay. There were two of these refuges on Hawaii, there having been one at Waipio on the north. To these all might flee, whatever their condition or crime. The gates were ever open, and there the pursuer must stop. Non-combatants awaited there the issue of battles, and thither the vanquished fled and were safe. Honaunau is said to have had its origin as a city of refuge near three hundred years ago, in the reign of Keawe. A *macadamized* horse-road, five or six feet broad, leads to it across a field of clinkers, made by breaking down the smaller masses and reducing them to fragments. The refuge is an enclosure upon the seashore, more than seven hundred feet in length, and four hundred broad, with high, thick walls of lava, and two enormous heaps of stones. These heaps were *heiaus*, and one had an altar for human sacrifices. The walls were formerly surmounted in their whole extent with images four rods apart. Cocoanut trees abound within and without. A rock is shown within the walls, beneath which Kaahumanu, when a young wife, is said to have hid herself from her royal spouse, his anger having been kindled against her. It is called by her name.

On our way to this place Mr. Paris directed our

attention to the plain of Kuamu, between us and the shore, where the forces of Liholiho fought the battle for the suppression of idolatry in 1819. How much depended on that conflict! Was the favorable result an answer to the prayers of Obookiah, Mills, Worcester, Evarts, and the company of missionaries then on its way? It was thus the way was prepared for the joyful announcement to the missionaries, soon after, as they approached the coast not far from this spot, "*The Islands are at peace — the tabu system is no more — the gods are destroyed — the temples are demolished!*" Even savage warfare is among the instrumentalities for good, in the hands of an all-wise and infinite Providence.

A mile or more beyond the Refuge, we came upon a great natural curiosity. The molten lava of a remote age had flowed over a precipice of still more ancient lava, seventy or eighty feet high, and had the appearance of being suddenly indurated, looking as we might suppose the Falls of Niagara would look were the waters to be at once congealed. A vaulted avenue of considerable length is thus formed beneath. Doubtless there was the terrific spectacle of a wide, unbroken fiery stream down this lofty steep. But no sudden induration of it was possible. What we now see doubtless came into existence near the close of the eruption, when the fall of lava would be in detached, semi-fluid masses, which, resting upon each other, would form a column gradually rising to the top; and then the fluid lava would flow over the outside of the arch to the plain below.

There are four substantial stone churches in South Kona, erected by the inhabitants, and capable together of seating twenty-five hundred people. The largest of these is the central one, near the Kealakekua side of the bay. There, on the Sabbath, I addressed a good-looking native congregation, which filled the house. I saw their manner of taking up a monthly concert collection. I learned from Mr. Paris that it is a way of their own devising, and which they prefer. Just before the sermon two leading men took their seats at the table in front of the pulpit. The whole people having been divided into classes, somewhat after the Methodist custom, each with a *luna*, or leader, the presiding deacon called the name of the *luna*, when all of his division who chose to contribute came forward to the table, and laid down their money, while the other took note of the contributions, and the names of the donors. This practice has a singular resemblance to the habit of our forefathers. In the Life and Times of William Brewster, it is said that, after the sermon, "the deacon puts the congregation in mind of the duty of contributing for the poor and the support of public worship, when the governor and all the others *go to the deacons' seat, deposit their gifts, and return.*"

On Friday, April 10th, we heard that the king and

queen had left Kailua, in an English war steamer, which had been there for several days, on their return to Honolulu. We had planned to spend the Sabbath at Kailua, and found nothing there to divide the attention of the people. The distance is twelve miles, and all the way is in full view of the ocean. The Pacific seemed then rightly named; but far different was our experience in the rough passage from San Francisco to the Islands, and far, far more in the terrible hurricane we experienced on our homeward voyage from San Francisco to Panama! Kailua was a favorite resort of the old chiefs; mainly, it would seem, on account of the smoothness of the sea, which gave them a more abundant supply of fish.

The king has a fine summer-house at Kailua, on the sea-shore, built by Kuakini. But, excepting the Protestant church opposite the royal dwelling, and the Roman Catholic church, this is the only respectable building. The village, which is said once to have contained three thousand inhabitants, is now but a poor remnant of its former self. Mr. Paris *ma* (as the islanders express it, *ma* here meaning *family*) accompanied us; all, excepting our daughter and myself, going in a four-wheeled carriage, presented to Mr. Paris by a relative in New York. We found a tolerable road nearly all the way. Along the shore it was good, and passed through several villages and cocoanut groves. We stopped a while in one of the groves. The people came around to shake hands, and boys climbed the tall trees, and threw down green nuts, that we might refresh ourselves with the water they afforded. We were then in North Kona. The arable uplands in both the Konas are owned chiefly by foreigners, who, on this part of the island, are for the most part Englishmen. One of them, a well-informed, gentlemanly man, has a large orange plantation. Indeed, the best of the lands on all the Islands appear to be fast going into foreign hands; and one of the allegations made to me by a foreign resident against the missionaries was, that their influence was against such a transfer. Mr. Paris told me, however, that to prevent the lands immediately about him, once owned by the admirable Kapiolani, from going to strangers he knew not who, he had felt obliged to invest his own private funds in them. It darkens the prospects of the native race that so small a portion of their territory is held by the common people, and that so many of the chiefs, the great landholders, have been improvident, and become involved in debt and mortgages, to the consequent loss of their possessions. I have more apprehension on this score than from the revelations made by the census; for how can the native race maintain itself in the presence of another and superior one, after this has come into the ownership of the soil?

It has been already stated that the first station on the Islands occupied by the mission was at Kailua. Mr. and Mrs. Thurston landed there on the 12th of

April, 1820, from the brig Thaddeus, and made Kailua their home until the recent failure of Mr. Thurston's health. They had been absent more than a year on that account, and were then in California. We occupied their house, situated on the black lava above the old village, and found much to remind us of these venerable servants of God. The village had in great measure disappeared, the people having removed to the more elevated grounds. Cultivation is scarcely possible near that shore, except in small patches. Indeed, there was little except a surface of lava to be seen around the village. We learn from Mr. Ellis that the point running three or four miles into the sea, making the northern boundary of the bay, was formed only twenty-three years before his time (that is, about the year 1800), by an eruption from one of the craters on the top of Mount Hualalai, which filled up a deep bay twenty miles in length. Of this there were still living witnesses. There was a similar occurrence on the coast in the year 1859, about thirty miles to the north, only from a different volcano.

Our Sabbath at Kailua, being the 12th of April, was the forty-third anniversary of the commencement of that station, and indeed of the mission. It was one of our most interesting days. The native preacher had given notice from the pulpit of our coming, and at an early hour the people were seen galloping in from all quarters, — for almost every Hawaiian is the owner of a horse or two, and they ride on the gallop, — the women riding as fast and in the same manner as the men, but with such an adjustment of robes as renders the position becoming. Between the first and second bells the *lunas*, or principal men of the church, as many as could

NATIVE WOMAN ON HORSEBACK.

be seated in Mr. Thurston's study, assembled there for prayer, and to talk over church matters, as their custom is. When they had completed their business, I was invited in, and received a very cordial greeting. They were well-dressed men, not a few were in middle age, and some were younger. Only one remembered the landing of Mr. Thurston, and he was the main pillar of the church. It was hopeful to see so many comparatively young men holding a prominent place in the church. The meeting-house is a large stone building, with high galleries and a high pulpit. It now greatly needs repairs and alterations, which would cost so much that it is not clear what ought to be done. On our way to church we found horses tied in every direction; there were hundreds of them, — Mr. Paris thought there were five hundred. The Lord's Supper was celebrated, in the afternoon, by as many as six or seven hundred communicants, — the congregation in the morning having been somewhat over a thousand, — and my feelings were drawn out while I dwelt on the grand object of the Supper as substantially the same with that of the mission we had so long maintained among them — namely, TO SHOW FORTH THE LORD'S DEATH. I know not that I was ever more conscious of being in fellowship with God's people.

CHAPTER IX.

HAWAII.

Landing at Kohala. — Mr. Bond's Opinion of his Church. — Congregation on a rainy Day. — Over the Mountains of Kohala to Waimea. — Desolated Fields and Villages. — Former Games and Sports. — Cause of their Decline. — Effect of radiated Heat. — Fine View of Mauna Kea. — Mauna Loa, and the Eruption of 1859. — Enthusiastic Meeting. — Address by Timotéo. — Original Hymn by Liana. — Version by Mr. Bingham. — Native Customs. — Mr. Bond's District. — District of Mr. Lyons. — Estimate of his Field. — Kawaihae and the Great Heiau. — Incident in the Life of Timotéa.

Bidding an affectionate and grateful farewell to our missionary friends, we embarked in the steamer, at an early hour on Monday morning, for North Kohala, the district under the care of Mr. Bond, where we landed at noon. Mr. Bond was waiting with horses for myself and daughter, and a friendly neighbor of German origin with a wagon for my wife. We had to face a strong trade-wind, but moved rapidly along a good road, seven miles, to Mr. Bond's. We met a shower, and rain kept us in-doors during most of the week. But I found most useful and agreeable occupation in conference with my missionary brother, especially with regard to the morals of the church-members, on which he had written us more freely, and perhaps more disparagingly, than any others. We also had much conversation on the proposed change in our plan of operations, now that the Islands have been Christianized. Mr. Bond is strong in his belief of the existence of piety among his people. He has as much certainty of meeting many of his church-members in heaven, as he can have of anything, and believes that as large a portion of his church give evidence of piety — the proper allowance being made — as is usual in our churches at home. Knowing how anxious he had been in his letters to prevent our having exaggerated views of the progress of the work, it was very pleasing to me to hear these opinions. The easily besetting sins of these Islands are impurity and intemperance; but he perceived no hesitation in his church to discipline for these sins, "cut where it will." He had never known a case where discipline was not carried through, and by the people themselves. Impurity was so universal among the people in their late heathen condition, and the manners, habits, and language became so corrupted by it, that there has not yet been time to form a strong public sentiment and to create a sufficiently sensitive conscience in respect to it, even in the church. I called Mr. Bond's attention to the Corinthian church, as it is spoken of by the apostle Paul in his Epistles, and he had no doubt that there were fewer evils, and of less magnitude, in his own church, than there would seem to have been in that noted church of the apostolic age. He said there had been great progress in the morals of the church during the twenty-two years of his residence in Kohala, and a still greater progress in intelligence. The people are poor, but they take as many as eighty-five copies of the "Kuokoa," — a semi-religious newspaper in the native language, published by Mr. Whitney at Honolulu, — though paying two dollars a year for it, *in advance.* The morning of the Sabbath was exceedingly rainy, and Mr. Bond doubted whether many of his people would assemble at the place of worship; but, to our mutual surprise, the house was well filled, and I had not a more attentive audience on the Islands.

The next day he went with us part of the way to Waimea, in South Kohala, where Mr. Lyons met us. The distance to Waimea is nearly thirty miles on the road we took, which led over the mountains of Kohala. Our German friend again came with his wagon for my wife, and went fifteen miles, — as far as the road permitted. The remainder of the distance she travelled on horseback. The North Kohala station was at first situated on one of these heights, where now there is not an inhabitant. It was affecting to see the large open country, most of which had evidently been once under cultivation, now given over to foreign pasturage, and the villages nearly all gone.

We passed a long, steep declivity, with the evident

marks upon it of the down-hill slides of former generations. This tropical counterpart of the winter sport of our own young people was on narrow sledges, with polished runners, from seven to twelve or eighteen feet long. The runners were separated four or five inches at the hinder part, but at the foremost end approached to within about two inches. They were connected together by cross-pieces, and two long, tough sticks were fastened to these on either side, extending the whole length of the cross-pieces.

"The person about to slide grasps the small side-stick firmly with his right hand, somewhere about the middle, runs a few yards to the brow of the hill, or starting-place, where he grasps the other stick with his left hand, and at the same time throws himself forward flat upon it, and slides down the hill, his hands retaining their hold of the side-sticks, and his feet being fixed against the hindermost cross-piece of the sledge. Much practice is necessary to assume and keep an even balance on so narrow a vehicle; yet a man accustomed to the sport will throw himself, with velocity and apparent ease, one hundred and fifty or two hundred yards down a gradually sloping hill."[1]

Those who slide farthest are the victors. This is one of the sports which seems to have passed away with the race of chiefs. There were others. Among the curiosities brought from the Islands is a

[1] Ellis's Tour, p. 265.

circular stone, adapted to rolling, made of compact lava, or a white alluvial rock, three or four inches in diameter, an inch in thickness around the edge, but thicker in the centre, and polished. These were bowled along a smooth surface, thirty or forty yards, the effort being to throw the stone between two sticks stuck in the ground only a few inches apart, but without striking either, or else to reach the greatest distance. At other times, the game of strength and skill being substantially the same, a blunt kind of dart or javelin, ingeniously made of heavy wood, was used instead of the bowls. Another popular game was the finding of a small stone hid under some one of five pieces of native cloth.

Much having been said, in certain quarters, of the calamity that has come upon the natives in consequence of the loss of these and other games of sport, I quote the remarks of Mr. Ellis on the subject, made nearly forty years ago: —

"Were their games followed only as sources of amusement, they would be comparatively harmless; but the demoralizing influence of the various kinds of gambling existing among them is very extensive. Scarcely an individual resorts to their games but for the purpose of betting; and at these periods all the excitement, anxiety, exultation, and rage, which such pursuits invariably produce, are not only visible in every countenance, but fully acted out, and all the malignant passions which gambling engenders are indulged without restraint. We have seen females hazarding their beads, scissors, beating mallets, and every piece of cloth they possessed, except what they wore, on a throw of *uru* or *páhe*. In the same throng might be seen the farmer with his *oo*, and other implements of husbandry; the builder of canoes, with his hatchets and adzes; and some poor man with a knife and the mat on which he slept, — all eager to stake every article they possessed on the success of their favorite player; and when they have lost all, we have known them, frantic with rage, to tear their hair from their heads on the spot. This is not all; the sport seldom terminates without quarrels, sometimes of a serious nature, ensuing between the adherents of the different parties.

"Since schools have been opened in the Islands, and the natives have been induced to direct their attention to Christian instruction and intellectual improvement, we have had the satisfaction to observe these games much less followed than formerly; and we hope the period is fast approaching when they shall only be the healthful exercise of children, and when the time and strength devoted to purposes so useless, and often injurious, shall be employed in cultivating their fertile soil, augmenting their sources of individual and social happiness, and securing to themselves the enjoyment of the comforts and privileges of civilized and Christian life." [1]

Our road down the mountain towards Waimea was through a forest, and chiefly along a horse-path. The mission premises are twelve miles from the sea, on the upper and elevated part of what seemed a vast plain as beheld from the mountain, but which

[1] Tour, p. 171.

is really broken into hills and valleys, with a continued descent towards Kawaihae. During the last hour or two of our ride we had a striking illustration of the effect of radiated heat upon the clouds. A mountain ridge ran along our left from west to east, and the dark rain-clouds, coming up to the mountain ridge, threatened constantly to pass over and pour down a deluge upon us. But there was a line beyond which the clouds could not hold together, and that was the line of radiation from the southern slope of the mountain.

I should not forget to mention the snowy summit of Mauna Kea, towards the east, of purest white, looking out from among the clouds, and sparkling in the sunbeams; carrying our thoughts to a brighter, purer world than the one in which we were travelling. This noble mountain is seen to great advantage from Waimea, the residence of Mr. Lyons, swelling majestically from across the plain. We have here, also, a good view of Mauna Loa, on the south, and may trace the whole, or nearly the whole, of the black lava-stream of the eruption in 1859, which broke out near the summit, and ran down thirty miles to the sea. Mr. Lyons describes the long river of fire, which he saw distinctly from his house, as terribly sublime.

A meeting of the native Christians of the districts of South Kohala and Hamakua had been called for Wednesday. The rain kept many away, or the neatly-cushioned meeting-house would not have contained half the multitude. The house was full; and both pastor and people had studied to make the most of the occasion. Two poetic pieces had been composed by Liana and Samuela, native church-members, which were sung with much animation by a large choir; and Timotéo, the senior deacon of the church, delivered an address of his own composing. The meeting of two hours, for variety and enthusiasm, would have met the requirements of the best missionary districts in our own country. The address is valuable as an original testimony to the work of grace in that region, and I insert a translation of it made for me by Mr. Lyons. While there was no effort to preserve the native idiom in the expression of thoughts, the rendering is understood to be otherwise literal. The address was as follows: —

"The church-members of the highlands of Waimea, the old men, the aged women, the strong men, the youth and children, tender, through me, their salutation to you, the Secretary, your companion, and daughter. Great, indeed, is our joy in being permitted to see you, to welcome you to our land. You have been sent by the learned Missionary Society of great America, as its delegate, to see the works of the gospel heralds you have sent to us.

"We, the ancient men of Kamehameha's time, were once idolaters, murderers, guilty of infanticide, polygamy, and constantly quarrelling one with another.

"On the death of Kamehameha, the kingdom devolved on his son Liholiho. He abolished idolatry, broke the tabus; men and women for the first time ate together, and the temples and gods were burned to ashes.

"Still we lived on in poverty and darkness, and in secret worship of idols, and were without the knowledge of the living and true God. Men, women, and children were promiscuously devoted to the most sordid pleasures, heathenish dances, and revelries, day and night. In the year 1820, the missionaries, Mr. Bingham and company, came to these Islands to proclaim the blessed gospel to us, who knew not God, nor had heard of the death of Jesus, the Messiah, the Saviour of the world.

"It was you, the Missionary Society you represent, that loved us, and sent the good missionaries to our dark land.

"The king and his premier allowed the missionaries to dwell with us; to introduce a new order of things; to teach us first the twelve letters of the alphabet; then spelling, then reading and writing.

"During the forty-three years the missionaries have resided on the Islands, much seed has been sown, much labor performed, and wonderful have been the results. We were once all dark, buried in darkness, sunk to the lowest depths of ignorance; roaming about the fields and woods, like wild beasts; without clothing; our naked bodies most shamefully exposed and blackened by the sun; without books, without Bibles, without Christianity; plunging into the darkness of hell. Now, we are clothed, like civilized beings; we are Christianized; we are gathered into churches; we are intelligent; we are supplied with books, Bibles, and hymn-books; and are living for God and for heaven. And this through the labors of the missionaries you have sent us.

"Our joy is inexpressible in seeing you; and we beg you to carry back to your associates, to the Missionary Society, to all the American churches connected with it, the warmest salutations of the churches of Waimea and Hamakua."

The poem by Liana I submitted to the inspection of the Rev. Mr. Bingham, since my return, and he pronounces it a gem in Hawaiian literature, and has sent me a metrical version, designed to be a faithful expression of the original. I copy both the original, and the English version.

THE ORIGINAL.

"Nani ke aloha la!
Me ka olioli pu
I ka malihini hou —
E aloha, aloha oe.

"Holo oia a maanei,
Mai Amerika mai no,
Eia no! ua komo mai —
E aloha, aloha oe.

"A, ma keia la maikai,
Hui aloha pu kakou,
Ma ka Luakini nei;
E aloha, aloha oe.

"E hauoli, oli pu,
E na hoahanau a pau,
Kane, wahine, keiki no,
E aloha, aloha oe.

"Na ia nei i hoouna mai
I na misioneri nei,
E ao mai ia kakou nei;
E aloha, aloha oe.

"E ala, oli kakou pu,
A kokua aloha no
Ka makua o kakou; —
E aloha, aloha mau."

METRICAL VERSION.

"Wonderful that love sincere!
Great our joint rejoicings here,
For the stranger guest we see;
Cordial welcome, friend, to thee.

"Sailing far to reach our homes,
From America he comes;
Lo! in peace he enters here;
Welcome to our hearts sincere.

"Now, on this delightful day,
We, in love, unite to pray:
Here, beneath our temple spire,
We our welcome give thee, sire.

"Jointly chanting, now rejoice;
Brethren, all unite your voice;
Husbands, wives, and little ones,
Greet this friend with grateful tones.

"This is he who hither sends
These true missionary friends,
To enlighten our dark mind;
Thanks and love to one so kind.

"Let us then all rise and sing,
And our grateful succor bring
For our sire our love to prove —
Love, good will, unceasing love."

The meeting closed with a formal introduction of the deacons and the representatives from the several parts of the district, and with a universal shaking of hands. Not a few, also, put small coins into the hands of myself and wife, according to an old custom on such occasions, which we were obliged to accept at the time. The ten dollars thus contributed were devoted to the purchase of Bibles for the use of the Bible-class and female prayer-meetings at Waimea.

Mr. Bond's district is North Kohala; that of Mr. Lyons includes South Kohala and Hamakua. The station in the former was begun by Mr. Bliss, in 1838, on the high top of one of the hills, where the chief resided, and where he built a great grass meeting-house. The trade-winds, rushing furiously across those hills, at length demolished the building, and the missionary was then allowed to remove lower down, near the sea. Mr. Bailey was here for a time. Mr. Bond came in 1841, and was the means of building the present house of worship, which is made of stone, and has a tower and bell. More than two thousand hopeful converts have been received into the North Kohala church, and its present members are nearly a thousand, or about one third of the population. A small boarding-school for training teachers, begun in 1842, and supported without any direct resort to public funds, has sent forth a hundred and fifty pupils. Among these are many schoolmasters. They are taught only in the vernacular.

The Hawaiian Waimea was originally a health resort, being some three or four thousand feet higher than the sea. The resident missionaries, at different times, have been Messrs. Ruggles, Baldwin, Knapp, and Lyons. The history of the church in that district is chiefly connected, however, with Mr. Lyons, who, for thirty years, has labored there with apostolic zeal. It is due to him, as it is also to the work at the Islands, that I go somewhat into a statement of facts. Like Mr. Coan, Mr. Lyons has been a bold operator. In the first year of the great awakening (1838) he admitted 2600 to the church, whom he regarded as hopeful converts, and nearly as many more in the following year. The whole number of persons admitted is 7267; of whom 3760 have died, and 1752 are now in regular church standing. The population of his district in 1860 was 3448; consequently somewhat more than half of the inhabitants are church-members, which must be a large part of the adult population. This is certainly an extraordinary state of things; and I was ready, with some of my brethren residing elsewhere, to apprehend that the matter of a public profession of religion had been carried too far, especially as I was told, though by one not residing in the district, that intemperance was considerably prevalent among church-members in Hamakua.

I frankly stated the case as I had heard it to Mr. Lyons. The facts on the other side were briefly these. Mr. Lyons possesses a most amiable and pious spirit, and may have been led to judge too charitably. But he is very active and self-denying, and has been accustomed to make the tour of his large district several times in a year, notwithstanding its mountains, ravines, and copious rains. He has always travelled on foot, until the recent decline in his health. He was usually accompanied by a deacon, and by one or two men to carry his bedding, clothing, food, and cooking apparatus. In each of these tours he has preached much, and conversed with large numbers; and he believes that he understands the nature of his field and the character of his people. He declares their standard of morals to be as high as can reasonably be expected, and that such is always his feeling on returning from his tours. He says, also, that we should judge his people by their fruits. Within six years they have expended almost twenty thousand dollars in building thirteen meeting-houses, and furnishing them with bells. Government schools are taught in six of these, towards the building of which the government afforded aid to the extent of two hundred dollars for each; and there were subscriptions in the other island churches amounting to five hundred dollars. For each of these houses of worship a church had been partially organized, but no native had yet been ordained to the pastorate. Two *hakus*, sub-pastors, or licensed preachers, had been appointed to each, and Mr. Lyons thought the time had come for instituting a more thorough native ministry. The greater portion of the native families own the New Testament, and are able to read it, and many have the whole Bible. More than a hundred copies of the "Kuokoa" are taken in this district.

The house of worship at Waimea, both within and without, would befit any of our own smaller country villages. In olden times, when the people from all quarters were accustomed to assemble there, the wall now enclosing the yard of the church formed the sides and ends of a vast thatched meeting-house. The congregation we met in the present building was certainly as Christian in its aspects as any one we saw on the Islands. Nor will the reflecting reader think lightly of the fact that, up to the thirtieth year of Mr. Lyons's labors, the church gathered in his district has declined no farther in numbers than has the population, has had no marked apostasy, no violent disruption, and is in as good repute as it was twenty years ago.

Such are the prominent facts; and while it is probable that there is chaff, and perhaps no small amount of it, among the wheat, it seems to me not improbable that our active, impulsive, devoted Christian brother will have an unusual number of stars in his crown of rejoicing.

Thursday we went down to Kawaihae, on the coast, accompanied by Mr. Lyons. The descent was along a valley of great width, with Mauna Kea behind, the Kohala mountains on one side, Mauna Loa on the other, and Mauna Hualalai and the ocean in front. On approaching the shore we ascended the great *heiau* of Kamehameha, built before his invasion of Oahu; one of the largest, and probably the latest, of the heathen temples. It was dedicated to Tiari, his god of war. Its length is upwards of two hundred feet, and its breadth a hundred feet — a huge mass of loose, black lava stones. On the top is a fine view of the sea. Somewhere upon it stood the idol, surrounded by images of inferior deities. We were shown the place where human victims were offered. The images have all long since disappeared; nor did the natives who accompanied us feel any alarm as they entered the once dreaded precincts.

The inhabitants of the island were summoned from all quarters for the erection of this heiau. The deacon Timotéo, author of the address at Waimea, was born in Hamakua, while his parents were on their way from Hilo in obedience to this order, and would have been killed, his father not knowing what to do with him, but for the compassion of an uncle, who adopted the child and took it to Hilo.

We were very hospitably received and entertained by Mr. Allen, son of the excellent Chief Justice, to whom we had a letter from the father. The steamer brought Mr. Bond, on his way to the Oahu College, where his son was recovering from a dangerous sickness; and also Mrs. Hitchcock, one of our missionary widows, who was to accompany Mr. Lyons on his return home.

CHAPTER X.

MAUI.

Wailuku. — Historic Facts. — Soil and Productions. — Meeting-houses. — Sabbath Congregation. — Native Address. — Station of Mr. Green in East Maui. — Mountain Scenery. — Field of branching Coral. — Lahaina. — Church building. — Lord's Supper. — Historical. — The Queen-Mother Keopuolani. — Beautiful Instance of filial Love in the King. — The Queen's Baptism. — Crisis made by her Death. — Native College at Lahainaluna. — Made over to the Government. — Native Clergymen from the Graduates. — Commencement. — Alumni. — Dinner. — Schools at Lahaina. — Hana. — Molokai. — Monthly Concert. — Steam Sugar Mill. — Roman Catholics.

We were bound to Wailuku, situated near the western side of the isthmus connecting West and East Maui. After crossing the channel the wind increased, and so rough was the sea that our landing seemed not quite safe. Mr. Alexander met us on the shore, but in such a sand-storm that we were obliged to veil our faces. We breasted the gale for a dozen miles, and near Wailuku were wet to the skin by a storm of rain.

It is forty years since Messrs. Richards and Stewart brought the gospel to this island, and thirty years since Mr. Green first broke ground at Wailuku. He labored here four years. After him came Mr.

Armstrong, six years; then Mr. Clark, for five, and Mr. Conde, for eight. Mr. Alexander took charge of the station at the close of 1856, having received a unanimous call from the church, and was installed its pastor. Mr. Bailey, a lay-teacher, began to reside here in 1841, in connection with a boarding school for females, commenced in 1836, in which he had Miss Ogden for a valuable assistant. I found so many proofs of the utility of this school in our progress through the Islands, that I deeply regretted its discontinuance in 1849, and that its buildings were too dilapidated to be ever restored.

The soil of Wailuku is rich and deep, and the sugar-cane is extensively cultivated. The rains, though copious, are not sufficient, and channels are therefore cut along the foot of the hills, for conveying the waters of the mountain streams where they may be diffused over the entire plantations. Good cane lands have here been sold for eighty dollars the acre. Along the streams are numerous *taro* patches, of course covered with water. This district is one of the chief producing regions for that indispensable article of native food, out of which the *poi* is manufactured. Upland taro is cultivated on Hawaii, but the best taro is grown in water. This vegetable seemed to me equal to the Irish potato, and better than the large sweet potato of the Islands. I very much preferred it to the bread-fruit grown on the Islands. Poi is taro baked, pounded, mixed with water, and more or less fermented. With the natives it is an indispensable article in all their meals.

The meeting-house at Wailuku is a neat stone building, of considerable size. Mr. Alexander informed me that there are seven such in his district, all built by natives, and all finished save one. There were, however, but two organized churches, and one of these had a native *assistant* pastor. On the Sabbath I twice addressed a large congregation, thoroughly Christian in its aspects; also a Sabbath school of two hundred boys and girls. The music was conducted entirely by natives, and was as good as I remember in my early days in New England. The choir had the aid of a melodeon. Two addresses were here placed in my hands, and Mr. Alexander kindly translated them. One was to myself, the other to the American Board; and both were composed, as I understood, by a native lawyer. The one to the Board is as follows: —

"May it please you, true Christian Fathers: We send by the hand of your representative the greetings of the brethren of the district of Wailuku, on the Island of Maui, and also of ourselves, the committee who write this.

"We are glad to declare to the American Missionary Society the blessings that have come upon the Hawaiian Islands from the messengers sent to us.

"1. God has had mercy on us, and given us his Spirit to believe on the Father, Son, and Holy Ghost.

"2. We have learned to read in our own language, to write, and also arithmetic.

"3. There have been enacted, passed, and confirmed a constitution and laws, securing peace under a royal administration.

"4. We have been released from a condition of serfdom, under oppressive and robbing masters.

"5. We have learned to know that it is shameful for men, women, and children to go naked; as was the case with our ancestors down to the time of Kamehameha II.

"And we bless God, the eternal Father, for discovering to us his kind love, that we might obtain the blessedness detailed above."

Mr. Green, who commenced this station, has been long laboring at Makawao, on East Maui, in connection with the American Missionary Association. I had fully purposed visiting my old friend and correspondent, and greatly regretted my inability to do so, especially as I was informed that his district is among the more interesting portions of the Islands. The last report I have seen of the churches under his care states the number of members at 1100.

Behind Wailuku there is very interesting scenery. What long ago was a crater, with raging fires, is now a beautiful mountain recess, having lofty perpendicular walls with sharp outlines, covered to the top with a soft, velvety verdure, the result of perpetual irrigation from the clouds. Seen from the central table-land, it is a splendid amphitheatre. A break towards the sea forms a ravine of four miles, down which once flowed the lava, and now flows an unfailing stream of water.

Wednesday was the time set for going to Lahaina. To avoid the fatiguing ride across the mountains, a whale-boat was to meet us early, at the southern shore of the isthmus, seven miles distant. So we rode thither. No boat was there, and we had to return; but we were refreshed by the ride along a good road, in a very fine morning. We had a clear view of Haleákala, on East Maui, the "House of the Sun," a grand, symmetrical, noble mountain, having a base of thirty miles, and a height of more than ten thousand feet. The crater on the top of this mountain ceased long since to be active, but is regarded as the largest in the world. It is eight miles by twelve in diameter, and thirty-two in circumference, and has a depth of more than two thousand feet. New York, with all its buildings and parks, might be hid within it.

More effectual arrangements saved us next day from a second disappointment, and a sail of fifteen miles brought us to Lahaina. Part of our way was over fields of beautifully branching coral, apparently not far beneath the surface of the water. Mr. Alexander accompanied us.

Lahaina, as beheld from the sea, presents a luxuriant mass of tropical foliage, chiefly the cocoanut, kou, and banana trees, but with barren heights in the background, swelling into a mountain. Seen from Lahainaluna, two miles above, it appears a well-watered garden, spreading itself three miles along the shore. The streets are narrow, and the town, though greatly improved from what it was, has less appearance of civilization than Honolulu. In former years, when a large number of whaling ships came to the Islands for supplies, Lahaina rivalled the metropolitan port as a place of resort. Its chief dependence at present is on the sugar-cane, growing to great perfection in its rich alluvion. Its well-conditioned stone church, with galleries, tower, and bell, and its burying-ground adjacent, where lie the honored dead, together with the large Christian audience on the Sabbath, interested me not a little. Some hundreds of communicants were present at the Lord's Supper. I noticed that a few of them, as at Kailua, drank more of the wine, or what was in place of it, than is customary with us on such occasions. At Wailuku, to prevent that impropriety, the deacons hold the cup to the lips of the recipient. I could see how the abuse, so strongly reprehended by the apostle Paul, might have grown up in the Corinthian church. Proprieties are the result of education, and do not all come at once.

Messrs. Richards and Stewart, as already stated, were the first to occupy this ground. Dr. Baldwin, the present resident missionary, came in 1837. In the intervening period, Messrs. L. Andrews, Green, and Spaulding, Dr. Chapin, Miss Ogden and

Miss Ward, were here for short terms. More than two thousand have been admitted to the church, and more than eight hundred of these have died in good Christian standing. The present membership is six hundred and forty-five.

The first person baptized in this place, and indeed the first baptized by the mission, was in some respects the most remarkable of all the native converts. This was Keopuolani, wife of the first Kamehameha, and mother of the second and third kings of that name. From my first arrival I had looked forward with interest to a visit to her burial-place, it having been one of my early missionary duties to edit a small memorial of her. The stone house said to contain her mortal remains is in full view from the Protestant church. She was born at Wailuku, in the year 1778, and her descent was more illustrious than that of any other person on the Islands. Her father's family had governed the Island of Hawaii for many generations. Her grandfather Kalaniopu was the king of Hawaii at the time of Captain Cook's death; and her grandmother Kanona, who adopted her as a daughter, was the wife who threw her arms about Kalaniopu's neck while he was walking with Cook, constraining him to desist from visiting the ship, and so furnished an opportunity to the natives for their fatal assault. The family of her mother had long governed Maui, and, at one time, Lanai, Molokai, and Oahu; and the two families were intimately connected by means of intermarriages. At the early age of thirteen she became the wife of Kamehameha I. He had four other wives; and it illustrates the times, that he permitted her to have a second husband while he was living, and that such was the custom among women high in rank. Kalanimoku sustained this relation for some years; after him, Hoapili, till her death. Both these men have a somewhat distinguished place in the history of the mission, as well as in their nation's history. Being the highest chief on the Islands, Keopuolani's person was peculiarly sacred. I have elsewhere spoken of her as the daughter of a race of kings, wife of a king, mother of two kings, and the first person received into the visible church at the Islands.[1] She was every way a remarkable character. When the first missionaries arrived, she approved of their being allowed to stay, and was friendly to them. She favored the *palapala*, as the system of instruction was called, though she did not at first yield herself to it. In 1823 she gave evidence of piety. Having two husbands, she said,—

"I have followed the custom of my country, but we have been a people of dark hearts. I have had two husbands, but since I thought it was wrong, I have not desired more than one. I wish now to obey Jesus Christ, and to walk in the good way. Hoapili is my husband, my only husband. The other I will now cast off."

[1] Page 60.

She then called him, and said,—

"I have renounced our old religion — the religion of wooden gods. I have embraced a new religion — the religion of Jesus Christ. He is my King and Saviour, and Him I desire to obey. Hereafter I must have one husband only. I wish you to live with me no longer. In future you must neither eat with my people, nor lodge in my house."

It was at her request that Messrs. Richards and Stewart came to reside at Lahaina, and she brought them with her from Honolulu. It is due to our estimate of the native character, that I copy Mr. Stewart's very interesting account of King Liholiho's manner of parting with her when she left Honolulu, and of meeting her when he came to Lahaina.

"There was something," Mr. Stewart says, "in the attentions of the king to his mother, when leaving Honolulu, that had a pleasing effect on our minds. This venerable lady was the last person that came on board. After we had reached the quarter-deck of the barge, she appeared on the beach, surrounded by an immense crowd, and supported by Liholiho in a tender and respectful manner. He would let no one assist her into the long-boat but himself, and seemed to think of nothing but her ease and safety, till she was seated on her couch, beneath an awning over the main hatch. The king continued to manifest the utmost affection and respect for her till we got under way, and, apparently from the same filial feelings, accompanied us fifteen miles to sea, and left the brig in a pilot-boat in time barely to reach the harbor before dark."

Again, at the meeting; —

"The parting of the mother and son, when we left Honolulu, had interested us so much that we felt desirous of witnessing their first interview, after a month's separation. The chiefs had assembled, and were formally seated on their mats in a large circle, before the tent of Keopuolani, waiting the approach of their monarch. He entered the circle opposite to his mother, and where Wahine-pio, the sister of Kalanimoku, and mother of his youngest queen, was seated. Dropping on one knee, he saluted her, on which she burst into tears, and, springing from her mat, led him to that of his mother. He knelt before her, gazed silently in her face for a moment, then pressed her to his bosom, and, placing a hand on each cheek, kissed her twice in the most tender manner. The whole scene was quite affecting. I scarce ever witnessed an exhibition of natural affection where the feelings were apparently more lively and sincere. The king is a fine-looking man, and graceful in his manners. While gazing on him, the queen's heart seemed to float in her eyes, and every feature told a mother's joy."

As Messrs. Richards and Stewart had not yet acquired the language, having but recently arrived in the second reënforcement, the coming of Mr. Ellis, and of Auna, the Tahitian, already mentioned, was a most seasonable, perhaps essential, help in leading her to Christ. The latter was her chosen teacher. Both were at Lahaina, in her last sickness, and Mr. Ellis baptized her just previous to her death, which occurred September 16, 1823.

16*

Her death formed a crisis in the nation. Until now every restraint had been cast off by the people when a high chief died. No regard was paid to the rights of person or of property. It was the time for redressing private wrongs. Grief was expressed by personal outrages, such as knocking out their own teeth, pulling out their hair, and burning and cutting their flesh. Almost every old man and woman we met with on the Islands had thus been deprived of the front teeth. There was also the most unrestrained drunkenness and debauchery. But Kalanimoku assured the missionaries that they need then be under no apprehension; for the departed queen had forbidden every heathen practice at her death, and the people had received the strictest orders against all the former customs, except wailing. This, considering the rank of the deceased, and the affection of the people towards her, could not prudently be restrained.

Her wishes were fully carried out in the funeral solemnities. Her flesh was not cut from her bones and burned, as had been customary aforetime, but her body was placed in a coffin, and, after appropriate religious observances, was followed to a tomb by an orderly Christian procession, all dressed in the European style, generally in black, with badges of mourning. There were also the tolling of the bell and the firing of minute guns. Thus early was inaugurated a great, radical, most influential change in the national customs.

"What fools we have been," — Kalanimoku was heard to say, as he afterwards took his seat by the king, — "to burn our dead, and cast them into the sea, when we might thus have committed their bodies to the tomb, and have had the satisfaction of still dwelling near them!"

The impulse given to the work of God on the Islands, about the year 1829, by the outpouring of the Spirit in sundry places, led to an important measure for raising up native preachers and helpers. This was the commencing of a High School at Lahainaluna, in 1831, under the instruction of Rev. Lorrin Andrews. It began with twenty-five scholars, and gradually increased to ninety, with ages varying from fifteen to thirty-five. A small stream running down from the hill above enabled the pupils to make taro grounds and gardens; and thus a system of manual labor was incorporated into the school, and still remains there. Mr. Andrews continued in the school about ten years, and I had the pleasure of seeing him at Honolulu, where he is much respected. Of his literary labors I shall speak elsewhere. I recall to mind a remark of his, made almost thirty years ago, respecting the great trial it was to his faith and patience, when, looking around upon his half-dressed, uncivilized pupils, seated upon a floor of dried grass, he endeavored to see in them the future schoolmasters, physicians, lawyers, and preachers of the Sandwich Islands. Such many of them have in fact become. The first school-building was erected by the pupils, under the active superintendence of the principal; and they had to drag most of the beams and rafters for it, or else carry them on their shoulders, from East Maui, a distance of twenty-five or thirty miles. There was a large outlay of funds, however, by the American Board, before the three school-buildings and two dwelling-houses were completed. From 1835, when Mr. Clark became associated with Mr. Andrews, to 1852, when Mr. Pogue became the principal, Messrs. Dibble, Rogers, Bailey, Emerson, Alexander, Hunt, and C. B. Andrews, were connected with it for longer or shorter periods. In 1849 the Board made over the institution to the Hawaiian government, on condition that it should be sustained "for the cultivation of sound literature and solid science," and that no religious doctrine or tenet should be taught contrary to what had been taught by the mission. To this the government agreed, and it has been faithful to its engagement. The whole number of pupils, from the beginning, has been seven hundred and seventy-one, and more than half were connected with it while it was sustained by the Board. Ten of its graduates have been ordained as ministers of the gospel, and have lived without reproach. The institution is the native college for the Islands. I was present at a part of the annual examination, at the commencement exercises in the Protestant church, and at the subsequent meeting of alumni, and was pleasantly reminded of like occasions in my own country. Most of the addresses were in the native language; but a few were in English, that language being embraced in the college studies. The graduating class were dressed like ourselves. The commencement dinner was in the open air, under the shade of trees near the church. The students had a table by themselves, served with poi and its accompaniments. The table prepared for the guests of foreign origin was in accordance with our peculiar tastes and habits. Certainly I have never attended a more satisfactory commencement. Mr. Pogue's associates in the instruction are a son of Mr. Alexander and a competent native graduate. The institution is controlled by the Board of Education, and Mr. Pogue spoke of Prince Kamehameha, brother of the king (now the reigning monarch) as among its best friends. The school buildings were burned in 1862, but a large one in place of them has been built by the government. A year spent in theological study with a missionary is thought sufficient to prepare a pious graduate of Lahainaluna for the pastoral office.

I must not forget to speak of the younger portion of the Lahaina community. Mr. Dwight Baldwin, son of the missionary, was principal of a government school for teaching the English language; and I met, by invitation, this school and two others, numbering two hundred and eighty of both sexes, in his schoolroom. It may seem a strange remark, — nevertheless it is true, — that the young children of these Islands reminded me, by their self-possession in speaking, and by the rapidity of their arithmetical solutions, of what I had formerly seen of Greek children in the Levant.[1] On the present occasion there were declamations, dialogues, and singing. The children were hearty in their singing; every one appeared to sing, and I heard no discordant voices.

With two weeks more at my command, I might have visited Hana, on the eastern shore of Maui, Molokai, the island adjacent to Maui, and the small island of Lanai, opposite Lahaina. Though Lanai is little better than a sheep-pasture, the Mormons have a settlement upon it. Rev. S. E. Bishop, son of a missionary, is the resident missionary at Hana. Messrs. Conde, Ives, Rice, Whittlesey, and W. O. Baldwin, were his predecessors. The district is supplied with meeting-houses, but I infer from Mr. Bishop's report that it has suffered for want of culture. The church-members are one thousand and eighteen,

[1] "At the schools it has been observed that the scholars are extremely fond of calculations in arithmetic, and possess extraordinary talent in that way. So great is their fondness for it, that in some schools the teachers have had recourse to depriving them of the study as a punishment." — *Com. Wilkes, in U. S. Expl. Exp.*, vol. iv. p. 54.

"I witnessed, at the mission schools, the remarkable universal talent and fondness for mathematical pursuits, about which so much has been said." — *Dr. Pickering, in U. S. Expl. Exp.*, vol. ix. p. 88.

and two of the churches at outstations are under the care of native preachers.

The population of Molokai is two thousand eight hundred and thirty, and the number of church-members is eight hundred and nine. The total of admissions to the church exceeds two thousand, and the island is well supplied with meeting-houses erected by the people. Mr. Forbes, who is a missionary's son, has been the resident missionary since 1858. The previous laborers for longer or shorter periods were Messrs. Hitchcock, Lowell Smith, Munn, Gulick, C. B. Andrews, and Dwight. Mr. Hitchcock began the work in 1833, and labored with great faithfulness and success till his death, which occurred August 29, 1855.

Monday afternoon, in company with Dr. Baldwin, I attended the monthly concert at the church, where a goodly number were present. In the evening I baptized the three children of the younger Mr. Baldwin, at his house. Next day I visited a steam sugar mill, nearly completed, and a neatly-furnished Roman Catholic church, at which Dr. Baldwin thinks the Sabbath attendance may be a hundred.

CHAPTER XI.

OAHU.

Social Intercourse. — Mr. Corwin and the foreign Church. — Mr. Damon, Seamen's Chaplain. — President Mills and Mrs. Mills. — A native Judge. — Honolulu. — First Church. — Second Church. — Interesting Ordination. — Rev. Hiram Bingham. — Levi Chamberlain. — Royal Cemetery. — Oahu College. — Tour of the Island. — Ewa. — Waialua. — Journey along the Northern and Eastern Shore. — Sugar Plantations. — Lassoing. — Kaneohe. — The Pali. — Unexpected Danger.

EMBARKING at evening, the rising sun of Wednesday, May 6th, found us at Honolulu. As before, we were guests in the hospitable family of Mr. Clark. Next day Mr. Wyllie, Minister of Foreign Affairs, made a friendly call. The remainder of the week was devoted to social intercourse.

We saw much of the Rev. Mr. Corwin, pastor of the Fort-street Church; of the Rev. Mr. Damon, seamen's chaplain, and pastor of the Bethel Church; and of President Mills, of the Oahu College. The first and last named of these gentlemen were graduates of Williams College. The other was from Amherst College. Mr. Corwin has been at Honolulu since October, 1858, and has a convenient house of worship, which cost near fifteen thousand dollars, a respectable and well-satisfied foreign congregation, an ample support from his people, and rare opportunity for exerting a religious influence. The Rev. T. Dwight Hunt had preached to a foreign congregation in 1847, but the Fort-street Church dates from June 2, 1852. Mr. Corwin's predecessors in the pastoral office were the Rev. T. E. Taylor and Rev. J. D. Strong, both of whom are now in California.

Mr. Damon preached his twentieth anniversary sermon on the 19th of October, 1862. Until the year 1833 the wants of the seamen resorting to Honolulu were partially met by the missionaries of the American Board. The Rev. John Diell then went there to reside, as one of three foreign chaplains sustained by the American Seamen's Friend Society. He died at sea, on his way home, in January, 1840, and the present chaplain was his successor. Mr. Damon seemed to me well adapted to his post, which is, and must continue to be, one of importance.

President Mills and his excellent lady were formerly connected with the Batticotta Seminary, in Ceylon, until failing health compelled them to leave. I believe they have found their experience in that remote part of the world a valuable training for their present post of duty. Oahu College being designed for males and females, they both find here not only a healthful climate, but also a genial occupation; and I was glad to know that they gave universal satisfaction.

The Hon. John Ii had returned from San Francisco, whither he went with others, on behalf of their own government, to save the life of a Hawaiian sailor, erroneously accused of murder on the high seas. In this they were successful. There was no one among the native Christians whom I was so desirous of seeing as this judge of the Supreme Court. Both of us were prepared for a cordial meeting, and there was but one drawback. I had supposed, from his long intimacy with the missionaries, that I should be able to communicate with him without the help of an interpreter. And so it doubtless would have been but for the excellent habit among our missionary brethren of always making the native language their medium of intercourse with the people. The name of John Ii appears very early in the history of the mission, and he has long preserved a consistent Christian character. Having been connected with the government for so many years, he must needs be conversant with Hawaiian legislation.

I have already spoken of the ten or twelve thousand inhabitants of Honolulu, and of its city-like appearance. The crooked and filthy lanes of thirty years ago have passed away, and so have the huts of dried grass, with low, contracted entrances. With no great appearance of wealth, there is an air of civilization in the houses, streets, and sidewalks. The finest of the streets is the one up the Nuuanu Valley. It is open for carriages as far as the *pali*, or precipice, six or seven miles, where it terminates. The upper part is unfinished.

HARBOR OF HONOLULU.

Honolulu stands on the south-western side of Oahu; and the harbor, one of the best in the Pacific Ocean, is formed by a coral reef. It admits ships drawing twenty-four feet of water, and has a safe anchorage within for at least a hundred vessels.[1] The palace is a story and a half, and the square in which it stands is enclosed by a stone wall, not in very good repair. The native Protestants have two churches, and the Roman Catholics one. There is also the Fort-street Church, and a Seamen's Chapel, and the Episcopalians, or "Reformed Catholics," as they call themselves, have also a church. It was built by a Methodist missionary from the United States, who did not succeed in collecting a congregation. I was told there are at least a dozen houses for Protestant worship, of different sizes, in the Honolulu district, all built by the people. Three of them are of stone; but generally they are wooden buildings, with an average cost of about six hundred dollars. The walls and tower of the first church in Honolulu are built of coral blocks, and the church, having extensive galleries, will seat a very large congregation. A clock

[1] The engraving of the harbor is from one of a series of photographic views taken some years since, and for sale in Honolulu. The Bethel Church is seen, but neither of the others. The stone church lay too much to the right, and probably the Fort-street Church was not then built, or its steeple would appear in front, beyond the Bethel Church. The mountains forming the Nuuanu Valley rise behind the city.

in the tower strikes the hours. The second church has *adobe* walls, three feet in thickness, twelve feet high, plastered within and without, and a wide veranda all around, but no tower. It will seat twelve hundred. Mr. Smith has been the pastor since 1838, at which time this separate enterprise was commenced. Mr. Bingham was the original pastor of the first church; after him Dr. Armstrong; then Mr. Clark; now Mr. Parker, a son of the venerable missionary at Kaneohe. This church numbers 2516 members, the second, 1006; and the total of their membership from the first is 7192.

The ordination of Mr. Parker occurred on Sabbath, the 28th of June, and was one of the most interesting events that came under my observation. It was in the afternoon, and the two native congregations united, forming an audience of scarcely less than twenty-five hundred. Mr. Parker had preached during the year as assistant to Mr. Clark, much to the satisfaction of the people; and the old pastor had resigned in favor of his younger brother, because of the inadequacy of his own health and strength to meet the demands of so great a people. Under advice from their pastor the people made out a call; promised a salary of a thousand dollars, to be raised by themselves; called a council by letters missive; were present by their committee at the examination of the candidate in the native language; and the church officers had the care of preserving order in the assembly. The vast audience, its becoming appearance, the interest, the attention, the singing, — every thing indicated an established and true Christianity. The right hand of fellowship was given by the Rev. Mr. Kuáea, a graduate of the native college at Lahainaluna, and then the respected pastor of a church on the east side of the island. He has since taken Mr. Emerson's place, whose health has failed, as pastor of the church at Waialua.

On the Sabbath preceding my departure from the Islands I met the two congregations, and nearly as large an audience, in the same church, and made my farewell address. To this there was a response from Judge Ii. He ascended the pulpit, and spoke with dignity and fluency for half an hour, without a note before him.

Anything like a history of the Honolulu station would occupy too much space. But I ought to say that it was here Mr. Bingham had his home till the failing health of Mrs. Bingham, in 1841, constrained them to return to the United States. It gratified me to see with what interest his memory was cherished by the old people of both sexes, not only at Honolulu, but on all the Islands. He had sent me a sentence in Hawaiian, containing his *aloha* to his island friends, and this was usually read at the opening of my addresses; and in no way could I have better awakened attention among the old people. This respected brother, during the whole of his twenty years' residence on the Islands, was an active, enterprising, fearless, faithful laborer in the cause of his Master; and I know of none who will have more reason to be thankful for the agency allowed to them in the work of God there than this honored pioneer.

There is another, who drew to himself less of public attention, but exerted an influence second in importance to that of scarcely any other. I refer to Levi Chamberlain. In 1821 he was a young merchant in Boston, and as sure as any young merchant could be of acquiring a fortune. But he had an overpowering inclination, implanted, no doubt, by the Holy Spirit, to engage in the missionary work; and that was his call of God to relinquish the pursuit of wealth. Coming myself from the Andover Seminary, early in 1822, to spend a few months at the Missionary Rooms, while Mr. Evarts, the Corresponding Secretary, was absent, I found Mr. Chamberlain in the Treasury department. And when I came again, in the autumn of that year, for what has proved a long stay, he was still there, and we labored together until the latter part of 1823. He then joined the first reënforcement of the mission at the Sandwich Islands. Only the threatened failure of his health induced the Prudential Committee to give him up for the foreign service. He went as a layman, to take the superintendence of secular affairs in the mission. I know not that I ever was conversant with a better judgment than that of Mr. Chamberlain, and all his private interests were held in strict subordination to those of Christ's kingdom. Consequently he was trusted by his brethren in matters deeply affecting their private interests and feelings as scarcely any other man would have been; and to him, under God, the mission is greatly indebted for its safe navigation, in its early period, through the rocks and quicksands of the common stock and depository systems, into which it was inadvertently, perhaps inevitably, drawn at the outset. His death took place July 29, 1849. In the last month of our sojourn at the Islands we were happy to be guests in the family of Mrs. Chamberlain, where we saw most of the children, and some of the grandchildren, of our beloved and lamented friend. While there I baptized the two youngest of his grandchildren.

Calling on Kanaina, — one of the old chiefs, who occupies a spacious stone house in a square contiguous to that of the palace, and whose wife, not now living, was the distinguished premier whose portrait has been given, — Prince William, his son, invited us to see the royal cemetery. This is a stone house, with one large room, standing on the other side of the square. The prince speaks our language well, and did the honors with ease and dignity. The first thing attracting attention, as we entered, was a table standing in the centre of the room, covered with a cloth, upon which was a cushion supporting the Hawaiian crown. Elegant coffins stand beyond, and, on either side, some of them covered with scarlet and gold. The prince pointed us to the coffins of Liholiho (Kamehameha II.) and his queen, in which their remains were returned from England; of Kamehameha III.; and, among the high chiefs, to that of Paki, remarkable for its length, he having been a man of extraordinary stature. But the one which interested me most was that in which rest the remains of the good Queen Kaahumanu. Much of historic and religious interest is concentrated in this narrow house. Here lie, silent in death, kings, queens, and chiefs, both men and women, who, when living, controlled, for weal or woe, the affairs of the nation.

Two miles from Honolulu, over the plain, — a favorite drive skirting the hills, — is Oahu College, looking out finely upon the sea, which, however, is far enough off to make no disturbance with its roar. It is a beautiful place, and the college seemed to me to be a gem of the Islands. Here the children of the missionaries, male and female, and other foreign youths, and natives speaking the English language and paying their expenses, may receive almost as effective an education as was given by American colleges in my early years. I repeatedly visited the institution, with my family, at the invitation of the respected President and his lady. Besides the President and Mrs. Mills, there are Professor Alexander and wife, Mr. Bailey, and Miss Coan, college teachers; the four last named being children of missionaries. Perhaps one would hardly recognize a college in the buildings seen at Punahou, but they surpass the visible beginnings of either Harvard or Yale. The charter, obtained from the Hawaiian government in 1853, embraces a preparatory school as well as college. The school was commenced in 1841, and for a time was exclusively for the children of missionaries. It was opened to others in 1851. The charter has this important provision: —

"No course of instruction shall be deemed lawful in said institution which is not accordant with the principles of Protestant Evangelical Christianity, as held by that body of Protestant Christians in the United States of America which originated the Christian mission to the Islands, and to whose labors and benevolent contributions the people of these Islands are so greatly indebted."

There is also an additional security for the institution in the following article, namely: —

"Whenever a vacancy shall occur in said corporation, it shall be the duty of the Trustees to fill the same with all reasonable and convenient despatch. And every new election shall be immediately made known to the Prudential Committee of the American Board of Commissioners for Foreign Missions, and be subject to their approval or rejection; and this power of revision shall be continued to the American Board for twenty years from the date of this charter."

When the college had become incorporated, the American Board made over the buildings and other property to the Trustees, to the value of $25,000. The buildings stand on a lot of one hundred acres, enclosed by a good stone wall, with an unfailing fountain on the upper side, sufficient to irrigate the whole; whence the name "Punahou." Another hundred acres adjoining are also enclosed by a stone wall, and devoted to pasturage; and there is still another large lot of woodland two miles distant. The buildings meet the present wants of the institution. There is a two-story house, containing a hall and class-rooms; also, a long block, forming two dwelling-houses, which face the sea, having two wings, and a projection from the centre, all in front, for lodging-rooms, dining-room, kitchen, etc. On the right stands the President's house, now occupied by the Professor. The President and Mrs. Mills dwell in the midst of their pupils, which is an admirable arrangement for the young people.

The Rev. Daniel Dole had charge of the school in its first years, and was an excellent instructor. Rev. Edward G. Beckwith, now pastor of a church in San Francisco, was its first President, and greatly esteemed. He came to the United States in 1857, with Dr. Armstrong, to secure an endowment of $50,000, of which the island government engaged to give $10,000. Those who were at the annual meeting of the American Board in that year will remember his eloquent and effective speech on behalf of the college. Owing to an extraordinary commercial revulsion, the agency was suddenly arrested, though not until $12,000 had been secured, besides the grant of the Hawaiian government. To this James Hunnewell, Esq., of Charlestown, Mass., a contributor to the first endowment, and an officer of the brig Thaddeus when it conveyed the first missionaries to the Islands, has recently added $5,000. The number of pupils in the college and preparatory school is seventy-nine.

I was present at the annual examination, on the 16th and 17th of June, which was held in the spacious hall of the college building. The walls were ornamented with evergreen, and with maps and drawings executed by the pupils. I noticed that the flags of Hawaii and the United States floated upon one and the same staff. The Hawaiian Evangelical Association, then holding its sessions in Honolulu, and comprising the parents of the greater part of the students, had adjourned to attend the examination, and the hall was filled with students, teachers, and an intelligent audience. The examination was admirably conducted, and completely successful. The President examined in geometry, meteorology, algebra, elements of criticism, and intellectual philosophy; Professor Alexander, in the Latin Reader, Sophocles, Virgil, and analytical geometry; Mrs. Mills, in chemistry, geology, botany, natural theology, and

18

English grammar; Miss Coan, in history and rhetoric, while the paintings and drawings executed by her pupils were seen upon the walls; and Mr. Bailey, in arithmetic and geography, including the exhibition of neatly executed maps. There were, moreover, exhibitions in calisthenics, beautifully performed: and in vocal music, to which a portion of the pupils had evidently given much attention. Several compositions were read by their authors, which the audience heard with interest. On each day of the examination the visitors were refreshed by a collation, which did credit to the young ladies having charge of the domestic department of the institution.

The commencement performances were on Thursday evening, June 18th, in the great Stone Church of Honolulu. The speakers acquitted themselves well, and the singing by the pupils, under a German professor, was of a high order. Notice having been given in the native congregations, there was a large attendance of natives, in addition to the foreign residents drawn perhaps by curiosity to hear the singing, for they could not understand the speakers. On Friday evening there was a re-union at the college, and after a social evening, refreshments were tastefully served in the large hall of examination.

Altogether the institution appeared to be in a prosperous condition, and I cannot help regarding it as one of the more important elements of safety and prosperity for the Hawaiian nation.

A tour around Oahu is not much short of a hundred miles. Dr. Judd generously proposed arranging and providing for our journey, and to accompany us, with his daughter. The distance to Waialua is thirty miles, the country open, the road for the most part good. Excepting a slight shower — while we were looking at a salt lake, five or six miles from Honolulu, on a level with the sea, but with no visible connection — the day was pleasant. Ewa is twelve miles from the capital, and has a spacious and deep harbor, but rendered almost useless by the shallow entrance across the coral reef. The village has the appearance of decay. Should the harbor ever be opened, as it may be, the place will doubtless rise into importance. It would then greatly exceed that of Honolulu. Mr. Bishop formerly resided here, and had assembled an audience of about a hundred to meet me in the large adobe church situated on a hill — the small remnant of his former people. After lunch we resumed our ride. Mountains rose on each side, with wide intervening spaces, and we had an extended prospect before us. The ancient lava was generally concealed by soil and grass, except in the deep gorges, where mountain streams crossed our way. At five P. M., we reached the dwelling of Mr. and Mrs. Emerson, and received from them a cordial welcome. The fact that a physician was with us must have added to the pleasure of our arrival; for we were sorry to find Mr. Emerson seriously ill —

too much so to converse with me on the object of my visit.

Waialua is on the windward side of the island, and of course is well watered. Mr. Emerson came here as early as 1832, and is the father of the station. Messrs. Clark, Locke, A. B. Smith, Wilcox, and Gulick were here at different times. A son of Mr. Emerson, and one of Mr. Levi Chamberlain, reside in the neighborhood, as citizens, the former a grazier, the latter a planter. More than thirty square miles in the Waialua district, it is said, can be cultivated without artificial irrigation.

The site of Mr. Emerson's house is well chosen. The ground is fertile. A perennial spring flows just below, between the house and the river, and an hydraulic ram throws a stream of water into the house-yard. In the garden are tamarinds, dates, bananas, and cocoanuts. The meeting-house is a good building, and it was filled with a respectable congregation on the Sabbath, Dr. Judd being my interpreter. Mrs. Emerson has long taken a lead in the singing, and that part of the service was excellent. Mr. and Mrs. Chamberlain brought their infant child to church for baptism. The communicants at Waialua number three hundred and forty-eight, and the two outstations have four hundred and twenty-five. The number from the beginning, in this district, exceeds two thousand. The period of our visit was represented to be a season of spiritual declension.

Tuesday morning we resumed our journey, and all day had a beautiful ride. The mountain range of Konahuanui leaves only a narrow strip of land along the sea, varying from half a mile to two miles in width. The first district we traversed, after leaving Waialua, was Koolauloa. The scenery is bold, beautiful, and various. A native church once existed here, with Rev. J. Kekela for its pastor, now a highly valued missionary at the Marquesas. Both as pastor and missionary he has adorned his profession; but the church in this district no longer exists. I believe the causes of its extinction have some connection with the tenure by which the lands are held for pasturage; but I am not sufficiently informed to go into the subject. A part of us were on horseback. A four-wheeled vehicle, drawn by two horses, was with us all day for the ladies, furnished the first half of the way by the younger Mr. Emerson, who accompanied us, and the other half by Mr. Charles Judd, who came to meet us from his plantation at Kualoa. We had received a polite invitation to lunch with Mr. Moffitt, an English gentleman, largely interested in flocks and herds, who gave us a hospitable reception.

Having pledged ourselves to meet an assembly at the residence of Mr. Kuaea, the native pastor already mentioned, and being short of time, I sallied forth with Dr. Judd, after lunch, and told him, as he owned both the horses, he might go as fast as he pleased, and I would follow. We went the whole distance of eight or ten miles in fifty minutes. There was no one on the way to observe us. It was the least fatiguing of all my rides; and I could understand how, with changes of fine horses, a vigorous man might ride ninety or a hundred miles in a single day. The meeting-house at Hauula is a long, narrow, stone building, plainly finished within. Kuaea and his amiable wife received us in a comfortably furnished house, and had prepared a dinner: but we were too late to dine before the meeting, and afterwards the rising tide in a river we were to ford obliged a part of us to hasten away. A small congregation had waited patiently, and gave the customary attention. The pastor followed us to the younger Mr. Judd's, where I had an interesting conference with him on various points connected with the native ministry.

We were now on the eastern side of the island, open to the trade-winds and frequent rains. Here the Messrs. Judd and Wilder are bringing forward a plantation of sugar-cane; and farther on they are cultivating rice, notwithstanding the depredations committed by armies of rats. We spent the greater part of Wednesday at the house of Mr. Wilder, where we saw, for the first time, the process of lassoing horses and cattle. It is exciting both to men and animals. Our young friends were the performers, and showed much activity and skill. A mountain rises near Mr. Wilder's house, with basaltic-looking sides, resembling a majestic old cathedral; and there is a curious island just off the shore, near the house of Mr. Judd, of pyramidal form, that may once have been a volcano.

The ride of ten miles, next day, to Mr. Parker's at Kaneohe, was necessarily on horseback, owing to the nature of the country. We passed a small, neat church soon after starting, which is within Mr. Parker's district. Then came the rice-fields. Sometimes our road was along the beach; then over hills; always with the mountains rising steeply not far off on our right. Kaneohe is pleasantly situated, two or three miles from the pali, already mentioned as forming an abrupt termination of the Nuuanu Valley. The pastor and his lady have resided here since 1834. They are the parents of the young man who was soon after ordained as pastor of the first church in Honolulu. A daughter was at home, engaged in the instruction of a native school. About a thousand hopeful converts have been admitted to the church in the Kaneohe district, and there are now four hundred members. Three meeting-houses have been built for Sabbath worship, and two for lectures on week days; two of stone, three of wood; all by the people. The central church cost six thousand dollars; the southern, one thousand five hundred dollars; the northern, one thousand and fifty dollars. The district extends twenty miles along the sea, and has two thousand seven hundred inhabitants. I addressed the people on Thursday.

Next day, May 29th, we took horses with Dr. Judd for Honolulu, ten miles distant. The road passes over the pali, once wholly impracticable for horses, and nearly so for men. The government has expended much upon it, and will ultimately make it practicable (which is all, I fear, that can ever be said) for carriages, by means of a zigzag road with sharp turns. But it will never be comfortable looking a thousand feet down the steep side. Our greatest danger came where we least expected it, as is often the case in human life. When half way to the foot of the precipice, along a fine road, our baggage-horse took fright, ran, and tore our travelling bags to pieces. But though he dashed through a river, and into wet taro grounds (where he was caught), our most valuable effects were either dropped on the dry upland, or remained in the bags, and were uninjured, while nearly every article was recovered. The horse on which my wife rode was frightened as the animal rushed by, but was kept from running by Dr. Judd, who sprang from his own horse, letting him run, while he held hers firmly by the head.

Our thoughtful friend had directed a chaise to be in waiting for her on the other side of the pali, and five or six miles more completed our interesting tour of Oahu. Connected with it will be a grateful recollection of the kindnesses of Dr. Judd and his family.

CHAPTER XII.

KAUAI.

The Voyage. — The Island. — Waioli. — Congregation in a Kukui Grove. — Beautiful Plantation at Hanalei. — Fertility of the District. — Touching Incident. — Hospitality. — Governor Kanoa. — Koloa. — Fearful Deluge. — Waimea. — Old Jonah. — Island of Niihau. — Return to Honolulu. — Delicate Testimonial.

It was convenient to make the tour of Kauai before that of Oahu, but I conform my narrative to the geographical order. Kauai is the remotest of the large islands towards the north-west. Its distance from Oahu is a hundred miles.

Among the more painful recollections of former times, retained by our brethren, are those of the sufferings they frequently endured when voyaging in small crowded schooners from island to island. Of this they said we could have no conception from our experience in the "Kilauea." There was, however, some approximation towards it in the "Annie Laurie," a small schooner plying between Honolulu and Kauai, especially on our return passage, when, with head winds and a rough sea, we lay helplessly seasick on the deck for two nights and a day. This vessel had a small auxiliary propeller, or we should perhaps have been a week on our passage. Our captain and fellow-passengers showed us every kindness. Our companions in this tour were the Rev. Mr. Corwin, of the Fort-street Church, and Mr. Wilder, a planter and son-in-law of Dr. Judd. We were favored, also, on the outward voyage, with the company of Mr. Wyllie, the Foreign Minister of the government, then going on a visit to his sugar plantation at Hanalei. At the end of the voyage he kindly sent us to our landing-place in the boat that had come off for him. Mr. Johnson and Mr. Wilcox, and two sons of the latter, met us there with horses for Waioli, not far distant. We were glad to enjoy the hospitality of these two families, though the time was shorter than we could have wished.

Kauai is regarded as the most fertile of the Islands, and it seemed to me that it must be the oldest of them, since the process of lava-disintegration is there farthest advanced. But the geologist says, this only proves that the fires of the more northern volcanoes were first extinguished.

"The mountains and the valleys are covered with forests; and the high shore plain, which forms a broad border to the island on the southern, eastern, and northern sides, is mostly a region of grass and shrubbery, shaded with occasional groves of pandanus and kukui. The lower lands of the island lie all to the windward of its mountains, and this is sufficient cause of the prevailing fertility. The lofty summits and the mountain plain of the west are in a region of frequent mists and rains, and the declivities are often marked

Congregation in a Grove of Kukui Trees, 1840.

with white, thready cascades, streaming down their almost vertical surface, sometimes through one, two, or even three thousand feet, in uninterrupted lines. The island is, consequently, well watered, and the lower country seldom fails in its productions. The district of Waimea, to the south-west, is the only exception to these remarks; and this is owing to its leeward situation." [1]

The station of Waioli was commenced by Mr. Alexander, in 1834, and he remained nine years. The view here given of the beautiful grove of kukui-nut trees forming the shade in which Mr. Alexander frequently preached to the natives prior to the year 1840, and of his rural congregation, is copied from the "United States Exploring Expedition." Few places in the open air could have been found so well adapted for holding divine service. This congregation may be viewed in connection with the one seated on the bare lava of Hawaii, ten years earlier, delineated by Mr. Ellis.[2] The close observer will perceive a slight improvement in dress in the congregation of more recent date.

Mr. Rowell succeeded Mr. Alexander, and labored here till 1846. Mr. Johnson began as a teacher in 1837, and became Mr. Rowell's successor in the pastorate, having been ordained for that purpose. Mr. Wilcox took Mr. Johnson's place, and at the time of our visit had a select school of forty-five pupils. Almost a score of his former pupils are schoolmasters

[1] Dana's Geology, p. 265. [2] See p. 295.

on Kauai and Niihau. The Board of Education pays a part of his salary, in consideration of his making the English language a study in his school. An incendiary not long since burned his school-house, and the Education Board furnished materials for a new building. Mr. Johnson's church contains four hundred and twenty-one members, and has a good house of worship.

After my address on Wednesday, we accepted an invitation from Mr. Wyllie to visit his celebrated plantation. I had heard much of the beauty of Hanalei, and it is certainly one of the loveliest spots on the Islands. It is seen to great advantage from the plantation house. The mountains in the distance had the deep verdure common to the windward side; and out of them comes this charming vale, with its river, and its rich bottom lands, extensively covered with luxuriant sugar-cane. Here and there portions of the cane had been removed, and scores of people were gathering it for the large new steam mill on the river bank, whither it is conveyed in scows. At the mill we had ample opportunity for observation. The ponderous rollers are fed by an endless cane-carrier, which also drops the cane outside the building after the juice has been expressed. The engine was powerful enough to send more than six hundred gallons of cane-juice into a clarifier in twenty minutes. This costly mill is said to be the most complete on the Islands; and we saw the process of sugar-manufacturing in all its stages, from the expressing of the juice until the granulated mass is packed in barrels, weighed, and marked for exportation.[1]

The Annie Laurie was to return in a week. We were therefore obliged to hasten from Waioli, which is on the north side of the island, to Koloa, on the side opposite, distant about forty miles. The morning of our departure was beautiful, and Messrs. Johnson and Wilcox, and two of the young men, accompanied us some distance. The vale of Hanalei at one time opened in full view, with its surpassing loveliness. Towards noon we had a pleasing surprise. As we approached a school-house near the small village of Koolau, the master of the school came out, followed

[1] "The eastern portion of the district of Hanalei is watered by at least twenty streams. Many of these are large enough to be termed rivers, and might be employed to turn machinery. It is elevated from three to eight hundred feet above the sea, and comprises about fifty thousand acres of land, capable of producing sugar-cane, cotton, indigo, coffee, corn, beans, the mulberry, and vegetables in every variety. It now produces taro, sweet potatoes, yams, bread-fruit, bananas, plantains, squashes, melons, beans, Indian corn, and cocoanuts. Sugar-cane grows spontaneously. Mulberry trees flourish, of which there are four kinds, the Chinese, the multicaulis, the white and the black. The latter variety has a small leaf. The vegetation is extremely luxuriant from the frequent rains. The sugar-cane and mulberry, both Chinese and multicaulis, are the staple articles of culture. The mulberry has here a most rapid growth, and, being sheltered from the strong winds, it succeeds well. Some of the leaves of the multicaulis are of the enormous size of fifteen inches in length by twelve in breadth." — *U. S. Expedition*, vol. iv. p. 70.

by all his pupils, who arranged themselves by the road we were to pass. Seeing they designed it as a token of respect, I dismounted, and then saw that a very little girl, the smallest in the company, had an orange in each hand, as large as she could hold, which she was to give me as a present from the school. They then sang a couple of hymns in their native language, and, after their *alohas*, returned to the school-house. Mr. Corwin pronounced it the most touching scene he had witnessed on the Islands.

We were handsomely entertained at night by Mr. Knill, an intelligent gentleman from Hamburg, who has a large, well-ordered dairy. His grass houses were perfect in their kind, and well furnished, and his grounds tastefully laid out. He is a member of the Lutheran church. After tea he laid the Bible on the table, and we had family worship. Near noon, on Friday, we were met by a barouche from Lihue, kindly sent by a German gentleman at the request of Mrs. Rice, of which several of our company were glad to avail themselves. The carriage had two horses, and a curiously contrived auxiliary force for the hills. A smart native rode a horse on each side of us, with a long rope attached to the pommel of his saddle and also to the carriage, and the aid was afforded by each rider spurring up his horse at the proper moment, and bringing a strain upon the rope.

The gladness of our reception by Mrs. Rice and

her interesting family could not be exceeded. I had designed to go myself, that night, ten miles farther to Koloa, leaving the rest of the company to follow next day, but was constrained to relinquish my purpose. Mr. and Mrs. Rice were formerly connected with the secular department of Oahu College, where their services were very useful. Mr. Rice, for some time previous to his death, which occurred early in 1863, had the oversight of a sugar plantation at Lihue. Kanoa, governor of Kauai, resides near Mrs. Rice. He went to Waioli to meet us, was with me a long time here, and I saw him again at Koloa, whither he brought his wife and a married daughter to hear my statement. The old man shed tears when we parted. He and others were desirous of having a native pastor at Lihue; and as there are communicants enough to form a church, and a good meeting-house, and they are ten miles from Koloa, measures have very properly been taken to gratify their wishes.

Saturday morning I had a refreshing ride to Koloa, before breakfast, in company with one of the Misses Rice. The country is open, and the road tolerably good. Mr. Marshall, the American gentleman who met us the day before, was to bring the others over during the forenoon. Dr. Smith rode out to meet us, and conducted me to his house. He combines the clerical and medical professions, and his district includes Koloa and Lihue, and about five hundred church-members. Mr. Dole, formerly principal of the Punahou School, also resides at Koloa, preaching to the foreigners at the places above named, and teaching a school for children of foreign origin. Mrs. Smith has a small boarding-school for girls. One of my most interesting Sabbaths was at Koloa. The customary addresses occupied the forenoon, with an evidently interested congregation. In the afternoon the Lord's Supper was celebrated. After this I preached to Mr. Dole's foreign congregation.

The Koloa station was commenced by Mr. Gulick in 1835, who remained till the arrival of Dr. Smith, in 1844. Dr. Lafon was here from 1838 to 1841, and Mr. Pogue from 1845 to 1848. The latter came near losing his life, while here, from an extraordinary rise of waters in the night. Awaked by their rush past his dwelling, he assayed to reach the house of Dr. Smith near by, but was borne away by the flood a full half mile down towards the sea. When near perishing, a kind Providence threw him upon a heap of stones, where he remained till morning and the subsiding of the waters. It was a fearful night.

Monday morning we started for Waimea, sixteen miles across an open country, with the sea always in sight. Dr. Smith, Mr. Dole, and two ladies accompanied us a part of the way, and we were met by Mr. Rowell.

The mountains shut off Waimea from the trade-winds and from clouds, and make it a dry and thirsty land. There had been no rain since December, and none was expected until November. The grass was dead, and the few trees gave signs of suffering. The people obtain their food from two ravines not far off, watered by mountain streams, where the taro and other esculent fruits are grown, and where Mr. Rowell has a garden. The church is built of a whitish sandstone, obtained near the sea-shore, and is one of the best looking on the Islands. The cost to the people was nearly five thousand dollars, besides the labor at the quarry and in the construction of the house.

Waimea was the favorite residence of Kaumualii, king of the island when Messrs. Whitney and Ruggles commenced the station, in the first year of the mission. Mr. Whitney was alone at the station in 1824, but the rulers had even then acknowledged the Sabbath, and forbidden drunkenness and infanticide. The early coöperation with the missionary by the rulers on these Islands is one of the remarkable facts in their religious history. Mr. Gulick went to Waimea in 1829, and resided there some years. Mr. Whitney remained at the station till his death, in 1845. Mr. Rowell removed thither in the following year. Mrs. Whitney, now in the forty-third year of her residence, still occupies the house built by her husband, preferring it from long habit, and having no fear to dwell alone. How changed the habits, manners, and morals among that people, since she and her excellent husband began their Christian labors! Mr. Whitney always had great influence over the chiefs and people. Mrs. Whitney's simple narrative of their early trials was very affecting. An incident on the outward voyage of course retained a strong hold upon her feelings. It was the escape of her husband from the sea, into which he had fallen from the ship; and she showed us the rough bench, carefully preserved, that was thrown to him, and to which he clung till a boat came for his rescue. Mr. Rowell has a large and intelligent family.

I was specially interested, while addressing the people on Tuesday, in "old Jona," who sat directly in front of the pulpit facing the people. He is Mr. Rowell's right-hand man, and about seventy-five years of age. He was an agent of the old chiefs in every species of service, and still possesses a governing mind, and his piety is unquestioned. While I was speaking of Jerusalem and other places of which he had read in his Bible, he turned up his old, expressive face toward me with such a glow upon it, and such a twinkle in his eye, as almost disturbed my self-possession. After the service I asked him what he thought had been accomplished by the mission. Pausing a few moments he replied, that the first period was one of luxuriant growth, but the time of sifting had now come, and it was seen what was good. Mr. Corwin regards "old Jona" as the most remarkable native on the Islands.

The Island of Niihau, included in the missionary district of Waimea, is separated from the latter island by a channel of fifteen miles, is twenty-two miles long, from four to eight broad, and has a population of six hundred. Mr. Rowell can visit the island only once or twice a year; and, though there are two hundred communicants, I did not learn that a separate church has yet been organized. Of course they have no native pastor. The *lunas*, or leading men, preach, as has been customary at most out-stations on these Islands. The Waimea church numbers four hundred and twenty-one members.

Wednesday was our last day on the island. A visit to Mr. Rowell's garden made my ride back to Koloa about twenty miles. But I had an excellent horse, through the kindness of Dr. Wood, the gentlemanly owner of a large sugar estate at that place. He was then absent at Honolulu; but, with his niece, was a fellow-passenger with us on our return to San Francisco, contributing materially to the happiness of our voyage.

At night we went on board the Annie Laurie, with our good friends Mr. Corwin and Mr. Wilder, and after two nights and a day, which we shall not soon forget, landed at Honolulu early on Friday morning.

Mr. Corwin proposed walking to his house, and asked of me the loan of a sandal-wood stick, given me by Mrs. Rice, "to keep off the dogs." Not many days after he returned me the stick in the form of a beautiful cane, having a large ivory head, but made no explanations. To my great surprise it proved, that the ivory head was hollow, and filled with gold pieces, and small circular papers written over in this manner: —

"Good for ——, for the A. B. C. F. M., a gift from —— ——, towards the expenses of your visit."

The amount in gold was three hundred and fifty dollars. Two of the principal donors had never sustained any connection with the Board, but the remaining seven had formerly been missionaries. The delicacy of the testimonial, as well as its value to the Board (which, with the premium, was four hundred and twenty-five dollars), gave me very great pleasure.

III.

PEOPLE OF THE ISLANDS.

PEOPLE OF THE ISLANDS.

CHAPTER XIII.

THEIR SOCIAL AND CIVIL CONDITION.

Aim of the Mission. — Improved Social Condition of the People. — Relations of Missionaries to a Barbarous Government. — Declaration of the Mission. — No Improper Influence. — Mr. Richards the chosen Counsellor of the Government. — *Magna Charta.* — Constitution. — Code of Laws. — Christian Tone of the Constitution. — Laws at first necessarily Imperfect. — Exemplary Punishment. — Revision of the Statutes. — The National Religion. — The Religion free. — The Christian Sabbath. — Churches and Parsonages. — Days of Fasting and Thanksgiving. — Structure of the Government.

THE pioneers of this mission were instructed by their Board "to aim at nothing short of covering the Sandwich Islands with fruitful fields, and pleasant dwellings, and schools and churches, and of raising the whole people to an elevated state of Christian civilization." Considering what the Hawaiian people were at that time, it must be admitted that great progress has since been made, through a kind Providence, in the work assigned to the mission. The preceding chapters afford numerous illustrations of the improved social condition of the people. The Hawaiian people have been *humanized* by the gospel. When travelling among them it was hard to conceive how their murderous war-spirit, so universally prevalent only a few years before, had given place to a spirit so apparently mild and peaceful, or how they could have become so obedient to written laws, so observant of the rights of property.

Their social condition, though far from what it should be, is yet a great improvement on the past. Scarcely forty years have elapsed since the first marriage. Prior to that there was no connection between man and woman that could not be sundered at any moment by the will of the parties; and this led to frequent crimes and great misery. Among the earliest blessings on a large scale, introduced by missionaries, was Christian marriage. Two thousand marriages were solemnized in the single year following June, 1830. The number reported during the last ten years is six thousand seven hundred and nineteen; and the contract has been recognized and confirmed by the laws for more than thirty years, so that it could not be annulled by the parties.

Civilization does not precede the gospel among a barbarous people, nor even keep pace with it in its early stages. The arts of domestic life have, as yet, made slow progress among the masses of the islanders. The chiefs are the principal holders of property; some are the owners of large landed estates. These have houses and furniture like their foreign neighbors, especially in the towns. This is more or less true, also, of not a few among the common people, who have the means, and reside in the towns. But natives in rural districts, whatever their rank, continue to love grass houses, which, besides their small cost, are certainly adapted to the climate. Even the late king had one within the enclosure of his country-seat at Kailua. But the grass houses of the common people are now larger and better built than they once were, with a more convenient entrance. Their furniture, for the most part, is still very simple, consisting of a few mats spread on the ground for sleeping, a few calabashes for food and water, and means for pounding the *taro*, which is their main reliance for food after it has been manufactured into *poi*.

I am not able to say how far they are adepts in the mechanic arts. But I was assured there are natives, in most parts of the Islands, who are able to make doors, chairs, chests, tables, bedsteads, cupboards. And females, taught in the first instance by ladies of the mission, succeed well in the manufacture of bonnets and hats from the cocoanut and palm-leaf, or a fine flexible grass; while not a few are able to cut and make garments for themselves and their children. At any rate, many of the females must have learned the art of making clothes, for they are everywhere seen wearing loose but appropriate garments of foreign cloth.

While the instructions to the first missionaries enjoined upon them the grand aim "of raising up the whole people of the Islands to an elevated state of Christian civilization," they were also required to "withhold themselves entirely from all interference and intermeddling with the political affairs and party concerns of the nation." This they have done. But they were not thus shut off from all attempts to enlighten and elevate the government of the Islands, since that was indispensable to the attainment, by the people, of an elevated Christian civilization. The government could not remain unchanged, and the people become free and civilized. The people must own property, have acknowledged rights, and be governed by written, well-known, established laws. This was far from their condition before the year 1838. The government was then a despotism. The will of the king was law, his power absolute; and this was true of the chiefs, also, in their separate spheres, so far as the common people were concerned. All right of property, in the last resort, was with the king. How were the people to attain the true Christian position? Obviously the rulers had duties to learn and to perform, equally with the people; and the missionaries were the Christian teachers of both classes, with God's Word for their guide.

The nature of their teaching was distinctly and

admirably set forth by the mission, in a series of resolutions adopted June, 1838 — resolutions which Mr. Wyllie, the well-known Minister of Foreign Affairs, pronounced worthy "to be printed in letters of gold, and hung up in the house of nobles." These resolutions, entitled, "Duties of the Mission to Rulers and Subjects as such," deserve a permanent record. They were, with a few unimportant omissions, as follows: —

"1. Though the system of government, since the commencement of the reign of Liholiho, has been greatly improved, through the influence of Christianity and the introduction of written and printed laws, it is still so very imperfect for managing the affairs of a civilized and virtuous nation, as to render it of great importance that correct views of the rights and duties of rulers and subjects, and of the principles of jurisprudence and political economy, should be held up before the king and the members of the national council.

"2. It is the duty of missionaries to teach the doctrine, that rulers should be just, ruling in the fear of God, seeking the best good of their nation, demanding no more of subjects, as such, than the various ends of the government may justly require; and if church-members among them violate the commands of God, they should be admonished with the same faithfulness and tenderness as their dependents.

"3. Rulers are such by the providence of God, and also, in an important sense, by the will or consent of the people, and ought not to shrink from the cares and responsibilities of their office; and the teachers of religion ought carefully to guard the subjects against contempt for the authority of their rulers, or any evasion or resistance of government orders.

"4. The resources of the nation are at its own disposal for its defence, improvement, and perfection; and subjects ought to be taught to feel that a portion of their time and services, their property and earnings, may rightfully be required by the sovereign or national council, for the support of government in all its branches and departments; and that it is a Christian duty to render honor, obedience, fear, custom, and tribute to whom they are due, as taught in the 13th of Romans; and that the sin of disloyalty, which tends to confusion, anarchy, and ruin, deserves reproof as really and as promptly as that of injustice on the part of rulers, or any other violation of the commands of God.

"5. While rulers should be allowed to do what they will with their own, or with what they have a right to demand, we ought to encourage the security of the right of subjects to do what they will with their own, provided they render to Cæsar his due.

"6. Rulers ought to be prompted to direct their efforts to the promotion of general intelligence and virtue as a grand means of removing the existing evils, gradually defining, by equitable laws, the rights and duties of all classes; that thus, by improving rather than revolutionizing the government, its administration may become more abundantly salutary, and the hereditary rulers receive no detriment, but rather advantage.

"7. To remove the improvidence and imbecility of the people, and promote the industry, wealth, and happiness of the nation, it is the duty of the missionary to urge mainly the motives to loyalty, patriotism, social kindness, and general benevolence; but while, on the one hand, he should not condemn their artificial wants, ancient or modern, because they depend on fancy, or a taste not refined, he should, on the other, endeavor to encourage and multiply such as will enlist their energies, call forth ingenuity, enterprise, and patient industry, and give scope for enlarged plans of profitable exertion, which, if well directed, would clothe the population in beautiful cottons, fine linen, and silk, and their arable fields with rich and various productions suitable to the climate; would adorn the land with numerous comfortable and substantial habitations, made pleasant by elegant furniture, cabinets, and libraries; with permanent and well-endowed school-houses and seminaries; with large, commodious and durable churches; and their seas and harbors with ships owned by natives, sufficient to export to other countries annually the surplus products of their soil, which may at no very distant period amount to millions."

The chief rulers, after their conversion, were open to instruction and influence from the missionaries on all points affecting their religious characters and duties. This was especially true of the Regent, Kaahumanu. It was also true, to a great extent, of Kamehameha III., who, though not professedly pious, and not always temperate in his habits, had excellent points of character, and was beloved as a father to his people. The assertion sometimes made, that "the missionaries individually wormed themselves into the confidence of the king and chiefs, in order to exercise an influence favorable to themselves and to the United States," the Minister of Foreign Affairs, a native of Great Britain, declares to be "a bold and unscrupulous assertion, without even a shadow of truth."

It was subsequent to the year 1837, and in the reign of Kamehameha III., that the government received its present form, and avowedly came upon a high Christian basis. A brief reference to the facts, as presented in the printed Laws and Rules, and in the Statute Laws of Kamehameha III., is all that comports with our limits; and less than this would not satisfy the intelligent reader.

The application of the king and chiefs to their American patrons, in 1836, for teachers in agriculture and the arts, and in Christian government, is given in the second chapter, as also the response of the American Board. It was there stated how the Rev. William Richards became their adviser in respect to all matters on which they chose to consult him. Mr. Richards was probably the best man for them at the outset. I knew him well. Though not from the same college, he was my classmate in the Andover Theological Seminary, and I afterwards corresponded officially with him until his death. With intelligence such as a liberal education affords, with a sound judgment, the utmost disinterestedness, and the confidence of king, chiefs, and people, Mr. Richards took a release from his connection with the Board and the mission in 1838, that he might guide the infant steps of the government, as it went forward, relaxing the bands of despotism, and forming relations with the great Christian world. His duties were performed amid very trying embarrassments, from the opposition of foreigners, who wished to use the government for their own selfish purposes. Not that he was free from all errors of judgment; that were too much to expect; but when he died, the gratitude of the nation decreed a pension to his widow, which was regularly paid until her decease not long since.

The following Bill of Rights was signed by the king on the 7th of June, 1839, and was the first essential departure from the ancient despotism:

"God has made of one blood all nations of men, to dwell on the face of the earth in unity and blessedness. God has also bestowed certain rights alike on all men, and all chiefs, and all people, of all lands.

"These are some of the rights which he has given alike to every man and every chief, namely, life, limb, liberty, the labor of his hands, and the productions of his mind.

"God has also established governments and rulers for the purposes of peace; but, in making laws for a nation, it is by no means proper to enact laws for the protection of rulers only, without also providing protection for their subjects; neither is it proper to enact laws to enrich the chiefs only, without regard to the enriching of their subjects also; and hereafter there shall by no means be any law enacted which is inconsistent with what is above expressed; neither shall any tax be assessed, nor any service or labor required of any man, in any manner at variance with the above sentiments.

"These sentiments are hereby proclaimed for the purpose of protecting all alike, both the people and the chiefs of all these Islands, that no chief may be able to oppress any subject, but that the chiefs and people may enjoy the same protection under the same law.

"Protection is hereby secured to the persons of all the people, together with their lands, their building lots, and all their property; and nothing whatever shall be taken from any individual, except by express provision of the laws. Whatever chief shall perseveringly act in violation of this constitution, shall no longer remain a chief of the Sandwich Islands; and the same shall be true of the governors, officers, and all land agents."

This *Magna Charta* of the Hawaiian Islands was conferred voluntarily, without the intervention of armed barons and their retainers; and perhaps it might be difficult to find such another instance of the cheerful surrender of arbitrary power, purely out of regard to the welfare and happiness of the subjects.

On the 8th of October, 1840, Kamehameha conferred a constitution on the people, recognizing the three grand divisions of a civilized monarchy, — king, legislature, and judges, — and defining, in some respects, the duties of each.

It is not certainly known what agency Mr. Richards had in securing these invaluable concessions to the people; but no one can doubt that they were the direct consequence of the enlightening, humanizing, Christianizing influence of the mission. It is an historic fact, that Mr. Richards, in 1842, collected from detached fragments, and translated into the English language, the declaratory and penal ordinances which had been made by the king before the constitution was declared, or afterwards enacted by the legislature. The constitution of 1840 declared that "no law shall be enacted which is at variance with the Word of the Lord Jehovah, or with the general spirit of his Word," and that "all laws of the Islands shall be in consistency with the general spirit of God's law." The laws must of course have been imperfect, because they were framed with reference to the low condition of the people, and what it seemed then possible to carry into effect. They were severe upon the prevalent and destructive vices of intemperance and licentiousness. And was it not something to succeed (as they did) in driving those shameless vices into concealment? One of the first inflictions of the death penalty, for the infraction of these laws, was upon a chief of high rank, a favorite of the king, for murdering his wife by poison. He and his accomplice, after a regular trial and condemnation in a court composed of Kekuanaoa, governor of Oahu, as presiding judge, and a jury of twelve Hawaiians, were hung on the walls of the fort.

As the nation progressed and its relations multiplied, it became necessary to secure the services of some one who had received a legal education, and such a man was found in Mr. John Ricord. From what country he came I do not know; but he made, for the time, an efficient legal adviser to the government, occupying the post of attorney-general. In June, 1845, he was requested to prepare a digest of the existing laws, with such improvements and additions as the circumstances of the country demanded. This code of laws was adopted by the "nobles and representatives of the Hawaiian Islands, in legislative council assembled," April 27, 1846.[1] A few of the more important statutes concerning religious matters will be quoted.

"1. The religion of the Lord Jesus Christ shall continue to be the established national religion of the Hawaiian Islands. The laws of Kamehameha III., orally proclaimed, abolishing all idol-worship and ancient heathen customs, are hereby continued in force, and said worship and customs are forbidden to be practised in this kingdom, upon the pains and penalties to be prescribed in the criminal code.

"2. Although the Protestant religion is the religion of the government, as heretofore proclaimed, nothing in the last preceding section shall be construed as requiring any particular form of worship, neither is anything therein contained to be construed as connecting the ecclesiastical with the body politic. All men residing in this kingdom shall be allowed freely to worship the God of the Christian Bible according to the dictates of their own consciences, and this sacred privilege shall never be infringed upon. Any

[1] In the English language, the code occupies three hundred and eighty pages, and in the Hawaiian language, into which it was rendered by Mr. Richards, two hundred and twenty-eight pages.

disturbance of religious assemblies, or hinderance of the free and unconstrained worship of God, unless such worship be connected with indecent or improper conduct, shall be considered a misdemeanor, and punished as in and by the criminal code prescribed.

"3. It shall not be lawful to violate the Christian Sabbath by the transaction of worldly business. The Sabbath shall be considered no day in law. All documents and other evidences of worldly transactions dated on the Sabbath shall be deemed in law to have no date, and to be void for not having legal existence. It shall not on that day be lawful to entertain any civil cause in the courts of this kingdom. Every attempt to serve civil process on that day shall be deemed a trespass by the officer attempting it, and shall subject such officer to the private civil suit of the party aggrieved. Provided, however, that it shall, in criminal, fraudulent, and tortuous cases be lawful to issue compulsory process for the arrest of wrong-doers; and it shall, without such process, be lawful on that day for any conservator of the public peace and morality, to arrest, commit, and detain for examination a wrong-doer.

"4. Any adult male persons, not less in number than fifty individuals, living in the same vicinity and adopting similar doctrines and tenets of religious belief, and like form of Christian worship, shall be entitled to petition the minister of public instruction, through the general superintendent, in writing, for permission to erect, at their own expense, a church or other religious conventicle, and for land to be appropriated to a parsonage for the use and support of the clergyman employed with the approbation of said minister, on satisfactory evidence that he is in good and regular standing with his own denomination of Christians.

"When days of fasting or thanksgiving are proclaimed by the king in privy council, they are declared to be obligatory on all persons, according to their general spirit and intent."

It appears, therefore, that the Christian religion is "the established national religion of the Hawaiian Islands;" and the Protestant form of it is "the religion of the government." But this is without any connection, properly speaking, between church and state, since no one sect derives its support from the government, and all are equally free "to worship the God of the Christian Bible according to the dictates of their own consciences."

The government is a limited monarchy. By the amended constitution the crown was permanently confirmed to Kamehameha IV., "and the heirs of his body lawfully begotten, and to their lawful descendants in a direct line." Next to him was his Royal Highness Prince Lot Kamehameha, now on the throne; and next, their sister, the Princess Victoria. In the failure of all these, and of the king and House of Nobles to designate and proclaim some person during the king's life, a successor to the throne is to be elected by joint ballot of both houses of the legislature. To the king belongs the executive power, and his person is inviolable and sacred. His ministers are responsible. Laws passed by both houses of the legislature must be signed by His Majesty, and also by the Kuhina Nui, as the premier is called.

The House of Nobles is restricted by the constitution to thirty members, and at present has only fifteen, who hold their seats for life, by appointment from the king. Ten of them are natives. The popular branch of the legislature consists of twenty-seven members, who are chosen biennially by the people, and the representation is proportioned to the population. Less than one fourth of the representatives elected at the opening of the year 1864 were of foreign origin.

"No person is eligible for a representative of the people who is insane, or an idiot, or who shall at any time have been convicted of any infamous crime, or unless he be a male subject or denizen of the kingdom, who shall have arrived at the full age of twenty-five years, who shall know how to read and write, who shall understand accounts, and who shall have resided in the kingdom for at least one year immediately preceding his election, and who shall own real estate within the kingdom, unencumbered, of the value of at least two hundred and fifty dollars, or who shall have an annual income of at least two hundred and fifty dollars."

The Supreme Court has a chief justice and two associate justices. There are also Circuit Courts, with judges not to exceed three; and these two classes of judges hold office during good behavior. There are, besides, district judges, whose commissions expire at the end of two years. The Hawaiian kingdom has been greatly favored in the judges of its

Supreme Court. The first chief justice, William L. Lee, came from the United States to the Islands in 1846, I believe with some reference to the climate and his own health, and died at Honolulu, May 28, 1857. Chief Justice Lee must have been one of the best of men, and his sterling common sense, sound judgment, practical education, Christian virtues, and his deep concern in everything tending to the welfare of the nation, rendered him a most valuable citizen, and his death a great public loss. The judges of that court, at the time of my visit, were the Hon. Elisha H. Allen, chief justice, a native of the United States, Hon. G. M. Robertson, a native of Great Britain, and the Hon. John Ii, a native-born citizen. I saw enough of these gentlemen to entertain for them the highest respect — a feeling which I have reason to believe is universal on the Islands. It certainly speaks well for courts of justice, where the laws are everywhere felt to be a living power. In no country are life and property more secure than they now are on the Hawaiian Islands.

The independence of the Hawaiian nation was formally recognized by England and France on the 28th of November, 1843; and the two nations then engaged "never to take possession, neither directly nor under the title of protectorate, or under any other form, of any part of the territory of which they are composed." On the 6th of July, 1844, Mr. Calnoun, then United States Secretary of State, assured the Hawaiian Commissioners that the communication addressed to them by Mr. Webster, as Secretary of State, "dated the 29th December, 1842, and the proceedings thereon of the House of Representatives, the appropriation made for the compensation of a Commissioner of the United States, who was subsequently appointed, to reside in the Sandwich Islands, were regarded by the President as a full recognition on the part of the United States, at that time, of the independence of the Hawaiian government." And the United States has ever since treated that government as an independent power.

CHAPTER XIV.

INDUSTRY AND COMMERCE.

INDUSTRY: Arable Land. — Scarcity of Labor. — Coolies. — Cane Lands. — Taro and Rice Lands. — Capacity for sustaining Population. — Sugar Plantations and their Product. — Coffee. — Wool. — Cotton. — Oranges. — Hawaiians and Labor. — What is needed. — COMMERCE: Amount of Trade. — Merchant Vessels. — Whalers. — Coasting Fleet. — Conditions of National Prosperity.

THE Hawaiian Islands, though of volcanic origin and mountainous, have a large amount of arable land; and much of it is adapted to the culture of sugar-cane, and much to the growth of taro (*arum esculentum*) and rice. The drawback to the rice is in the ravages of field mice. In some districts there is a degree of uncertainty as to irrigation. This latter evil will be quite sure to increase, unless decisive measures are taken to prevent the mountain sides from being opened to the sunbeams by the unrestrained inroads of cattle and horses, and of the vast flocks of goats, which are so destructive to the undergrowth of the forests. There is also a deficiency of laborers; and a far greater amount of capital will be required for covering the lands with the sugar-cane, than moneyed men are yet disposed to invest there. Coolies were imported, some years since, from China, but they did not meet the expectations of the planters. It was affirmed, in a late meeting of the Planters' Society, that it is not safe for the plantations to depend wholly upon native labor, and that it is undesirable for a large proportion of the natives to be compelled to resort for support to the plantations. It was also stated, that the natives hold as much land in their own right (the *kuleana*, or freehold) as they are able to cultivate, even were none of them to work for the foreigner.

Mr. Wyllie not long since publicly declared his purpose to introduce a large number of carefully selected coolies for the use of his plantation. In April, 1864, the Minister of the Interior, by command of the king, requested the planters to state what number of Chinese, or other Asiatic laborers, each desired and would take; what monthly wages they would pay to each laborer, besides food and lodging; what each would pay on the arrival of the laborers in Honolulu; for what term of years each would require the laborers to be contracted for; and whether he would wish them to come with their wives and children. About the same time a joint committee from the government and the Planters' Association agreed to recommend to the government to make the attempt to import from fifty to a hundred laborers from the Polynesian Islands, with their women, to meet the present necessity. They stated that the attainable Chinese laborers are usually rogues, thieves, and pirates; that respectable Chinese women will not leave their native land, and that it is illegal to bring Chinese men or women away from their country. And they came to the conclusion that the Hill Coolies of India, who for many years have been sent from Calcutta to the West Indies and to Mauritius, would be the most desirable class of laborers to import, and that immediate measures ought to be adopted to obtain them. These facts are stated as bearing, for good or evil, on the future of the Islands.

I have the authority of one of the wealthiest and best informed of the planters for saying, that there are at least ten thousand acres of land on the Island of Maui adapted to the cultivation of the sugar-cane, and as many as fifty thousand acres of such land on the Islands. He regards most of Hilo and a part of Hamakua as good cane land. A far greater amount of land is capable of being cultivated by the plough, for the raising of wheat, etc. Large districts are adapted to grazing, and especially to the pasturage of sheep. The population which the Islands might be made to sustain would not fall much short of a million.

The opinion prevails, among persons most likely to be informed, that sugar is to become the grand staple of the Islands. In 1854 there were exported 513,684 lbs. of this article; in 1863, 5,292,121 lbs., and the quantity in 1864 will be greatly enlarged.

The principal sugar plantations now in operation

are the following. Their estimated products, in the year 1864, though given in round numbers, is believed to be substantially correct.

On Kauai.

	Tons.
Hanalei, producing	500
Lahue, "	250
Koloa, "	250

On Oahu.

Nuuanu Valley, a plantation four miles back of Honolulu.

On Maui.

Lahaina, — the cane produced by small cultivators, and either bought of them by the manufacturers, or manufactured on

	Tons.
Shares, producing	200
Waikapu, "	200
Wailuku, "	300
Makawao, two plantations, producing .	700
Haiku . . . . " . .	500
Ulupalakua . . . . " . .	800
Hana . . . . " . .	150

On Hawaii.

Two plantations in Hilo, owned by Chinese, each producing 250 tons, . .	500
Onomea, seven miles from Hilo, . . .	400
Metcalf plantation, in Hilo, ...	420

A few other plantations are in progress on each of the four principal Islands.

Excellent coffee is produced on the Islands. A blight discouraged the cultivation of it for a time; but that is now known to be a temporary evil, and coffee promises to be one of the staple productions. The export in 1863 was 138,171 lbs. Wool is also a staple; the export in 1860 was 70,524 lbs., and 283,163 lbs. in 1863. Among the new articles of export, I notice 3122 lbs. of cotton, "most of which," the newspaper says, "was choice sea-island cotton." Good oranges are grown, especially in the south-western district of Hawaii, where is a large plantation. The trees suffered for a time from the same cause as the coffee.

For a people living under a tropical sun, the Hawaiians do not seem to be especially chargeable with indolence. They are vivacious, sanguine, imitative. As their wants multiply with advancing civilization, they show a disposition to labor for the means of supplying those wants. But it is not always easy for them to make their labors productive. Were every valley and hill-side adapted to some particular culture, the masses of the native land-holding population want either the knowledge or the means for availing themselves of the advantages. Those combinations, by means of which results are obtained beyond the power of the individual, belong to a civilization which there has not been time for the islander to reach. If his *kuleana*, reserved to him by the laws, lies in the midst of huge tracts rented by government to graziers, then, not being able to fence it, his products are destroyed by animals. And this is the chief reason why certain districts have been depopulated. There is, moreover, the want of roads and bridges, and of safe anchorage for vessels, where the native farmer may promptly ship his produce for the market. These facilities are coming, but they necessarily come slowly.

The *Commerce* of the Islands is of course yet in its infancy. The traffic in sandal-wood lasted about thirty years, and yielded in that time perhaps a million of dollars. The collecting of it, in the mountains, became at length a grievous burden to the common people. The imports in 1863 were $1,175,493.25, and the exports $1,025,852.74. Of the exports, $744,413.54 were in domestic produce, and the balance, $281,439.20, was in foreign merchandise reëxported. The custom-house receipts, in the same year, were $122,752.68. A large portion of the export was sugar. The number of merchant vessels at the ports of the Hawaiian Islands in the same year was eighty-eight, with a tonnage of 42,936. Nine of these were Hawaiian, nine were British, and sixty were American, averaging nearly five hundred tons for each vessel. Besides these, one hundred and two whaling vessels visited the Islands, ninety-two of which were American.

In addition to the propeller named Kilauea and

the schooner-propeller Annie Laurie, the coasting fleet of the Islands consists of about a score of schooner-rigged vessels, of from fifty to one hundred and twenty tons. One of the finest of them, the Emma Rooke, lately drifted upon the rocky shore, and was wrecked where we made our landing at Kohala. We often had the pleasure of looking down from the mountain sides upon these brisk little commercial pioneers, as they were sailing along the smooth sea.

Three regular packets were plying between San Francisco and the Islands at the time of my visit. They were barks, very comfortable vessels, and made an average passage from San Francisco to Honolulu of fifteen days, and of sixteen days and six hours on their return voyage. In the former case they have the advantage of the north-east trades, and once or twice have made the passage in ten days; but, on returning to the American coast, it is necessary to go northward in search of westerly winds. The exports are chiefly to San Francisco, and the imports come, for the most part, from the same great and growing mart of commerce.

The remarkable geographical relations of these Islands to the commercial countries around the Pacific Ocean have already been pointed out.[1] Honolulu must become at least a great coaling and refitting

[1] See Chapter I.

station on the commercial route from Panama to Japan and China. Should the culture of sugar, rice, coffee, cotton — of any one or all of these — be successful, it will insure a population of some kind for the Islands, and a large capital. But this, again, must depend on the confidence reposed in the stability and wisdom of the government. The chief dangers of the nation are within itself. Its national life is to be preserved in the way in which it was created — by means of the gospel and gospel institutions, and those habits of temperance, purity, and sobriety which are inculcated by the gospel, along with the general culture of the native mind, through the medium of the native language. And a wise government will not fail to see that this is not compatible with measures tending to alienate the confidence and affections of the people from those excellent men, to whom, under God, they are indebted for all their personal, social, and national blessings.

CHAPTER XV.

SCHOOLS AND LITERATURE.

SCHOOLS: For the Young and Adults,— Their Number. — Teachers. — Readers. — Cheapness of Instruction. — The Youth brought into the Schools. — Their Number. — Schools for Teachers. — Government assumes the Support of the Common Schools. — Tabular View of Government Schools. — Their Cost. — School for the Chiefs. — The Government and High Schools. — Oahu College. — LITERATURE: Hawaiian Language. — Its Alphabet. — Amount of Printing. — Works in the Language. — Contemplated Progress. — Susceptibility of the People to be influenced by their Literature.

EDUCATION at these Islands began with the adults as well as with the children and youth. At one time a very large proportion of the adult population was embraced in the schools. In 1830 and the two following years, before the commencement of the great religious awakening, the pupils, for those years respectively, were thirty-nine thousand, forty-five thousand, and fifty-three thousand. The attendance was of course irregular, the people coming as their ordinary occupations would allow. The teachers were natives, who had obtained what they were able to impart to their pupils by spending a few months at the station schools, under the immediate supervision of the missionaries. In 1831 there were as many as nine hundred of these teachers. Their qualifications were of course extremely moderate; and after 1832 the schools declined rapidly, for want of teachers able to instruct beyond the mere rudiments. Yet, of the eighty-five thousand Hawaiians, more than one fourth part had then learned to read God's word, and some in every place were able to write, and not a few to use the elementary principles of arithmetic. Learning to read was easy with so simple an alphabet, and the cheapness of the instruction was wonderful. Not a dozen of the teachers were paid anything by the mission. The school-houses were the merest grass hovels. The supply of books was almost the only expense, and even these were not distributed gratuitously, though, for want of a circulating medium, the people could pay for them only with the products of the Islands, or by their labor.

Attention was at length directed to the higher education of the youth. A school had been commenced at Lahainaluna in 1831, for educating male teachers; another was opened in 1836, at Hilo; and in the same year a High School for females was commenced at Wailuku. In 1837 the number reported in the common schools was only about two thousand. In 1843 it was eighteen thousand seven hundred, which is larger than the average number since reported. Three years later, the Hawaiian government assumed the entire support of the common schools, including the wages of teachers. The following tabular view is taken from the one published by the Board of Education in 1860:—

Year.	No of Schools.	No. of Scholars.	No. of Days' Schooling.	Average Days each School.	Population.	Cost of Schools.	No. of English Schools.	No. of English Scholars.	Gov.Support to English Schools.	Natives and half-castes in Eng.Schools.
1846		18,644				$20,000.00				
1847	625	19,644				21,706.48	6	200	$3,411.04	
1848	527	19,028	76,663	145.8	87,063	22,318.84				
1849	540	15,620	88,996	164.1	84,165	21,989.84	8	306	None.	211
1850	543	15,308	83,290	153.3	83,988	25,890.06	6	208	567.40	125
1851	535	15,482	73,749	137.8	80,620	25,271.08	11	305	10,045.50	187
1852	440	13,948	57,212	30	79,650	24,049.07	10	353		156
1853	423	12,205	54,099	127.8	73,137	20,563.58		300	3,641.00	
1854	412	10,241	54,586	132.5	73,079	20,705.31	15	891	2,658.00	700
1855					73,032					
1856	332	8,671		143	72,740	25,827.27	27	1055	11,853.58	1019
1857	312	8,460		164	72,338	27,578.28	20	872	9,076.20	739
1858	293	8,628	52,476	192	71,954	29,215.02				
1859	289	8,628	54,656	179	71,275	34,165.47				

In 1839 the government resolved upon having a High School expressly for the young chiefs, to be supported by the nation. At the request of the rulers, Mr. and Mrs. Cooke were set apart by the mission to take charge of the school. Two well-educated young men, from the United States, were afterwards associated with them in the instruction. The late king, his queen, the present king, Victoria (their sister), and Bernice (the accomplished Mrs. Bishop), all received their education in this school, of which Mr. Wyllie thus speaks in his published Notes of 1848 : —

"Mr. and Mrs. Cooke, both by precept and the example of their own well-regulated family, enforced the utmost propriety of moral deportment, and every punctilio of cleanliness, dress, manner, and address, calculated to add polish and refinement to more solid and useful attainments."

It was stated, in connection with my tour on Maui, that the institution at Lahainaluna was made over to the government of the Islands in 1849, which henceforward assumed its entire support. In 1862 the government built three substantial school edifices, in place of the large one that had been burned down. It also shared with the Board and private benefactors in the expense of rebuilding the house for the High School at Hilo, which had been burned, and it now bears a part of the expense of instruction in that school. When the school-house at Waioli, on Kauai, had been destroyed by fire, in 1862, the government furnished the materials for a new building, and contributed towards the support of the principal, whose salary had hitherto been wholly paid by the American Board.

The account already given of Oahu College[1] supersedes the necessity of speaking of it here; except to say, that it needs a larger endowment, to be able to give a more liberal education to the children of missionaries, and other foreign residents of those Islands.

The Hawaiian language was so far reduced to writing by the missionaries in 1822, that they commenced printing in January of that year. Every syllable in the language ends with a vowel; and all the sounds of the language are expressed by five vowels and seven consonants. To give a proper expression to the names of persons, places, and things in other countries, with which the Hawaiians need to become acquainted, especially to Scripture names, nine consonants have been added — *b*, *d*, *f*, *g*, *r*, *s*, *t*, *v*, and *z*. The twelve letters of the proper Hawaiian alphabet are *a*, *e*, *i*, *o*, *u*, *h*, *k*, *l*, *m*, *n*, *p*, *w*. It was this simple alphabet that so soon made the ability to read almost universal. In pronouncing Hawaiian words, *a* has the sound of *a* in *father*; *e* of *a* in *pale*; *i* of *i* in *machine*; *o* of *o* in *no*; *u* of *oo* in *too*; and

[1] Chapter XI.

these vowels have names expressive of their power, *Ah*, *A*, *Ee*, *O*, *Oo*. The consonants have names alike expressive, following the sounds of the vowels, *He*, *Ke*, *La*, *Mu*, *Nu*, *Pi*, *We*. The full accent is usually on the last syllable but one, and there is a secondary accent two syllables before the full accent.

There have been published in the native language, besides the Old and New Testaments, more than two hundred different works, and more than two hundred million pages. A portion of the works may be thus classed: —

Religious.

	Copies.
The entire Bible (Baibala, 1451 pages), . .	20,000
New Testament, Hawaiian, ...	12,000
New Testament, Hawaiian and English, 727 pages (New York, 1860), ...	60,000
Daily Texts, ...	150,000
Doctrinal Catechism, ...	30,000
Other Catechisms and Bible Class Books, . .	40,000
Thirty Tracts, on various subjects, . . .	120,000
Baxter's Saints' Rest.	
Pilgrim's Progress, ...	10,000
Gallaudet's Treatise on the Soul.	
Volume of Sermons, ...	5,500
Clark's Scripture Promises.	
Natural Theology, ...	2,500
Evidences of Christianity, ...	500
History of Joseph.	
Church History, ...	2,500

	Copies.
Scripture History, ...	10,000
Tract Primer, ...	3,000
Tract for Parents.	
Hymns, with Music, for Children, ...	3,000
Hymn Books, ...	100,000
Child's Hymn Book, ...	10,000
Dying Testimony of Christians and Infidels.	
Keith on the Prophecies.	

School Books.

First Book (five or six kinds), and Pictorial Primer. Child's, Mental, Leonard's, and Colburn's Arithmetics; Algebra, and the Higher Mathematics. Linear Drawing, Geometry for Children, Legendre's Geometry, Trigonometry, and Logarithms. Surveying, Study of the Globes, Geography, Atlas, and Sacred Geography. Astronomy, Anatomy, and Chronology. Lyra Hawaii (a music book). Hawaiian Grammar, Hawaiian and English Phrase Book, and Hawaiian and English Vocabulary. Several school books, issued by the Board of Education.

General Literature.

Wayland's Moral Science, and Wayland's Political Economy. Compend of General History, Ancient History, Elements of History, and Hawaiian History. Military Tactics.

Government.

Statute Laws, 1846, two volumes. Civil Code, three volumes. Penal Code, one volume. Several volumes of Department Reports.

Newspapers.

Lama Hawaii, Kumu Hawaii, Elele Hawaii, Kumu Kamalii, Nonanona, Nu Hou, Hae Hawaii, Hoku Pakifika, Hoku Loa, and Nupepa Kuokoa. The two last named are the papers now in existence.

Recent events in the Islands, described in this volume, have given a wholesome influence in the direction of a Christian literature. It is proposed to publish a concordance of the Scriptures as soon as the revision of the existing version is finished, and the American Bible Society shall have completed the electrotype plates for it, upon which it purposes to enter before the close of the year 1864. Also, a commentary on the Scriptures, now greatly needed by the native ministry, together with a Scripture manual, and treatises on pastoral duties and homiletics. A compend of modern history is in contemplation, and a work illustrating the family medical practice, and another on the laws of health, of which the Hawaiians have a very imperfect understanding. There is a call among the people for religious biographies suited to their capacity, and for a more elaborate Scripture history and biography than is now in existence. The Pilgrim's Progress, so much appreciated among the Nestorian Christians, has not found a ready sale among the Hawaiians, for want of an easy comprehension of its story. A supply of illustrative engravings, it is thought, will render the book more attractive and intelligible.

The Hoku Pakifika (newspaper in the native language) is understood to take its tone from the government. The Nupepa Kuokoa (a weekly paper in the Hawaiian language, published by Mr. Whitney, son of one of the first missionaries) is professedly neutral in matters of religious controversy, but aims to promote the moral and intellectual progress of the nation. The Hoku Loa has been revived by the joint labors of the Rev. L. H. Gulick, Secretary of the Hawaiian Board, and the Rev. H. H. Parker, pastor of the first church at Honolulu, to meet the strongly felt want of a religious newspaper.

The question will arise, *How far the Hawaiian people are able and disposed to be profited by a literature in their native language.* This will best be answered by an extract from a well considered article, which was read by Judge Andrews before the Hawaiian Evangelical Association in June, 1863. His competence to testify on the subject is seen in the fact, that he is the author of the Hawaiian Grammar mentioned above, and also of a Dictionary of the Hawaiian Language, containing ten or twelve thousand words, which is about being published under the auspices of the Hawaiian government. It will be remembered that he was the first principal of what is now the Lahainaluna College.

"What are some of the things of specific value which Hawaiians have gained through the medium of instruction in their own language? Here we can go into a few specifications; and I shall draw largely on my own experience. In the summer of 1828 I commenced teaching, or rather hearing Hawaiians read, in their own language. That was about the time that the desire to learn to read became prevalent throughout the nation, and schools were established in almost every district on the Islands, and the great mass of the people (adults) began to *read* in their own language. It is true they did not read very fluently, nor had they much in their language then to read. But a great many learned to read, and in some measure understood what they read. It will be remembered that at that time, and for several years afterwards, no children were in the schools. The schools were composed entirely of adults, chiefs and people, men and women. Many who had passed the middle age of life were proud to stand up in classes, and read their *palapalas*. The masses read, and continued to learn to read, as fast as the missionaries could get out books for them. The first book was a small Spelling-book; then followed Thoughts of the Chiefs. The chiefs had not only learned to read, but to write their own thoughts. The Sermon on the Mount followed; then the History of Joseph; then a Sequel to the Spelling-book, a small Arithmetic, etc. As before, it is not pretended that the adult Hawaiians, as a general thing, became good or fluent readers; but they did read, were anxious to get books, and got ideas from reading.

"Again, simultaneously with reading, the people learned to *write*, just as far as they could get the apparatus, i. e., pen, or pencil, and paper (the ink they manufactured, or got from the cuttle-fish), or slates and pencils. My first efforts to understand the Hawaiian language, in 1828, consisted in reading and examining manuscripts written by Hawaiians. Letter-writing, even at that time, was considerably practised, and would have been much more but for want of materials. It was often said, — and I never heard it disputed, — that every Hawaiian who could procure a slate knew how to write. They did not write a beautiful clerk's hand, but they wrote that which was legible, and was of vast importance to them in conveying intelligence from one to another, and from island to island. Missionaries had a good opportunity to know, for in those days they acted as postmasters. This correspondence among themselves has been kept up to this day, as the present post-office department will show.

"In February, 1834, a Hawaiian weekly periodical (Lama Hawaii), of four quarto pages, was commenced at Lahainaluna, one condition of which was, that one full page of each number was reserved for the original thoughts of Hawaiians; and they filled it with respectable newspaper matter. And a Hawaiian periodical, of some kind, has been kept up from that time to the present, no inconsiderable portion of which has been furnished by Hawaiians themselves. Here, then, are readers and writers to no small extent. And here, to show the value I put upon instruction in Hawaiian, allow me to say, that the sources from which I formed the Hawaiian Grammar, and am now (1860) writing a Hawaiian Dictionary, are the letters, essays, compositions, etc., all manuscripts, besides thousands of printed pages, the matter of which was originally written by Hawaiians themselves. For authority in all cases (except the Hawaiian Bible, which in some sense is a Hawaiian book), I have drawn from Hawaiian manuscripts, or from printed pages written by Hawaiians. The ability to have done this — i. e., to have written so much — I consider of immense value to the individuals themselves, and to the nation.

"Another thing taught and learned, and in a good degree understood in native schools, is *arithmetic*; and it is of just the same value to Hawaiians, so far as mental improvement is concerned, as arithmetic is in any other language. All questions in arithmetic can just as well be solved, and the answers given, in Hawaiian as in English, and with the same degree of certainty. This has been done in thousands of cases, as all intelligent persons, both foreign and Hawaiian, know. And the treatises that have been prepared, and printed, and studied, are not mere *first books* for children, but such as are studied in common and higher schools in the United States and in England. I know not what the present text-books are, but I know that when I left the Seminary at Lahainaluna, seventeen years ago, common arithmetic was studied, and as well understood as in schools generally of that class. I know, too, that arithmetic has the effect of improving, enlarging, and strengthening a Hawaiian mind, as it has the mind of a person speaking another language.

"Again, in the higher schools of Lahainaluna, Hilo, and Waioli, neither teachers nor scholars have stopped at arithmetic, but have gone a step farther — into *algebra*. And any one, by examination, may be assured not only that the Hawaiian language is capable of expressing the terms of that science, but that Hawaiian minds are capable of understanding its principles and solving its problems; and that the value of such instruction in Hawaiian is of itself equal to what it would be if gained through the medium of any other language.

"Again, *surveying* has not only been theoretically taught through the medium of Hawaiian, but carried out in practice for several years past. No small part of the surveying of the Islands is now in the hands of Hawaiians, who have learned it entirely in their own language.

"*Geography* in former years, and perhaps now, is successfully taught in many schools, especially topographical geography. This, next to arithmetic, has been a favorite study. The shape of the earth, its divisions of sea and land, of countries and kingdoms, their boundaries, rivers, lakes, cities, nations, etc., etc., with the solving of problems on the globes, constituted a study calculated to enlarge their minds, excite their curiosity, and probably has led some to ship as seamen, that they might see foreign countries. But it has been done, and can be done, in their own language.

"As I have had but little to do with schools for the last fifteen years, I know not what *new* studies have been introduced at Lahainaluna, or Hilo, or elsewhere; but those I have mentioned I know to have been taught with success, for I have taught them myself, after having prepared a part of the text-books. And I have good reason to believe that the same branches are now more extensively and successfully taught than when I was there. In my opinion they have been of incalculable value to individuals and to the nation, and have laid such a foundation for a superstructure, as could not have been laid in any other way, in so short a time, and at so little expense.

"Hitherto I have spoken only of intellectual improvement, or simply the gain of knowledge. But the *moral* and *religious* instruction which Hawaiians have gained through the medium of their own language is, in my opinion, of vastly greater importance. They have received it in schools, from periodicals, from tracts, from reading the Bible, and from hearing the gospel preached from Sabbath to Sabbath.

From the beginning, the Bible, as fast as it could be translated and printed, has been a text-book in morals and religion, especially in the Protestant schools; and that not so much by catechism, or second-hand instruction, as by reading and questioning on the plain facts, and duties, and doctrines taught in the Scriptures. Simultaneously with teaching the people to read, they were taught, out of the Bible, the great truths relating to the character and attributes of Jehovah, as distinct from what they knew of their former gods. This was essential to the establishment of the Christian system. They learned from the Bible their relationship to God, and to one another, and the duties growing out of that relationship. They have learned, moreover, the plan of salvation through the obedience, sufferings, and death of the Son of God. It is true that in all ages people of very simple minds and very little mental improvement have understood enough of these truths to be a foundation for their hopes of a happy immortality. Hawaiians have done it, and continue to do it, through their own language.

"Besides the Bible, they have read many other moral and religious books, as they have been prepared or translated for them; such as Wayland's Moral Philosophy, Gallaudet's Treatise on the Soul, Baxter's Saints' Rest, etc., etc., besides the moral and religious lessons in the weekly publications. The value of this kind of instruction cannot be estimated in dollars and cents. We may see some of its effects in the morals of the people; the quieting of the war spirit for almost forty years; the general adherence to a written code of laws; the almost entire cessation of the murderous spirit; the adoption of the Bible Sabbath, instead of the ancient arbitrary *tabus;* the general safety of foreign residents; the peaceful possession of property; the liberty of any form of religious worship, etc., etc. All this state of things is not easy to be accounted for, except by means of the moral and religious instruction conveyed to the masses, through their own language, and primarily in native schools. The education, therefore, which Hawaiians have received, and are now receiving, in their own language, is, in my opinion, of inestimablé value to them."

CHAPTER XVI.

DECLINE OF POPULATION.

How far Civilization is responsible for the Decline. — Statement. — Sources of Information. — The Climate and Diseases of the Islands. — Small Number of Children. — Causes of the Decline. — These in Operation before the Gospel came. — Singular Effect of destructive Epidemics. — Influence of the Gospel.

It is the vices and diseases of civilization that prove so fatal to the savage, and not civilization itself. It has been so on the Hawaiian Islands. But for the timely intervention of the gospel, with its rich conservatism, the native population had ere this been nearly swept away. We see clearly enough what have been the causes of the great decline in numbers during the more than fourscore years since the discovery of the Islands by Captain Cook, though it is not easy to determine what is the share of each in the destructive agency.

One cannot travel through the Islands without discovering conclusive evidence, in the signs of former cultivation, of a far more numerous people than now exists; though the estimate of four hundred thousand, by the scientific gentlemen who accompanied Captain Cook, may have been excessive. The census of 1860 made the native population sixty-seven thousand and eighty-four, while that of 1853 made it seventy-one thousand and nineteen. In a tabular form, the case may be stated thus, as it appears in the results of the census for 1860:—

Natives.

Males,	35,379
Females,	31,705
Total,	67,084
Excess of males,	3,674
Married,	38,124
Unmarried,	28,960
Under twenty years of age,	20,829
Between twenty and sixty years,	40,409
Over sixty years,	5,761
Ages not reported,	85

Foreigners.

Males,	2,120
Females,	596
Total,	2,716
Married,	1,079
Unmarried,	1,637
Under twenty years of age,	647
Between twenty and sixty years,	1,969
Over sixty years,	100

Summary.

Total of population in 1860,	69,800
Total of population in 1853,	73,138
Decrease from 1853 to 1860,	3,338
Decrease from 1853 to 1860, in native population,	3,935

The following table, relating to different periods, is copied from the Pacific Commercial Advertiser: —

Years.	Foreign.	Native.	Total.		Decrease.
1779 (est'd by Cook),			400,000.		
1823 (estimated),			142,050,	44 yrs.	257,950.
1832 (off. census),			130,315,	9 "	11,735.
1836 (off. census),			108,579,	4 "	21,736.
1850 (off. census),	1,962,	82,203,	84,165,	14 "	24,414.
1853 (off. census),	2,119,	71,019,	73,138,	3 "	11,027.
1860 (off. census),	2,716,	67,084,	69,800,	7 "	3,338.

According to these estimates in the earlier years, and the census returns in the later, the decrease in the first period of forty-four years, from 1779 to 1823, — three years after the landing of the first missionaries, — was about sixty-five per cent., at the annual rate of five thousand eight hundred and sixty-two. From 1823 to 1853, a period of thirty years, it was about forty-nine per cent., at the annual rate of two thousand two hundred and ninety-seven. During the seven years preceding 1860, the decrease of the native population was three thousand nine hundred and thirty-five, at the annual rate of five hundred and sixty-two, or about five per cent. The decrease has diminished so greatly of late, as to encourage the hope, should the government not repeal the laws against the manufacture and sale of ardent spirits, that it will soon be altogether arrested.

In the Hawaiian Spectator for 1839 I find an article on the decrease of population, by David Malo, a Christian native of rare intelligence and excellence of character, who died some years since. This is one of the most reliable sources of information. So also is an article in the same periodical, about the same time, by the Rev. Artemas Bishop. The physicians connected with the mission made a report on the diseases of the Islands in the year 1839, in which they declared the climate to be eminently favorable to health. Notwithstanding this, they found an unusual amount of disease among the natives, especially of the subacute character, which, though not often very painful, tended to undermine the constitution. The immediate causes of most of the maladies were thought to be their low estimate of life, and consequent reckless habits of living; their wretched habitations; their practice of lying on the damp ground; their want of suitable clothing in exhausted conditions of the system; and their poverty, depriving them of the necessaries and comforts of life. This was twenty-five years ago. Mr. Bishop declares that, at the time of his writing, the majority of children born in the Islands died before they were two years old, and that perhaps not more than one in four of the families had children of their own alive.

This he attributes to the former practice of infanticide, to the former unrestrained licentiousness of the then older and middle-aged women, and to the ignorance and heedlessness of mothers. Then the government being at that time theoretically, practically, and oppressively the owner of the soil, the only means of defence the common people had was to remain idle and poor, and thus avoid many heavy exactions. But they could not thus protect themselves against the consequences of frequent desolating wars in the time of their heathenism.

In the opinion of Mr. Bishop, the two principal causes of the depopulation were ardent spirits, and diseases propagated through impure intercourse with white men.

"It is well known," he says, "that a barbarous or semi-barbarous people have no command over their appetites, and therefore they do not drink alcohol with any degree of moderation, but, so long as it can be obtained, use it to fatal excess. The consequences, therefore, are certain. This has been the case here to an alarming degree, and would be so again, were the restraints of prohibitory law removed. Not only was alcohol imported in great abundance, but every neighborhood had its distillery, and the materials for making it were spontaneously afforded in exhaustless quantities. The consequences were, that not longer ago than in the days of Liholiho, this was a nation of drunkards. Whole villages of men, women, and children would give themselves up, for days together, to drunkenness and revelry. To this day, a native, who gets a taste of the liquid fire, never stops short of drunkenness, if it is in his power to obtain a sufficient quantity. What, then, would have been the result, if this whole people had been permitted to go on, as they began, through the brief course of a few generations? Rum had slain its thousands ere the rulers were fully aware of its effects."

Of the second cause of depopulation he speaks thus: —

"These Islands, like others in the Pacific, were inhabited, at the time of their discovery, by a people of loose and licentious manners, but free from disease. This trait in their character formed the combustibles, to which the match only needed to be applied, and the conflagration followed. But to speak without a figure, their previous looseness of morals formed a ready conductor for the disease, which was introduced by the first ship that touched here; and, from the account given by the natives themselves, the consequences were incalculably more dreadful than had been feared by Captain Cook and his associates. The deadly virus had a wide and rapid circulation throughout the blood, the bones, and sinews of the whole nation, and left in its course a train of wretchedness and misery which the very pen blushes to record. In the lapse of a few years, a dreadful mortality, heightened, if not induced, by their unholy intercourse, swept away one half of the population, leaving the dead unburied for want of those able to perform the rites of sepulture." [1]

Among the causes of decreasing population mentioned by David Malo, were the great number of human sacrifices, and also of murders, before the time of the first Kamehameha; a universal pestilence in his reign, which destroyed a majority of the people; the increased oppression by the chiefs after his death, owing to their attention being diverted from

[1] Hawaiian Spectator for 1838, pp. 60, 61.

the care of the people to their own aggrandizement, by the sale of sandal-wood gathered on the mountains, also by the sequestration of lands, and other oppressive means; also, the poorness of the clothing, food, and sleeping places; the neglect of children; and in general, the "little regard paid to the law of God." "Foreigners," says he, "have lent their whole influence to make the Hawaiian Islands one great brothel. For this cause God is angry, and he is diminishing the people, and they are nigh unto destruction." But he adds, "If a reformation of morals should take place, and the kingdom should be renewed, then would it escape destruction."[1]

What was the nature of the destructive pestilence mentioned above, which occurred in the years 1803 and 1804, is not well known. Physicians have conjectured, from the descriptions given of it by the natives, that it was the Asiatic cholera, or some plague of as virulent a character. There was a great mortality in the four years subsequent to 1848, resulting from the whooping cough and the measles. The small pox was brought to the Islands in 1853, but its ravages were chiefly on the islands of Oahu and Maui.

Such are the facts, concisely stated, so far as I have been able to collect them. And it appears, and it is due to the gospel to state, that all the causes of the depopulation on the Hawaiian Islands, excepting

[1] Hawaiian Spectator for 1839, pp. 128, 130.

several of the foreign epidemics introduced by the shipping, *were in full operation before the arrival of the missionaries*. The epidemics spent themselves chiefly on the most decayed portion of the people, and so had the singular effect, on the whole, considerably to raise the national tone of morals. They were like the amputation of diseased members of the body.

All this while the gospel was struggling, and not in vain, to remove the *moral causes* of depopulation. The only war since the year 1820 — that on Kauai, resulting from rebellion — was not a war of extermination, as formerly, and the war-spirit of the nation now gives no signs of life. Infanticide, branded by the laws with the penalty of death, has ceased. Intemperance is kept down by legal and moral restraints, more effectually than in almost any other Christian nation. Life, being now more highly appreciated, is more cared for. The people are consequently exposed far less than they were to foreign diseases. And though, as the result of a law in God's government visiting certain sins of parents upon their children to the third and fourth generation, not a few of the Hawaiian families are without children, and the deaths still somewhat exceed the number of births, the hope is indulged that it may soon be otherwise.

CENSUS OF THE HAWAIIAN ISLANDS FOR 1860.

		NATIVES.						
ISLANDS.	DISTRICTS.	Males.	Females.	Married.	Unmarried.	Under 20 Years of Age.	Between 20 and 60.	Over 60 Years.
HAWAII,	1. Hilo,	2,507	2,096	2,755	1,848	1,270	2,873	460
	2. Puna,	1,087	1,068	1,174	981	776	1,125	254
	3. Kau,	1,130	1,069	1,422	777	763	1,280	156
	4. Kona Hema,	1,333	1,319	1,398	1,254	1,027	1,445	180
	5. Kona Akau,	1,759	1,689	1,898	1,550	1,327	1,785	336
	6. Kohala Hema,	673	595	706	562	431	753	84
	7. Hamakua,	1,136	1,074	1,346	864	661	1,377	172
	8. Kohala Akau,	1,281	1,320	1,493	1,108	881	1,391	298
		10,906	10,230	12,192	8,944	7,136	12,029	1940
MAUI,	1. Lahaina,	2,453	2,216	2,449	2,220	1,447	2,855	367
	2. Wailuku,	1,874	1,775	2,020	1,629	1,176	2,276	197
	3. Hamakua,	1,657	1,525	1,828	1,354	1,070	1,829	283
	4. Hana,	2,352	2,139	2,844	1,647	1,468	2,699	324
		8,336	7,655	9,141	6,850	5,161	9,659	1171
MOLOKAI,	5. Molokai,	1,463	1,367	1,610	1,220	939	1,587	304
LANAI,	6. Lanai,	342	303	338	307	221	316	108
OAHU,[1]	1. Honolulu,	6,871	5,800	6,921	5,750	3,258	8,587	826
	2. Ewa and Waianae,	1,120	967	1,227	860	647	1,281	142
	3. Waialua,	677	607	767	517	389	793	102
	4. Koolauloa,	636	545	672	509	355	705	121
	5. Koolaupoko,	1,223	1,051	1,337	937	616	1,409	212
		10,527	8,970	10,924	8,573	5,265	12,775	1403
KAUAI,	1. Waimea,	943	830	1,020	753	495	944	334
	2. Koloa,	731	525	638	618	421	730	105
	3. Buna,	928	782	1,012	698	485	1,024	201
	4. Koolau, } 5. Hanalei, }	869	731	921	679	477	962	161
		3,471	2,868	3,591	2,748	1,878	3,660	801
NIIHAU,	6. Niihau,	334	312	328	318	229	383	34
		35,379	31,705	38,124	28,960	20,829	40,409	5761

[1] Chinese are included in the number of the native population in the district of Honolulu.

CENSUS OF THE HAWAIIAN ISLANDS FOR 1860.

		FOR'S.		RESULTS.					
ISLANDS.	DISTRICTS.	Males.	Females.	Total Foreigners.	Total Natives.	Total Population.	Total Population of 1853.	Increase.	Decrease.
HAWAII,	1. Hilo, ...	115	24	139	4,603	4,742	7,748 (Hilo and Puna)		848
	2. Puna, . . .	3		3	2,155	2,158			
	3. Kau, ...	25	3	28	2,199	2,227	2,210	17	
	4. Kona Hema,	25	6	31	2,652	2,683	3,113		430
	5. Kona Akau, .	39	1	40	3,448	3,488	4,110		622
	6. Kohala Hema,	47	6	53	1,268	1,321	3,874 (Kohala Hema and Hamakua)		323
	7. Hamakua, .	20		20	2,210	2,230			
	8. Kohala Akau,	20	11	31	2,601	2,632	3,395		763
		294	51	345	21,136	21,481	24,450	17	2,986
MAUI,	1. Lahaina, . .	191	26	217	4,669	4,886	4,833	53	
	2. Wailuku, . .	40	6	46	3,649	3,695	4,463		768
	3. Hamakua, . .	106	22	128	3,182	3,310	2,947	363	
	4. Hana, . . .	16	2	18	4,491	4,509	5,331		822
		353	56	409	15,991	16,400	17,574	416	1,590
MOLOKAI,	5. Molokai, . .	33	1	34	2,830	2,864	3,607		743
LANAI,	6. Lanai, . . .	1		1	645	646	600	46	
OAHU,	1. Honolulu,	1198	441	1639	12,671	14,310	11,455	2,855	
	2. Ewa and Waianae, . . .	64		64	2,087	2,151	2,451		300
	3. Waialua, . .	23	2	25	1,284	1,309	1,126	185	
	4. Koolauloa, .	6		6	1,181	1,187	1,345		158
	5. Koolaupoko,	38	6	44	2,274	2,318	2,749		431
		1329	449	1778	19,497	21,275	19,126	3,038	889
KAUAI,	1. Waimea, . .	7	4	11	1,773	1,784	2,082		298
	2. Kolou, . . .	53	15	68	1,256	1,324	1,296	28	
	3. Puna, ...	17	11	28	1,710	1,738	1,615	123	
	4. Koolau, 5. Hanalei,	32	9	41	1,600	1,641	1,998		357
		109	39	148	6,339	6,487	6,991		
NIIHAU,	6. Niihau, . . .	1		1	646	647	790		143
		2120	596	2716	67,084	69,800	73,138	3,668	7,006

CHAPTER XVII.

CHARACTER OF THE PROTESTANT CHURCHES.

Rule of Judging. — Church of Corinth. — Church in Madagascar. — Church in India. — Whence unfavorable Views. — Civilized and Uncivilized Piety. — Favorable View of Piety at the Islands. — Contrast of Past and Present. — More easy for the Fallen to rise again. — Another Reference to the Corinthian Church. — Extreme Debasement of the Heathen World. — Cheering Fact in the Hawaiian Ministry. — Comparative View. — Family Prayer. — Morning Prayer-meetings. — Confidence in Prayer. — Addresses. — The People clothed. — How best interested. — Interesting Audiences. — The "Aloha." — Church Building. — Statistics of the Hawaiian Churches. — Benevolence. — Paganism no longer known.

THE Prudential Committee instructed me to make inquiry into the character of the native churches. I did so, and my inquiries in 1863 confirmed the testimony of the missionaries in 1848. The standard of comparison I had in mind was not so much the churches of my native land, as the primitive churches, and especially the church of Corinth, as set forth in the writings of the apostle Paul. In their morals, before conversion, the people of Corinth and of the Islands would seem to have been singularly alike; and the same may be said of their religious tendencies and liabilities after connection with the Christian church. It appears, moreover, to have been equally true of both people, that the Lord Jesus had many of his chosen ones among them. In this connection the reader will be interested in some passages from Conybeare and Howson's Life of St. Paul.

"One evil at least, we know," say these biographers, "prevailed extensively, and threatened to corrupt the whole church of Corinth. This was nothing less than the addiction of many Corinthian Christians to those sins of impurity which they had practised in the days of their heathenism, and which disgraced their native city even among the heathen. We have mentioned the peculiar licentiousness of manners which prevailed at Corinth. So notorious was this, that it had actually passed into the vocabulary of the Greek tongue; and the very word to 'Corinthianize' meant 'to play the wanton;' nay, the bad reputation of the city had become proverbial, even in foreign languages, and is immortalized by the Latin poets. Such being the habits in which many of the Corinthian converts had been educated, we cannot wonder if it proved most difficult to root out immorality from the rising church. The offenders against Christian chastity were exceedingly numerous at this period; and it was especially with the object of attempting to reform them, and to check the growing mischief, that St. Paul now determined to visit Corinth.

"He has himself described this visit as a painful one. He went in sorrow at the tidings he had received, and when he arrived he found the state of things even worse than he had expected. He tells us that it was a time of personal humiliation to himself, occasioned by the flagrant sins of so many of his own converts. He reminds the Corinthians, afterwards, how he had 'mourned' over those who had dishonored the name of Christ by uncleanness, and fornication, and wantonness, which they had committed.

"But in the midst of his grief he showed the greatest tenderness for the individual offenders. He warned them of the heinous guilt which they were incurring; he showed them its inconsistency with their Christian calling; he reminded them how, at their baptism, they had died to sin, and risen again unto righteousness; but he did not at once exclude them from the church which they had defiled. Yet he was compelled to threaten them with this penalty, if they persevered in the sins which had now called forth his rebuke. He has recorded the very words which he used. 'If I come again,' he said, 'I will not spare.'"

"But his censures and warnings had produced too little effect upon his converts. His mildness had been mistaken for weakness; his hesitation in punishing had been ascribed to a fear of the offenders; and it was not long before he received new intelligence that the profligacy which had infected the community was still increasing. Then it was that he felt himself compelled to resort to harsher measures. He wrote an Epistle (which has not been preserved to us), in which, as we learn from himself, he ordered the Christians of Corinth, by virtue of his apostolic authority, 'to cease from all intercourse with fornicators.' By this he meant, as he subsequently explained his injunctions, to direct the exclusion of all profligates from the church. The Corinthians, however, either did not understand this, or (to excuse themselves) they affected not to do so; for they asked how it was possible for them to abstain from all intercourse with the profligate, unless they entirely secluded themselves from all the business of life which they had to transact with their heathen neighbors. Whether the lost Epistle contained any other topics we cannot know with certainty; but we may conclude, with some probability, that it was very short, and directed to this one subject; otherwise it is not easy to understand why it should not have been preserved together with the two subsequent Epistles."

"Meantime some members of the household of Chloe, a distinguished Christian family at Corinth, arrived at Ephesus; and from them St. Paul received fuller information than he before possessed of the condition of the Corinthian church. The spirit of party had seized upon its members, and well-nigh destroyed Christian love."

"It is not impossible that the Antinomian Free-thinkers, whom we have already seen to form so dangerous a portion of the primitive church, attached themselves to this last-named party; at any rate, they were, at this time, one of the worst elements of evil at Corinth. They put forward a theoretic defence of the practical immorality in which they lived; and some of them had so lost the very foundation of Christian faith as to deny the resurrection of the dead, and thus to adopt the belief, as well as the sensuality, of their Epicurean neighbors, whose motto was, 'Let us eat and drink, for to-morrow we die.'

"A crime, recently committed by one of these pretended Christians, was now reported to St. Paul, and excited his utmost abhorrence. A member of the Corinthian church was openly living in incestuous intercourse with his step-mother, and that during his father's life; yet this audacious offender was not excluded from the church.

"Nor were these the only evils. Some Christians were showing their total want of brotherly love by bringing vexatious actions against their brethren in the heathen courts of law. Others were turning even the spiritual gifts which they had received from the Holy Ghost into occasions of vanity and display, not unaccompanied by fanatical delusion. The decent order of Christian worship was disturbed by the tumultuary claims of rival ministrations. Women had forgotten the modesty of their sex, and came forward unveiled (contrary to the habit of their country) to address the public assembly. And even the sanctity of the holy communion itself was profaned by scenes of revelling and debauch.

"About the same time that all this disastrous intelligence was brought to St. Paul by the household of Chloe, other messengers arrived from Corinth, bearing the answer of the church to his previous letter, of which (as we have mentioned above) they requested an explanation, and at the same time referring to his decision several questions which caused dispute and difficulty. These questions related, 1. To the controversies respecting meat which had been offered to idols. 2. To the disputes regarding celibacy and matrimony, the right of divorce, and the perplexities which arose in the case of mixed marriages where one of the parties was an unbeliever. 3. To the exercise of the spiritual gifts in the public assemblies of the church.

"St. Paul hastened to reply to these questions, and at the same time to denounce the sins which had polluted the Corinthian church, and almost annulled its right to the name of Christian. The letter which he was thus led to write is addressed not only to this metropolitan church, but also to the Christian communities established in other places in the same province, which might be regarded as dependencies of that in the capital city. Hence we must infer that these churches also had been infected by some of the errors, or vices, which had prevailed at Corinth. This letter is, in its contents, the most diversified of all St. Paul's Epistles, and in proportion to the variety of its topics is the depth of its interest for ourselves."

The importance of a correct appreciation of this subject, while directing our inquiries to churches that have been gathered from among the debasing superstitions and vices of heathenism, will justify the quoting of opinions recently expressed by the Rev. William Ellis, and the Rev. Joseph Mullens, D. D., both well-known writers of authority on the subject of missions to the heathen. Mr. Ellis writes from Madagascar, having in view the strange inconsistencies in the character of the late king. He says, —

"In England we naturally estimate the character of persons in other countries by the standards and proportions according to which we form our judgments of those at home, where the education and training, or moulding of character, have been going on for centuries, and where it has consequently attained a symmetry, compactness, and homogeneousness which would be looked for in vain in communities such as those which inhabit Madagascar. In such countries great force of character is often manifested, and strength of intellect may be found cramped and contorted by the ignorance around it, and the puerilities on which it is exercised, as well as by the debased habits and low social tone of the society in which it is formed. In a country where the elements of virtue in character are few and weak, and those of vice numerous, vigorous, and predominant, character will at times be monstrous, often exhibiting contrarieties difficult or impossible to reconcile according to any standard of judgment in more advanced or improved communities. Where these causes have been long in operation, and especially if the influence of superstition has been added, the difficulty will be increased.

"In England, if we found a person advancing towards middle life frank, good-natured, generous, affable, and, considering the state of society in which he moved, neither uneducated nor ill-informed, — and if we found, moreover, that such person entertained and exemplified high and just notions of civil and religious liberty, was interested in the improvement of society, in the promotion of education, and the great truths of Christianity, read the Bible daily, and was never absent from public worship on the Lord's day, and generally the most attentive hearer there, — we should conclude that there was little that was bad, and a great deal more that was good, in such a character, because it would be so in the state of society to which we are accustomed.

"Now, in Madagascar, and in countries similarly circumstanced, such characters are not rare: only the virtues are fewer and feebler, and the vices stronger and less restrained, — as must be the case in a country where chastity is said in most cases not to be expected, — where falsehood, for sufficient inducements, is inculcated, and commended as a duty, — where theft, undetected, is often applauded, — and where the intellect is darkened by superstition, though active and acute in the pursuit of gain. . . . Even the early growth of Christian principles, grafted on such a stock, though we may have reason to believe it to be the work of

God's Spirit, often presents, in the vacillation and weakness it reveals, such incongruities of Christian character, and such inconsistencies of conduct, as sometimes astonish, perplex, and sorely grieve the missionary."

Dr. Mullens, writing at Calcutta, in his admirable Review of Ten Years of Missionary Labor in India, between 1852 and 1861 (p. 97), speaks as follows: —

"How often have the faults of the New Testament churches reappeared in the churches of India, and been strangely mixed with undoubted excellences! But they are on the way to better things. They have quitted the swampy shores of idolatry. Like the rolling hill districts among the Ghauts, they exhibit great inequalities of character — lofty virtues by depths of sinfulness; but they have only to press on amid the difficulties of their pilgrimage, and at length they will emerge upon that elevated plateau of settled virtue, which, as a Christian people, even Englishmen have attained only after eight generations of Protestant teaching and Bible influence."

Unfavorable views of the character of native piety at the Hawaiian Islands may be found in not a few published works on the Islands, even in some cases representing the labors of the missionaries as a "failure." I had personal conferences with intelligent and candid men, residents or visitors at the Islands, who were more or less sceptical on this subject. Without questioning the accuracy of statements within the range of their personal observations, I often could by no means assent to their conclusions. They were traders, it may be, graziers, planters — had seen the worst class of the people, and the worst side of their character. Their vocation was unfavorable to charitable and decidedly accurate views of the native character. I could see that sometimes the Christianity they had in mind was very different from my own conceptions of it, — scarcely more than a refined civilization. When the Hawaiian people were spoken of as Christianized, they objected that the nation lacked vitality, and was dying out. Were this an admitted fact, what had it to do with evidences of piety in individual Hawaiians? Then it always seemed to me that these objectors, however intelligent and candid, however correct in their estimates of piety at home, judged Hawaiian piety by a wrong standard. They compared it with piety in their native land. How erroneous a standard! The civilization of centuries enters into the hourly manifestations of our home Christianity. Take from us all of mere civilization that is shared with the world around, and what rudeness and fitfulness, what seeming superficiality and instability, our piety would present to the casual observer! The objectors do not make allowance enough for a difference in circumstances, when judging Hawaiian Christians.

I found in the piety of those Christians, as I expected, but little of the art and polish which so set off piety in our own social state. The jewel with them has a very rough setting, but still it is there. On a rigid comparison of their evidences of piety, after making all proper allowances, I came to the conclusion — as the missionaries seem to have done sixteen years before — that the difference between their piety and ours is more *circumstantial* than real. They have their easily-besetting sins, and these are different from ours; but I know not that they are more heinous in the sight of God. Theirs are licentiousness and intemperance; ours, as a commercial people, are covetousness and luxuriousness. In Christian churches of every land there are easily-besetting sins, and it is hard to create a *sensitive* conscience in respect to them. It is scarcely more difficult at the Sandwich Islands, than it is with us.

I cannot help feeling much charity for those islanders. No foreign traveller ever had better opportunities for judging of the Christian character of our own favored land, than I had on the Hawaiian Islands. I heard all my missionary brethren had to say on the subject during four months. I saw and addressed the people by thousands. Everywhere, on those sunny Isles, I had the *same sort* of evidence (differing only in degree) that I was among a Christian people, which presents itself when travelling in my own country. And I feel assured that multitudes of those whom I had the happiness to address and take by the hand, how low soever they may stand on the scale of intelligence and social life, are to be numbered with the people of God.

Of course the reader will not understand me as claiming for these people a high place, either on the social or the religious scale. We must remember how lately they came up from pagan degradation. As compared with *their own past*, — which is the proper comparison, — they have been greatly elevated. Though the preceding chapters contain much that is descriptive of their heathen condition, I may remind the reader, that they were then without a written language. They were naked barbarians. Lying, drunkenness, theft, robbery were universal. So was licentiousness, and it was shameless in open day. There was no restraint on polygamy and polyandry. Mothers buried their infant children alive, and children did the same with their aged and infirm parents. As a consequence of this moral and social degradation, a deadly poison ran through the veins and arteries of the whole nation, opening the way for destructive foreign epidemics, and a rapid depopulation, which, though greatly checked by the influences of the gospel, is not yet wholly arrested. Such were the character and condition of the Hawaiian people in the early part of the last generation.

But the people have now a written language, and are generally able to read and write. They are clothed. The law forbids the manufacture and sale of ardent spirits, and the law — pronounced constitutional by the Supreme Court while I was there — is enforced. I did not see a drunken native while on the Islands. The law also forbids polygamy and polyandry, and they have passed away. Theft and robbery are less frequent there, than in the United States. We slept at night with open doors, had no apprehension, and lost nothing. Licentiousness still largely exists outside of the church, and is one of the easily-besetting sins within it; but it now everywhere shuns the day, and is subjected to the discipline of the church. Nor do mothers any more bury their infant children alive, nor children their aged and infirm parents.

If it be a fact that the native Christians fall before the debasing temptations more easily than is usual with us, they appear often to find it easier to rise again after having thus fallen. I was assured of cases where, after a terrible declension, the return had been with increased humility, experience, watchfulness, and zeal, so that the lapsed and recovered ones became at length pillars in the church. Indeed, we find there — as will be the case in many a demoralized portion of heathendom — an approximation towards the character of the Corinthian church. In that church the great apostle had to lament over false teachers, a disordered worship, the irregular observance of the Lord's Supper, neglect of discipline, party divisions, litigation, debates, envyings, wraths, strifes, backbitings, whisperings, swellings, tumults. Yet, after making proper allowances, and upon a view of the whole church, he declares it to be "enriched by Jesus Christ in all utterance and all knowledge," so that it "came behind in no gift." Such combinations can exist only in *Corinthian* communities; but then such are most parts of the heathen world. Read the first chapter of the Epistle to the Romans, and the journals of modern missionaries. Consider the decline of mental power in masses of people under the long reign of paganism; the paralysis of the moral sense and conscience; the grossness of habits, physical and mental, in speech and action, in domestic life and social intercourse. Consider the absence of almost all the ideas lying at the foundation of elevated character; the absence of words even to serve as pure vehicles of holy thought and sentiment; the absence of a correct public opinion on all things appertaining to manners and morals; and the constant, all-pervading presence of polluting, degrading, soul-destroying temptations.

Such singular combinations exist, to a greater or less extent, in the churches at the Hawaiian Islands; though with far less varied, far less positive and striking manifestations, than in the Grecian city, because of the more limited mental and social development of the people. And we ought, perhaps, hereafter to expect more of this among the island-churches, before there shall be less.

A statement by Mr. Pogue, Principal of the

Seminary at Lahainaluna, gives a pleasing prospect for the native ministry. It is, that the graduates of that institution who have received ordination as ministers of the gospel, have lived without reproach.

An impression was made upon me that there is more freshness in the religious development of Hawaii than there is on the other islands. The influence of the foreign population has been less on that island; the people are more isolated; they travel less. If my impressions are correct, these are among the probable causes. There must be something, moreover, in my having received on this island most of my first impressions of the people. There were no public assemblies, however, more interesting to me, than those of Lahaina and Wailuku on Maui, of Honolulu and Waialua on Oahu, and of Koloa on Kauai — places where I spent my Sabbaths.

I was informed that family prayer is a prevalent custom in the Protestant churches. Illustrations of this were given in my tour around Hawaii. In some districts, at least, morning prayer-meetings furnish an interesting feature in the religious life of the people. At Honolulu I was awaked, on the morning after my arrival, by the bell of the great Stone Church, before the day had fairly dawned. It was for a prayer-meeting. True, the attendance was small, and chiefly of the older people; but the meeting had held on its way since the great awakening, — more than a score of years. Mr. Thurston informed me of several such meetings in his district of Kailua, and that they had been kept up for many years. Rev. Mr. Taylor, son-in-law of Mr. Thurston, whom I saw at Petaluma, in California, related to me this fact. When residing on Hawaii, near Kailua, some years before, he employed a number of natives to work for him, and one morning they were all late. Upon inquiring the reason, they said they had been to the prayer-meeting; and when asked why their meeting was so late, they replied that the man was tardy whose business it was to blow the conch-shell, but still they thought they ought to attend the prayer-meeting. His only advice to them was, to look more carefully in future after the man whose business it was to call them together.

Occasionally my attention was called to small houses in solitary places, and I was told they were prayer-houses, erected by the people for their neighborhood meetings.

Their views of prayer were described to me as very simple. They expect, when they pray, to be heard, — in this resembling the primitive Christians. An illustration of their confidence in prayer was given me by Mr. Bond, at Kohala. As we stood in the pulpit of his church, at the close of the afternoon service, looking at the retiring multitude, he called my attention to one of his aged church-members, now a valued friend and co-laborer. That man, said he, some years ago, was off the coast with two other natives, in a canoe, fishing; and a monstrous shark came upon their canoe, which was merely a hollowed log, with the evident intent of upsetting it. They beat him away with their paddles. He went off to some distance, and came down upon them the second time. Again they drove him away, and he returned to renew the attack. Their courage then began to fail, and they said, the shark will have us. But this man proposed to the others that he should pray to God, while they used the paddles. To this they agreed, and he fell on his knees in prayer, while they stood on the defensive. Down came the monster, but when very near he sheered off, and was soon out of sight. The natives regarded this as an answer to prayer, and my excellent missionary friend was of the same opinion.

After having addressed a score of congregations, and more than twelve thousand of the people, I cannot be greatly mistaken in a general estimate of their intelligence. They everywhere received me with enthusiastic kindness, as the messenger and representative of their American patrons; and they always expected me to address them, which I generally did on the Sabbath, and occasionally on some other day in the week. Of course I spoke through an interpreter. The congregations at the stations varied from five hundred to twelve hundred.

The meeting-houses were generally filled, and the

NATIVE CONGREGATION IN 1823.

people well clad, considering their circumstances. One of my first surprises at the Islands was to find the people so generally and so well dressed. Thirty years before, the masses of the people scarcely felt the need of clothes. The climate did not require them, and the natives at first looked upon our dress as merely ornamental. It will illustrate this if I relate an anecdote, which I received from the best source. In one of the first years of the mission, a chief on Hawaii was reproved by a missionary for entering his house so nearly naked. Profiting by the rebuke, and aiming to give full satisfaction, next time he walked in with the addition of a pair of silk stockings and a hat!

The accompanying engraving of a congregation of natives on Hawaii, in the year 1823, drawn by the Rev. William Ellis, will give an idea of their appearance at that time.[1]

In seeking to interest the people, and fix their attention, I found nothing so effectual as relating facts with which I had become acquainted in my visits to our missions in India and Western Asia, and especially in Palestine. Indeed, they were delighted to

[1] The engraving is from a sketch, by the Rev. William Ellis, of one of the congregations, to which he preached while on his tour through Hawaii in the year 1823. It will be seen that the natives are seated on the lava, and nearly destitute of clothing. His companions were Messrs. Thurston, Bishop, Goodrich, and Harwood.

see one who had been in Jerusalem, and had stood on Mount Zion, on Olivet, on the shores of the Sea of Galilee. To those simple-minded people it was like a *new evidence of their religion.* Their intelligent attention implied of course some knowledge of geography, and of history, especially missionary and sacred history, as well as an interest, which they are well known to take, in the propagation of the gospel among ignorant and degraded nations. I found, too, that when I spoke of the civil war in the United States, which I sometimes did, they were on the *qui vive*, as they had read often about it in their native newspapers, and had strong sympathy for the loyal States.

I shall not soon forget those crowded audiences, those upturned faces, those beaming countenances; nor those trembling lips and speaking eyes, when, at the close of the meeting, they came around to shake hands, and say *Aloha.* And that word *Aloha* is their *characteristic* word. If they have not words to express some of the greater ideas, they certainly have a word expressing one of the sweetest, richest sentiments of the human heart — ALOHA. It means *Love to you.* I never wearied with the repetition, though I repeated it thousands of times.

The natives have built more than a hundred meeting-houses, or churches, with but little foreign aid. I understood Mr. Lyons to say that, towards a few of the dozen churches built under his supervision, the government made a small contribution, with the understanding that it should have the right of using them for schools, but for nothing else. In the building of the older, larger, more expensive churches, the government, as such, had no agency. The aggregate cost of the churches exceeded one hundred and fifty thousand dollars. Some of the largest are built of coral, or blocks of lava, and several of these have galleries; more are framed wooden houses, painted white; one, on Kauai, is of a light-colored sandstone; a few have *adobe* walls, that is, of mud hardened in the sun; and a few are of grass. They have slips, or pews. Most have bells; and the "sound of the church-going bell," among the hills and valleys of those Islands, seemed to me as suggestive, as delightful, as among the hills and valleys of my native land.

The statistical history of the Hawaiian churches deserves some notice. The first native convert admitted to the church was Keopuolani, in 1823, — as is stated elsewhere, but more fully in the chapter on Maui. Up to the year 1832, and including that year, the whole number of members received was 577. The admissions in the next ten years were 29,651. Of these 19,877 were received in the years 1838–1840; 2,443 in 1842; and 5,296 in 1843, — indicating the years of the great awakening. The average number for each of the ten years is nearly 3,000. The admissions in the next ten years were 12,325, or an annual average of 1,232. In the next ten the number received was 8,802, giving an annual average of 880 new members. The whole number from the beginning is 50,913, or an average for each year of more than a thousand. To this an addition of 1,500 should be made for the Protestant evangelical churches of Makawao, in East Maui, connected with the American Missionary Association, which would swell the sum total to 52,413.

The excommunications in this period of forty years, not including the churches of Makawao, were not far from 8,000. The deaths reported were 20,017. The excommunications, from the commencement of the revival, bore the proportion of one in thirteen to the admissions, and the deaths one to ten. In the second decade the proportion of the excommunications to the admissions was as one to five. In the third decade the former came but little short of being one third of the latter, and there were nearly as many deaths as there were admissions. These statements will show why the number of church-members never rose above 24,000 at any one time, and why there is a tendency to numerical decline. The largest number of church-members was in the years 1848 and 1856, when there were 23,796 and 23,652. The number in the year 1863 was 19,679.

The accessions to the Roman Catholic community,

especially in former years, are understood to have been largely from the excommunicated Protestant church-members. I found it was the opinion of some of the missionaries, looking back in the light of present experience, that the excommunications had, in some instances, been for insufficient reasons, and of course too numerous. It was thought, also, as perhaps an offset to this, that in some cases the church discipline had been too lenient.[1]

The benevolence of the church is an essential element in determining its Christian character. The reported contributions of the Hawaiian churches, in the last eight years, for the support of the gospel and its propagation, are stated in the following table: —

[1] "*Resolved,* That no local church in our connection can consistently adopt by-laws or rules of discipline for itself, which shall virtually excommunicate, or actually debar from communion, members of sister churches in good standing.

"That evidence of piety is the grand criterion of fitness for the ordinance of the Lord's Supper, and that professed disciples of Christ should not be excommunicated until they give positive evidence of impenitence and unbelief, after proper and scriptural measures have been used to reclaim them.

"Excommunicated members may, on giving evidence of repentance, be restored to the communion and fellowship of the church from which the excision was made, without entering anew into covenant; or they may be received into other churches by profession." *Hawaiian Association in* 1836.

CONTRIBUTIONS OF HAWAIIAN CHURCHES, 1855-1862.

	1855	1856	1857	1858	1859	1860	1861	1862
Hilo,	$3,000	$4,000	$3,500	$5,000	$6,000	$3,000	$3,700	$3,600
Kohala,		1,501	826		1,551	1,358	1,578	1,194
Waimea,	933	2,550		2,971	2,635	5,719	2,626	1,792
Kailua,	500	363	420	457	761	600	594	650
Kealakekua,	1,356	1,300	1,367	1,461	1,466			1,181
Kau,		675	585		925		1,380	
Lahaina,	2,923		4,051	1,600	3,824		1,715	1,085
Kaanapali,	160	242					51	126
Wailuku,	666	1,427	836	968	1,358	287	1,366	744
Honuaula,				381		618	237	463
Hana,		719	788	245	323			
Molokai,	2,927	190	4,106		598	1,999	893	657
Honolulu, 1st,	3,302	1,704	2,125	3,840	1,830	1,527	1,872	2,266
Honolulu, 2d,	1,967	1,691	1,052	1,222	1,285	803	1,668	1,380
Ewa,	243	240		145	188	200	261	225
Waialua,	695	524	297	232	447		228	330
Waianae,		139	114		88		200	
Hanula,	150	420	683	228	240	332	1,070	746
Kaneohe,	624	1,245	768	520	508	537	827	500
Waimea,	463		313	185	317		175	110
Koloa,	545	655	709	497	1,328	756	500	537
Waioli,	450		353	213	397	471	376	449
Totals,	20,909	19,582	22,893	20,165	26,069	18,207	21,317	18,035

There are no avowed pagans now on the Hawaiian Islands, and the idols have utterly perished; at least I saw none. They have either been destroyed (as most of them were) or carried away as curiosities. All in the temples that fire could burn has been consumed, and there remain of them only huge black heaps of volcanic stones, which the people are at liberty to use in building their stone walls. I dare not say that there is no superstition remaining, when I think how much there is of it in old Christian countries. It is most conspicuous, perhaps, in the treatment of diseases by native doctors, and in the apprehension of being "prayed to death," — implying a belief in a species of witchcraft. But the people, as a whole, have been weaned from their old idolatry, and much of their repugnance to the Roman Catholic worship is owing to its idolatrous aspects.

There cannot be a more suitable close to this chapter than the testimony of the Rev. Mr. Damon, the well-known seamen's chaplain at Honolulu, and editor of "The Friend" newspaper. It is from a review of Manley Hopkins's History of the Sandwich Islands, published in London in 1862, and intended to disparage the labors of the missionaries. Mr. Damon says, —

"We are not going to rebut Mr. Hopkins's assertions by statistics, or extracts from missionary reports; but, as an offset to his assertions, we conclude our remarks with some assertions of our own. Mr. Hopkins has never visited the Islands, and we have lived among the Hawaiian people for twenty years. We have visited every inhabited island of the group except Niihau; we have visited every missionary station on the Islands, and some of them repeatedly; we are personally acquainted with every missionary and his family; we have spent many Sabbaths at the outstations; we have travelled with and among Hawaiians on sea and land; we have slept in their houses; we are personally acquainted with hundreds and thousands of them; we have worshipped in their churches; we have sat with them around the 'table of the Lord.' Now, this is the honest conclusion to which we have come, as the result of our observation, that, in proportion to the population of the Islands, there are, upon an average, as many true Christians among them as there are among the people of America or Europe: we will not except New England, Scotland, or England, or any other particularly favored portion of those countries."

IV.

ECCLESIASTICAL DEVELOPMENT.

ECCLESIASTICAL DEVELOPMENT.

CHAPTER XVIII.

ECCLESIASTICAL DEVELOPMENT PREVIOUS TO 1863.

Business transacted at first by the Mission as an organized Body. — An Association formed for Ecclesiastical Matters. — Much other Business. — The Native Churches a Development of the Mission Church. — Association reorganized, and all Business transferred to it. — How Ecclesiastical Government came to be exercised by the Missionary Body. — Difficulties in the Way of a Change. — The Time for a Change come. — The Ends to be secured.

In all my tour of the Islands I had reference to a meeting of the Hawaiian Evangelical Association, to be held in the month of June; and my object was to become conversant with the subjects which were then to receive attention, and to do what I could towards promoting an intelligent unity of opinion and action when the Association should come together.

The meeting was held at Honolulu, in a school-house not far from the rear of the Stone Church, built, many years since, by the mission.[1] The Asso-

[1] The school-house is seen to the right of the Stone Church, in the engraving at page 119.

ciation derived its distinctive features from the religious exigencies of the Islands. At first, the whole business was transacted by the mission, as an organized body; but in 1823 the Hawaiian Association was formed, "for mutual improvement and aid in laying the foundation and building up the house of the Lord." From this time, all matters purely ecclesiastical were reserved for the Association. But the mission, properly so called, had still a large amount of other business, of which there is ample evidence in its printed proceedings.

The native churches were a development of the mission church, composed of the missionary company that was organized in Boston, October 15, 1819. This appears from the proceedings of the Association in the year 1830. It was then arranged, —

1. The original mission church was to receive new missionaries, and have them under its supervision, and also to have the ecclesiastical supervision of all churches formed among the natives.

2. Native churches were then recognized at seven of the stations, and the missionaries residing at those stations were constituted their pastors.

3. The pastors were authorized to admit members to the church, to rebuke, censure, or exclude offending members, according to the nature of the offence; subject, however, to revision by the original church, on a complaint being entered by a member of said church; and members of those churches had also the right of appeal to the mission church.

4. It was not then deemed expedient to admit native members to a participation in the government of churches. Nevertheless one or more church-members were to be selected, and placed under instruction, with special reference to becoming helpers in the government of the churches; and they were to be set apart for this business when they had attained the requisite knowledge, gravity, etc.

5. There was to be an annual meeting of the original church, to transact its own business, and also to consult for the best interests of the other churches.

In consequence of the radical change made in the mission in the year 1848, already described,[1] the brethren agreed, in 1854, to reorganize their Association, enlarge its sphere, and no longer to do business in their corporate capacity as a mission. The Association then combined in itself all the duties which it had before shared with the mission; and this arrangement remained in force until the changes of 1863, which were not only in the constitution of the Association, but in that of the entire Protestant Christian community of the Islands.

How there came to be such powers vested in the missionary body, and in what manner they were exercised to create a religious independence and self-government among the Hawaiian people, will now be explained.

The mission had necessarily, for a time, much

[1] Chapter V.

influence with the government of the Islands, but never what may properly be denominated power. The influence was moral, religious; and there have been times when it would have been well had this influence been greater in the highest places of authority even than it was. Its beneficial tendency will not be questioned by well-informed and candid observers. But for the missionaries, and the foreign residents who acted with them, the native rulers could never have overcome the hostile agencies which were so long and fiercely arrayed against the progress of the native mind towards law and order. Such was the opinion, already quoted, of Mr. Dana.[1]

The effect of the gospel upon the Hawaiian people, in their civil life, was to enlighten, civilize, and greatly improve their already existing government. Upon the *religious* life, it was altogether a work of creation. The religion and its institutions were all new, and therefore all, for a time, was necessarily in the hands, and under the direction, of the missionaries. For a considerable period they were the only ones who could be the rulers in matters appertaining to religion. Native converts, churches, preachers, pastors, were all infantile. For many reasons it was not advisable to connect church and state, nor were they ever connected at the Islands. But had they been, the civil rulers were less competent to govern the churches, than the churches were to govern

[1] Chapter IV, p. 101.

themselves. The missionaries, in their efforts to train the native Christians to self-government in matters ecclesiastical, found it necessary, for a longer time than they expected, to retain a superintending, controlling influence over the churches. The Islands were divided into districts, and each district was committed to the care of one or more missionaries, appointed by the mission, or by the central Association, and responsible to it. Whatever subdivisions were made in the districts, there was really but one church in each of them (with the exception of Honolulu), and the resident missionary was the pastor, or spiritual overseer, of that church. When native pastors were constituted, — and they were few, — they held a position subordinate to the missionary; and it was so because the missionaries had not come to regard it as safe to constitute independent churches and pastorates. Of course I am speaking of the Protestant portion of the native community, comprising more than two thirds of the nation. The missionaries, as presiding over particular districts, or in the local ecclesiastical bodies, or in the general annual convocations, decided upon all ecclesiastical arrangements and appointments.

Of late, foreshadowing the events of the summer in 1863, the native churches were encouraged, on some of the islands, to send lay delegates to the Island ecclesiastical body, where, I believe, they had a vote. Among the missionaries there was considerable diversity of opinion as to the bringing forward of a native ministry, and consequently their practice varied on different islands. There was certainly much need of caution; but I do not doubt that the caution became at length somewhat excessive. Moreover, there was a serious obstacle in the way of dividing the district churches, and introducing a native ministry which should receive its support from the people, in the fact that many of the missionaries looked to their churches for a part or the whole of their own support. To obviate this difficulty, it was recommended to all those who had been missionaries of the Board, to relinquish entirely their dependence on the native churches for support, and look henceforward to the Board for what should be necessary to a comfortable subsistence at the Islands, in addition to what might be made available from their private property.

I went to the Islands with the impression, which was also entertained by the Prudential Committee, that the time had arrived for giving compactness and efficiency to the Protestant Christian community, and for devolving upon it the responsibilities of self-government in all ecclesiastical matters; thus preparing the way for committing to it the duty of working all its religious charities. Should it appear that the people had not been sufficiently trained for this result, then it might be feared, considering the delicacy and difficulty of the enterprise, and the advanced age of most of the missionaries, that there would not be enough left of superintending power to insure success. What I saw in my progress through the Islands, and still more what I heard from my brethren, awakened both hope and fear; but it seemed obvious, that if the native clergy and people did not soon have conceded to them as much agency in the management of their religious affairs as they already had in the affairs of the state, serious evils must ere long arise. Nor could I discover any prudential reasons of much weight in favor of a longer delay. The reverence for missionary authority, so far as it grew out of the former reverence for chiefs, could not long survive the relinquishment or loss of authority by the chiefs themselves. Nor was its continuance deemed favorable to the creation of a self-reliant, self-governing, self-supporting Christian community. The object immediately aimed at was *self-government*,— leaving the matter of *self-support* to come as the result of progress in civilization,—the two things being by no means inseparable.

Various ends were to be secured. The very delicate relations of the foreign and native pastors were to be adjusted, so as to leave no seriously conflicting interests. A method of self-government was to be devised, which should be efficient, and at the same time acceptable to the native pastors and churches. The Protestant churches on the different islands, though separated by rough ocean channels, were to be made to feel that they were one body in Christ, and one in interest, by means of appropriate bonds of union. It was moreover needful, that heavier responsibilities should rest on that community; that — comprehending, as it did, the missionaries and their families — it should be made *self-governing in the largest sense*, and assume the whole direction of the work of building up Christ's kingdom on the Hawaiian Islands, and on the numberless groups of islands lying farther west; while it should be relieved of the support of the old missionaries, and assured of such pecuniary aid, from time to time, as would enable and embolden it to assume the new responsibilities.

CHAPTER XIX.

THE RELIGIOUS CONVOCATION AND ITS RESULTS.

Organization of the Body. — The Topics under Discussion. — Great Unanimity. — The Results. — Native Churches and Pastors. — Ecclesiastical Control no longer with the Missionary. — Native Pastors and Laymen to come into all Ecclesiastical and Charitable Bodies. — Deliberations to be in the Native Language. — Education of the Native Ministry. — Female Boarding Schools. — The Press. — Home Missions. — Children of Missionaries. — Older Missionaries no longer supported by Native Churches. — Reorganization of the Hawaiian Evangelical Association. — Formation of a Hawaiian Board. — Correspondence to be maintained with the American Board. — The Responsibilities of the American Board to be transferred to the Hawaiian Board. — Micronesia Mission. — The Grand Result. — A Glorious Triumph of the Gospel. — A Protestant Christian Nation. — Well governed. — The late King. — Letter to him.

THE meeting of the Hawaiian Evangelical Association commenced June 3, 1863, and closed on the 1st of July. The Association spent twenty-one days in discussions, — the first half hour of every day being devoted to religious exercises. The following persons were present: —

FROM HAWAII. — Rev. John D. Paris, from South Kona; Rev. O. H. Gulick, from Kau; Rev. Titus Coan, Rev. David B. Lyman, and Charles H. Wetmore, M. D., from Hilo;

and Rev. Elias Bond, from Kohala. Rev. Asa Thurston, of Kailua, and Rev. Lorenzo Lyons, of Waimea, were absent, in consequence of sickness.

FROM MAUI. — Rev. Dwight Baldwin, from Lahaina; Rev. John F. Pogue, from Lahainaluna; Rev. William P. Alexander, from Wailuku; and Rev. Sereno E. Bishop, from Hana.

FROM MOLOKAI. — Rev. Anderson O. Forbes, from Kaluaaha.

FROM OAHU. — Rev. Ephraim W. Clark, Rev. Lowell Smith, Rev. Peter J. Gulick, Rev. Artemas Bishop, Rev. Lorrin Andrews, Rev. E. Corwin (Pastor of the Foreign Church), Rev. S. C. Damon (Pastor of the Bethel Church), Rev. Henry H. Parker, and Messrs. Gerrit P. Judd, M. D., Henry Dimond, Edwin O. Hall, Samuel N. Castle, and Amos S. Cooke, from Honolulu; Rev. Cyrus T. Mills (President of Oahu College), and Prof. William De Witt Alexander, from Punahou; Rev. Benjamin W. Parker, from Kaneohe; and Rev. John S. Emerson, from Waialua.

FROM KAUAI. — Rev. George B. Rowell, from Waimea; Rev. James W. Smith, M. D., and Rev. Daniel Dole, from Koloa; and Rev. Edward Johnson and Mr. Abner Wilcox, from Waioli.

CORRESPONDING MEMBERS. — Rev. Rufus Anderson, D. D., Foreign Secretary of the A. B. C. F. M., from Boston, U. S.; Rev. Edward T. Doane, from Ebon, Micronesia Mission; and Rev. J. Bicknell, formerly connected with the Marquesas Mission.

The wives of most of the above-named persons were present; also Mrs. Mercy Whitney, Mrs. Clarissa Armstrong, Mrs. Maria Chamberlain, Mrs. Rebecca Hitchcock, Mrs. Mary S. Rice, and Mrs Jane Shipman, widows of deceased missionaries; and Miss Maria Ogden and Miss Lydia Brown.

Mr. Alexander was chosen Moderator, and Mr. O. H. Gulick Scribe; and after an introductory address of considerable length, by the Foreign Secretary, the meeting proceeded to business. Nine committees were appointed on the same number of topics suggested by the Secretary, who were to draw up reports after their respective topics had been discussed, embodying the sense of the meeting. The topics were these: —

"1. How far it is desirable to form distinct churches throughout the Islands, independent of each other, but under the supervision of the Island ecclesiastical bodies; — how far it is desirable and practicable to obtain and constitute native pastors for the several islands; — whether the time has come when a purely ecclesiastical control of the native pastors should take the place of that which has grown out of the missionary relations; — and to what extent this ecclesiastical control should be exercised.

"2. Whether it be not expedient, hereafter, to educate natives expressly and avowedly for the pastoral office; and also native females, of suitable age and character, in such a way that they shall be fitted to become the wives of pastors; — what education these two classes should receive, and where and from whom; — also, should any part of the funds of the American Board be employed in teaching the English language.

"3. State of the religious and moral literature of the

Islands; — what are its deficiencies; — and what ought to be done in this department.

"4. How far the foreign missions, sent from these Islands, have exerted a beneficial reactionary influence on the evangelical community, carried on, as they have been, with no corresponding system of home missions; — and the nature and extent of the call, on these Islands, for home missions.

"5. Whether it be expedient for the American Board to send out more laborers from the United States, to occupy the more important centres when the missionary fathers are called to leave them; — or whether the children of the mission will be disposed and able to exert the needful conservative influence after the fathers are gone; — also, how far the children of the mission are conversant with the native language, and what means are used, and ought to be used, to acquaint them with it.

"6. Whether the new Christian community should now assume a leading responsibility in building up the kingdom of Christ on these Islands, aided by grants from the United States; — and the probable effect of the proposed change in the relations of the American Board to this community.

"7. The proposed arrangement for the support of the former missionaries of the American Board, without further dependence on the contributions of the native churches; — and the basis and amount of the various salaries.

"8. Whether it be desirable for the Hawaiian Evangelical Association to represent the entire evangelical community on the Islands, both foreign and native; — in what way this should be done; — and the use which should be made of the Hawaiian language in its records and deliberations; — also, whether it be not expedient for the Association to appoint a

Board, to act in the intervals of its meetings, for the prosecution of home and foreign missions, for the education of native ministers and their wives, and for the publication of books; — and to report the necessary modifications of the constitution of the Association.

"9. Whether, and how far, the proposed changes in the mission to Micronesia will enable the Board of the Hawaiian Evangelical Association to assume the conduct of the mission to those Islands."

Whatever may have been the diversity of opinion at the outset, the results were reached with entire unanimity, and the committees were successful in their reports. The limits of this volume will admit of only a concise statement of the results; which is indeed all that is essential to our purpose.

1. It was resolved to form as many as forty new churches in the fifteen missionary districts, as fast as it should be possible to obtain native pastors for them, leaving the missionaries, for the present, — most of them somewhat advanced in life, — in the pastoral care of churches at the central places where they reside.

2. While the age, experience, and superior attainments of the older missionary must secure to him no small degree of influence over native churches and pastors near him, the ecclesiastical control is no longer to be with him, but (so far as any is needful) with the ecclesiastical bodies. Those bodies are to organize the churches, define their territorial limits,

ordain and install the pastors, and remove them when it is desirable so to do; and their supervision extends to doctrine, discipline, and practice. — The details of this supervision are left to the ecclesiastical bodies of the several islands, and from their decision there is, ordinarily, to be no appeal. Yet the island organization is allowed to refer cases of peculiar difficulty to the central body, meeting annually at Honolulu, for advice and counsel. The missionaries thus divested themselves of a governing power in their several districts, which they had exercised from the beginning, and which government was needful for those infant churches at the first. They relinquished it for the sake of the still higher training and development of the new Christian community. But such is still the immaturity and weakness of the religious life on those Islands, as to create a necessity, at least for a time, for an authoritative religious superintendence by local ecclesiastical bodies. To these the pastors, foreign and native, all belong, and in them the churches are represented by lay delegates, though the bodies differ considerably in form and name. The whole matter was necessarily discussed from the *missionary* stand-point, rather than the *ecclesiastical;* since the native Christian community had not yet risen to the level of strictly denominational proceedings, as they are determined at home.

3. Native pastors and laymen are to be appointed, along with those of foreign birth or origin, on all the

ecclesiastical and charitable bodies on the Islands, and the deliberations of these bodies are to be in the Hawaiian language. — This amalgamation of the two classes was a necessity. The state of things at the Islands is peculiar. They have been Christianized. The missionaries have become citizens. In a technical sense they no longer are missionaries, but pastors, and as such on an official parity with the native pastors. The objections, therefore, which lie against missionaries elsewhere becoming members of native ecclesiastical bodies, do not apply to them.

4. Pious graduates from the native college at Lahainaluna, and others recommended by local ecclesiastical bodies, are to spend a year or more with some competent missionary, where they will be prepared for the ministerial and pastoral office.

5. There are to be boarding schools, in rural districts, for females above a certain age, where they may obtain a good common education, in the Hawaiian language, with a thorough domestic training, and thus be fitted to act as teachers, and to become the wives of native pastors.

6. Greater efficiency is to be given to the press in the several departments of literature.

7. While the foreign missions are to be prosecuted with zeal, home missions are to have a more prominent place than heretofore.

8. There was declared to be no present need of sending more laborers to the Hawaiian Islands from

the United States; and should a want of this sort arise, it would probably be but an exception to the general rule. The children of the missionaries are nearly all hopefully pious; four are already in the pastoral office; others are teachers, agriculturists, etc.; and as many as eighty of them can speak the Hawaiian language with considerable ease and fluency. The missionaries believe that a sufficient number of their children will be prepared, through grace, to fill the places of their fathers, when those places need to be thus filled.

9. That there may be no unnecessary hinderance to dividing the churches, multiplying native pastors, and obtaining their support from the native community, the American Board, from the year 1864, resumes the support of its former missionaries residing at the Islands, so far as it shall be necessary to supplement their private means.

10. The Hawaiian Evangelical Association, which has heretofore consisted only of missionaries and other evangelical ministers of foreign birth who sympathize with them, is henceforth to consist of all clergymen, both native and foreign, of the Congregational and Presbyterian orders, on the Hawaiian, Micronesia, and Marquesas Islands; and also of lay delegates, appointed annually by the local ecclesiastical bodies, and of laymen elected by a two-thirds vote of the Association.

11. A Board was formed, called "The Board of the

Hawaiian Evangelical Association." It is to consist of a Corresponding Secretary and Treasurer, and not less than eighteen members, chosen annually by the Association, one third of whom are to be natives. This Board takes charge of home missions, the education of native ministers, and females who may become teachers and the wives of pastors; of the preparation, publication, and circulation of useful books and tracts; and of foreign missions, so far as the conduct of them from the Hawaiian Islands is found to be practicable and expedient; together with the disbursement of all funds contributed for these objects, from whatever source.

12. Inasmuch as grants in aid of the several objects committed to the Hawaiian Board may be needed, to a certain extent, for years to come, and are to be sought from the churches at home through the American Board, the Association, its Board, and its ministers of foreign birth and descent, will continue to correspond with the Foreign Secretary of that Board; so that the interest of the American churches in the welfare of the Islands may be sustained, and the American Board be thus enabled to make the needed grants. And the channels of communication with the American churches are to remain open, as heretofore, to the brethren at the Islands.

13. In case the American Board should give its assent, the responsibilities of that Board for directing the work in the Islands of the Pacific are to be assumed by the Hawaiian Board.

14. It was recommended that the work in Micronesia, excepting Ponape, be carried on mainly by Hawaiian missionaries, who shall be visited periodically by agents of the Hawaiian Board. And because most of the islands in Micronesia are very low, and limited in their range of vegetable productions, so as to be unsuitable abodes for the superintending missionaries, it was believed that they might make the Hawaiian Islands the home of their families while going on their stated tours of inspection. Ponape, though too far west for a present centre, being a high island, should be cultivated, it was thought, as the centre of a future mission to the numerous islands beyond.

The Board of the Hawaiian Evangelical Association, or, more concisely, the Hawaiian Board, appointed four standing committees, — on Foreign Missions, Home Missions, Publications, and Education, — to prepare the business in their respective departments for the action of the Board.

The mission, having accomplished, through the blessing of God, the work specially appropriate to it *as a mission*, has been, as such, disbanded, and merged in the community. The Protestant Christian community, as in older Christian countries, has been organized for action. And the American Board, at its annual meeting next following, which was at Rochester, N. Y., performed the crowning act, by transferring to this new Hawaiian Board its own responsibilities for directing the work on the Hawaiian Islands. As has been intimated, it relieves the native churches of the support of the older missionaries, in order that those churches may be able to support their own native ministry and their different charities. It also holds out an encouraging hand to the infant churches, by engaging to make grants-in-aid, for a time, to the new Board.

What we are permitted to see, therefore, is a glorious triumph of the gospel through the labors of missionaries; and, it is believed, an effectual planting of gospel institutions on those Islands, for whatever people shall occupy them in the coming ages. There is now there an organized Christian government, with a constitution and laws as accordant with the Holy Scriptures as in the best old Christian nations. Nearly one third of the population are members of Protestant churches; the native education is provided for by the government; houses for the worship of God have been everywhere erected, and are preserved by the people; regular Christian congregations assemble on the Sabbath; and there is all the requisite machinery for the healthful development of the inner life of the nation, and for securing it a place, however humble, among the religious benefactors of the world. In short, we see a Protestant Christian nation in the year 1863, in place of a nation of barbarous pagans only forty years before, — self-governing in all its departments, and nearly self-supporting.

And the Hawaiian nation is on the whole well governed. The laws are good, and appear to be rigidly enforced. The king at the time of this meeting was in declining health, and died not long after. Better educated by far than any of his predecessors, more intelligent, more capable of ruling well, he was subject to strong feeling, and was said to be less an object of veneration and love to his people than was his immediate predecessor. Going from England to America in his foreign travels, he unhappily imbibed an anti-American prejudice, which became more apparent after the arrival of the English mission. To me, personally, he was courteous. He invited me to his palace on occasion of the presentation of Mr. McBride, our new minister resident, where his attentions were all that could have been expected. He, however, declined the customary public audience with the Hawaiian Evangelical Association, and made no response to an invitation to attend the commencement of the Oahu College.

Knowing that the proceedings of the Association were regarded with some interest by the government, I early sent to His Majesty, through his Minister of Foreign Affairs, a printed copy of the Address I made at the opening of the Association. This the king kindly acknowledged. And when the meeting was closed, and I was about leaving the

Islands on my return home, I took the liberty of sending him the following letter, —

"Honolulu, July 6, 1863.

"To His Majesty Kamehameha IV.

"Sire: As circumstances forbid a private audience with your Majesty before my departure from the Islands, I may perhaps be permitted, in view of my peculiar relations to a very large body of the best friends and benefactors of this nation, not to leave without my most respectful *aloha* to both your Majesties.

"Having labored assiduously during forty years for your people, and having, in my old age, visited the Islands, for the purpose of hastening their independence of foreign aid in the maintenance of their religious institutions, I rejoice in the belief that, with the kind protection of the government, this result is attainable. The important steps lately taken in this direction are perhaps sufficiently indicated in the printed Address, which I had the honor of sending through the Minister of Foreign Affairs, and the receipt of which he has duly acknowledged. I am happy to inform your Majesty that the plan there indicated has since been adopted, and is now going into effect, — with the best influence, as I cannot doubt, upon the religious welfare of your people.

"My visit to these Islands has impressed me, not only with the strength, but also with the beneficent and paternal character of your government. In no nation in Christendom is there greater security of person and property, or more of civil and religious liberty. As to the progress of the nation in Christian civilization, I am persuaded, and shall confidently affirm on my return home, that the history of the Christian church and of nations affords nothing equal to it.

"And now the Hawaiian Christian community is so far formed and matured, that the American Board ceases to act any longer as principal, and becomes an auxiliary, — merely affording grants in aid of the several departments of labor in building up the kingdom of Christ in these Islands, and also in the Islands of Micronesia. The needed grants we expect will diminish gradually, until they cease altogether. We shall, of course, rejoice when that time comes. Meanwhile we regard this Christian community, thus assuming the leadership and chief responsibility, as demonstrating the triumphant success of the gospel of our Lord and Saviour Jesus Christ. And in this we doubt not your Majesty will rejoice with us.

"Praying God to grant long life and prosperity to your Majesties, I am, with profound respect,

"Your Majesty's obedient, humble servant,

"R. ANDERSON,

"*Foreign Secretary of the American Board of Commissioners forForeign Missions.*"

V.

OTHER MISSIONS.

OTHER MISSIONS.

CHAPTER XX.

THE REFORMED CATHOLIC MISSION.

Name of the Mission. — Reason for the present Statement. — Such a Mission not originally requested by the King. — Official Letters. — Letter from Mr. Ellis. — Letter to Archbishop Sumner. — The Archbishop's Reply. — Bishop of London. — Opposition to the Measure. — Government License. — Consecration of Bishop Staley. — Statement of the Bishops. — Results. — Letter of the Dean of Windsor. — Desirableness of an Episcopal Presbyter at Honolulu. — Arrival of the Mission at the Islands. — High-church Stand taken by it. — Baptism of the Young Prince. — Difference in Doctrinal and Practical Religious Views. — Statements from Dr. Staley's two printed Sermons. — Leading Features of the Religion he is to propagate on the Islands. — The People hard to be interested. — The Worship too showy for them. — Public Discourtesy towards the Protestant Clergy at the Royal Funeral. — Influence of the New Mission in the Hawaiian Government. — Popular Unrest. — The Question for the American Board. — The Reformed Catholic Mission an Invasion in the Hour of Victory. — Another similar Movement in the Church of England. — Extracts from a Speech of the Earl of Shaftesbury.

The English mission lately sent to the Hawaiian Islands is known there by the name of the "Reformed Catholic Mission." It is so called in the official

"Court News," and its chartered rights are understood to be secured under the appellation of the "Reformed Catholic Church."

As nothing like an adequate account of this mission has been published in this country, nor, so far as I know, in England, I embody a statement of the facts connected with it, that have come to my knowledge.

The Report of the English "Colonial Church and School Society" for 1860 contains letters from Richard Armstrong, D. D., President of the Hawaiian Board of Public Instruction, and His Excellency R. C. Wyllie, Minister of Foreign Affairs, the former dated February 29, 1860, and the latter March 13th, both addressed to the Rev. William Ellis, of London. These letters are important, as showing that such a mission as the one now under consideration formed no part of the original design of the king and his legal advisers. Dr. Armstrong's letter is as follows: —

"Having been a resident of this place many years ago, and your name being yet fresh in the recollection of many here, both native and foreign, you will be prepared to appreciate the object of this letter. I will therefore make no apology for addressing it to you.

"Besides the two large native churches, we have here two of the Congregational order, — one of them in connection with the Seamen's Chapel, — and one Methodist, none of them large, for our foreign population is small, except in the fall season, when whaling ships resort to our ports.

"There are quite a number of persons here, and a few families, who are either members of the Episcopal church or partial to that church, and they have long been desirous to secure the services of an Episcopal minister, to break to them the bread of life.

"Several months ago, the king, who takes much interest in the subject, directed his Minister of Foreign Relations, R. C. Wyllie, a gentleman from Scotland, who also feels great interest in the matter, to write and guarantee to a suitable clergyman of the Episcopal church, who may come to Honolulu and labor for the spiritual good of its population, an annual salary of one thousand dollars, hoping that a full salary might be made up for him by this and what might be contributed for the object in England. Less than two thousand dollars would not be sufficient. And should the right man be obtained, he will have no difficulty in raising this amount here. The king has offered a lot of ground as a site for an Episcopal church; and there will, I think, be no difficulty in raising means here to erect one upon it.

"How to obtain just the *right man* is a question of great interest, not only to those of the Episcopal church, but to all who love Zion here. And here is just the reason for the liberty I take in addressing you now. You have lived here, and have associated with American missionaries. You would, therefore, know at once what kind of a man would be calculated to do good here. I may add, also, that I address you at the request of several Episcopalians, who are among our best people. They want a man of evangelical sentiment, of respectable talents, and most exemplary Christian life. A High Churchman, or one of loose Christian habits, would not succeed. He would not have the sympathy and support of the other evangelical ministers at all, but rather opposition, as you well know from personal observation.

"Could you see the Bishop of London on the subject, both in regard to a suitable man, and a portion of his support? — though I think, if acceptable, he will very soon get his entire support here.

"I send this through Mr. Wyllie, who will enclose it officially."

Mr. Wyllie wrote thus to Mr. Ellis: —

"I have the honor to enclose to you a letter from the Rev. Richard Armstrong, D. D., President of the Board of Public Instruction, which, he informs me, is on the subject of the establishment in this capital of an Episcopal Church.

"Their Majesties the king and queen prefer that form of worship, and were married according to the rites of the English Episcopal Church.

"The king himself, taking all the interest in the education, morals, and religion of his people which becomes him as a sovereign, believes that an Episcopal Church here, besides supplying a want long felt by many British and American families, would operate beneficially in narrowing the existing broad antagonism of the Calvinistic and Catholic creeds, and thereby promote that brotherly feeling between the clergy of both that so well becomes the followers of the same Lord.

"By order of His Majesty I have written fully upon this subject to Manley Hopkins, Esq., the king's Chargé d'Affaires and Consul-General in London. If you honor him with a call, he will communicate to you what further information you may desire."

I am not aware that Mr. Wyllie's letter to Mr. Hopkins has been made public; but it must be presumed it was in strict accordance with the letters to Mr. Ellis.

Mr. Ellis must have received his letters in the spring of 1860. A letter addressed by him to myself, dated July 24, 1861, somewhat more than a year afterwards, gives a continuation of the history. He says, —

"I immediately waited on Mr. Hopkins, the Hawaiian Consul, who expressed some surprise that I should have been applied to, and informed me that he was already in coöperation with parties in England, endeavoring to send out, not a simple clergyman, as desired by the king, but a bishop. I expressed my opinion that such a procedure would be a great mistake, as the bishop, if sent, would probably fail, while a respectable pious clergyman, who would coöperate with the Christian ministers already there in promoting the moral and spiritual benefit of the community, would prove a real blessing, especially to those who cherished attachment for the system of the Church of England, of which, excepting as one of the various forms of Christianity, the king must necessarily be ignorant.

"Mr. Hopkins then handed me a sort of circular, which he had prepared, and by the names attached to which I perceived that he was associated with that section of the Church of England from which the greatest number of perverts to

Popery has proceeded, and between whom and the Roman Catholics the difference is reported to be slight. I left Mr. Hopkins under the impression that any interference on my part was by him deemed unnecessary, and would not be welcome.

"Some time after, Mr. Hopkins wrote to me, asking the loan of my Tour of Hawaii, and any other information I would supply, as he was about to prepare a statement for publication in furtherance of the object. I sent him the Tour, and enclosed a copy of your last Annual Report, informing him that it would supply the most authentic account of the extent of religion among the people, and the amount of provision already made for their educational and religious improvement.

"I had, in the mean time, communicated the request which I had received from the Sandwich Islands to the 'Colonial Church and School Society,' placing the letters from Mr. Wyllie and Dr. Armstrong in the hands of the Secretary, with whom I left the circular of Mr. Hopkins. The Committee approved of the object, and when the letters were submitted to the Bishop of London, his lordship expressed his entire concurrence in these proceedings, and his readiness to aid in carrying them out. I forward you a copy of their last year's Report, by which (p. 98) you will learn their views and proceedings. I suggested that the clergyman should be married.

"Disappointed in one or two individuals, whom they deemed suitable, I now find that the section of the Church of England, of which the Bishop of Oxford, Mr. Beresford Hope, and some others of similar views, are the representatives, have appointed a Bishop of Hawaii, who is, I believe, about to proceed to his newly-made diocese. How far the king of the Sandwich Islands may approve of the territorial title when informed of its import, as no doubt he will be, and how far he may regard it as similar to the assumption of the Pope in appointing Cardinal Wiseman Bishop of Westminster, I do not pretend to guess. But I deeply regret that, instead of an unpretending clergyman, holding and preaching the simple truths of the gospel, which would have been beneficial to the souls of his flock, the section of the Church of England characterized by extreme ritualism, and supposed leaning towards the forms of Popery, should have thought it preferable to send a bishop, with all the paraphernalia appertaining to his office and functions, among a people just emerging from barbarism and idolatry, and to whom, heretofore, the simplicity in which the New Testament presents Christianity has been one of its attractions, as well as one of the chief characteristics which externally distinguish it from Heathenism and Popery."

As soon as information of this proposed mission to the Islands reached the United States (coming through a Hawaiian newspaper), it seemed proper to address the Archbishop of Canterbury; and the letter, dated September 3, 1860, with the reply of the archbishop, will be given here.

"My Lord: A newspaper published at the Sandwich Islands, called 'The Pacific Commercial Advertiser,' lately copied an article from an English paper, which is the occasion of this letter. The article was as follows: —

"'*Church of England in the Sandwich Islands.* — There is some idea of the introduction of Anglicanism, and, if possible, of its episcopate, into these Islands, which territorially do not belong to the English crown, and ecclesiastically pertain to the American missionaries. It is stated that an effort is being made by Mr. Manley Hopkins, Consul for Hawaii, in concert with the Society for the Propagation of the Gospel, to introduce a branch of the Church of England into the Sandwich Islands. Since the year 1827 the Church of Rome has made persevering efforts to establish itself among these interesting islanders, but without success until 1839, when the Roman Catholic faith was introduced under the pressure of a French admiral and the guns of a French frigate ; and now there is not only a Roman Catholic bishop and a staff of clergy, but a body of Sisters of Mercy, established at Hawaii. The leanings of the king and queen, who are themselves Protestants, have been always in favor of the English Church ; and they have requested the coöperation of this country in the work. The king offers to build a parsonage, and to give a site for a church at once, and to pay a salary of £200 a year to an English clergyman. It is ultimately hoped that Hawaii will become the see of an English bishop, with Polynesia for the sphere of his jurisdiction. The archbishop has given his encouragement to the plan.'

"Considering all the circumstances, it has seemed prudent to notice this article, though we do not regard it as conclusive evidence, and to address ourselves to your Grace, as having, perhaps, a governing influence over such an arrangement as is proposed, as well as being most liberal, and friendly in your feelings towards the missionary enterprises of other Christian bodies.

"It has been the policy of our Board to leave the islands of the *South* Pacific to be evangelized exclusively by means of the labors of our English brethren, and to confine our own efforts exclusively to the islands situated *north of the equator* — the Sandwich and Micronesia Islands.

"The Sandwich Islands being now virtually Christianized, we can have no objection to the people arranging themselves in different Christian denominations, as they please. If it be a fact, as stated in the article above quoted, that the king and queen prefer the Episcopal worship to the simple forms under which they have had their Christian training, they can have no difficulty in arranging for their own accommodation in this matter. They can easily secure for themselves this form of worship.

"But if the king's ministers have advised him to encourage the introduction of 'a branch of the Church of England into the Sandwich Islands,' we believe they have acted unwisely. Might not such a step by the Church of England, implying, as it must, the probable extension of British dominion, be regarded with jealousy by the government of the United States? We fear it would stimulate the French government to connect itself, more than it has done, with the Roman Catholic mission on those Islands. And we apprehend it would have the ultimate effect to distract the counsels of the native government, and to estrange it from the men who planted and have sustained the gospel institutions on those Islands; apart from whom, without a miracle of grace (as we apprehend), those institutions cannot long exist under a native government.

"It has been our constant aim, as a missionary institution, in planting churches at the Sandwich Islands, to preserve them free from all subjection to the ecclesiastical bodies in our own country; and the very large and respectable body of people in the United States who have now expended a million of dollars in imparting the blessings of the gospel to the Sandwich Islands, would earnestly deprecate such a measure as the one now under consideration. We entreat your Grace to exert an influence with the Society for the Propagation of the Gospel, to dissuade that venerable institution from extending its operations to the islands in the North Pacific, since the effect of such an extension, however well intended, would be to embarrass, weaken, and discourage the Christian missions of their American brethren, hitherto so signally crowned with the divine blessing.

"The apology for this letter is in the importance of its object, and also in the confidence that we are addressing an enlightened friend of all that concerns the kingdom of our blessed Redeemer; and your Grace will please accept the assurance of our profound respect and esteem."

To the foregoing, the archbishop returned the following reply: —

"Lambeth Palace, September 28, 1860.

"REVEREND SIR: In consequence of the letter dated 3d instant, which I had the honor of receiving from you, I have made inquiry on the subject to which it refers; and I find it to be quite true, that certain individuals have formed themselves into a committee, for the purpose of taking advantage of the proposal of the king of Hawaii, and with the ultimate view of establishing a bishop on the Polynesian Islands.

"The subject does not originate with the Society for Propagating the Gospel, to which it has not been hitherto proposed. And it is altogether untrue, that the archbishop encourages the plan, of which, in fact, he was ignorant until your letter arrived.

"Should an attempt be made to connect this object with the Society for Propagating the Gospel, I shall think it my duty to lay your letter before the persons who chiefly administer its affairs; and I shall be truly sorry if any circumstances shall occur calculated to create jealousy between parties who have the same great end in view — an object which would be counteracted by collision, in the same degree as it may be promoted by coöperation.

"With high respect for the Society to which you belong, and much thankfulness for the work which God has enabled it to effect, I remain,

"Reverend Sir, your faithful servant,

"J. B. CANTUAR.

"To the Secretary of the Board of Missions."

The Report of the "Church and School Society" states, that the plan proposed in the letters from Messrs. Armstrong and Wyllie had received the cordial concurrence of the Bishop of London. And it appears, from an editorial article in "The Evening Standard" (a London newspaper) of November 14, 1861, that he objected so decidedly to the plan of sending a bishop, as to come near defeating the measure.[1] On this becoming known, a letter

[1] From the same source we learn that the law officers hesitated as to the applicability to this case of a former decision. That decision appears to have been, that there were no legal impediments to consecrating missionary bishops *for parts beyond Her Majesty's dominions.* This decision was doubtless reached, in the first instance, in respect to pagan Africa or China. But would it apply to a *Christian, independent* nation, like the Hawaiian, whose independence had been

was addressed to the Bishop of London by the Foreign Secretary of the American Board. But before there was time for it to reach London, the Rev. T. N. Staley, D. D., had been consecrated "Bishop of the United Church of England and Ireland in the Hawaiian or Sandwich Islands, and all other of the dominions of the king of Hawaii," or, more briefly, "Bishop of the United Church of England and Ireland in Hawaii." This language is from the license of the Foreign Secretary, Earl Russell, on which Dr. Staley was consecrated. The following is a copy of the license: —

"Victoria, by the grace of God, etc., to the Archbishop of Canterbury, etc., greeting: —

"Whereas you, the said John Bird, Archbishop of Canterbury, have humbly applied unto us for our license, by warrant under our Royal Signet and Seal Manual, authorizing and empowering you to consecrate the Rev. Thomas Nettleship Staley, Clerk, Master of Arts, a British subject,

acknowledged and guaranteed by the British nation? No wonder the lawyers and the bishop hesitated. Their scruples seem to have been overcome at last by evidence that the Hawaiian king had given his assent to the plan. It is not known what influences were brought to bear upon him. But the Hawaiian government is as really a government of laws, as is that of England; and Hawaiian lawyers, if they felt free to speak, would probably declare that a request from their king, for an extension of the "United Church of England and Ireland" to their independent kingdom, lay beyond his legal powers. That the king was not self-moved to make such a request, we have evidence in the documents at the opening of this chapter.

to be bishop of the United Church of England and Ireland in the Hawaiian or Sandwich Islands, and all other of the dominions of the king of Hawaii, you have certified to us that you have fully ascertained the sufficiency of the said Rev. Thomas Nettleship Staley in good learning, the soundness of his faith, and the purity of his manners.

"Now, it is our royal will and pleasure, and we do, by this our license under our Royal Signet and Sign Manual, authorize and empower you, the said archbishop, to consecrate the said Thomas Nettleship Staley to be bishop of the United Church of England and Ireland in Hawaii.

"Given at our Court of St. James's the 11th day of December, 1861, in the twenty-fifth year of our reign.

"By Her Majesty's command. RUSSELL."

The recognition was on the 15th of December, and the consecrating prelates were Archbishop Sumner, the Bishop of London, and the Bishop of Oxford.

The Bishop of London replied in due course to the letter of the Secretary, and stated that "everything had been arranged in strict accordance with the expressed wishes of the king of the Sandwich Islands." He also expressed the hope, "as Bishop Staley goes forth with an ardent desire wisely and faithfully to bear his part in preaching the gospel of Christ, and advancing his kingdom," that "he may be found to strengthen the hands of all who have the same object at heart." The Bishop of Oxford, in his Preface to a work of Mr. Manley Hopkins, the

Hawaiian Consul-General, spoken of by Mr. Ellis (dated May 24, 1862), also declares the confirmation of the bishop to have been at the desire of the Hawaiian king.[1] From the preceding statement we draw the following inferences: —

1. The idea of sending a bishop to the Hawaiian Islands did not originate with the Hawaiian king. It was neither his idea nor desire, when his ministers wrote to England for an Episcopal presbyter. It must have originated in England.

2. Bishop Staley and his presbyters were selected neither by Archbishop Sumner, nor by the Bishop of London.

3. The opposition of the Bishop of London, in November, 1861, viewed in connection with his agency in the consecration in the following month, renders it probable that, up to November of that year, no assenting response had been received from the Hawaiian king. This conclusion is strengthened by the singularly vague language, otherwise unac-

[1] "Hawaii: The Past, Present, and Future of its Island-Kingdom. By Manley Hopkins, Hawaiian Consul-General, etc. With a Preface, by the Bishop of Oxford. London, 1862." It should be said of this work, that its author was never at the Sandwich Islands, and that he reposed undue confidence in authorities that were hostile to the American Mission. No apology can be made, however, for the dishonorable caricature-engraving of the Rev. William Richards — professedly "a sketch from memory, by the author." And one cannot but wonder, that so highly intelligent a prelate as Bishop Wilberforce should give his sanction to a work of so one-sided and partisan a character.

countable, employed by Mr. Hopkins at page 339 of his work, — printed, it may be, some time before the date of the Bishop of Oxford's Preface, — where, instead of saying that the king had asked for a *bishop*, he says the church and people of England were requested to "establish a *branch of the Reformed Episcopal Church*[1] in Hawaii;" and even this is more than can be gathered from the official letters.

4. As there was abundant time for an interchange of letters after the Bishop of Oxford and his associates had taken up the project of this mission, Bishop Tait's assent obliges us to suppose the young king to have at length acceded to the proposal of a bishop; and this is rendered the more probable by the cordial reception he is known to have given the mission on its reaching Honolulu.

Among the documents connected with this mission, important because influential with the reigning powers at the Islands, is the following letter from the Dean of Windsor to Dr. Staley: —

"Windsor, August 15, 1862.

"My dear Lord Bishop: The queen has desired me to express to you her regret at being unable, in consequence of her great affliction, and absence in Scotland, to communicate with you personally upon many most interesting circumstances connected with your episcopate.

[1] What is the "*Reformed* Episcopal Church"?

"Her Majesty preserves a lively recollection of the visit of the king of the Sandwich Islands to this country, eleven years ago; and more especially of the deep interest then taken by her beloved consort in his welfare. Since that time she has most gratefully appreciated and sympathized with all the exertions of the king with a view to the progress of Christianity in Honolulu, and has heard with much satisfaction of his attachment to the doctrines and discipline of the Church of England.

"For the queen of the Sandwich Islands, as springing from her own nation, Her Majesty entertains sentiments of peculiar regard, and considers her position as most propitiously exercised in furthering the good work of the English mission.

"But it is to the intention of the royal parents with regard to the crown prince that Her Majesty looks forward with the most hope and confidence. She has heard with great satisfaction that he will, in the first place, be intrusted to your justice and care; being assured that you will associate with the other duties of your episcopate, as one of its first objects, the instruction of the heir of the crown, early, in the sound and charitable views of religion which belong to the Church into which he is to be admitted. Her best wishes and prayers will attend the baptismal rites, with which, immediately on your arrival at Honolulu, you will receive the prince into our Church. Your episcopate will thus be inaugurated on the Islands with the most promising auspices.

"Her Majesty has already signified, through her Secretary of State for Foreign Affairs, her intention of being one of the sponsors to the prince, and has forwarded a suitable gift for the occasion.

"Her Majesty has commanded me to add, that, although now left alone, she shall continue to watch the progress of Christianity, and education, and social improvement, in the Sandwich Islands, with the same lively interest with which she has hitherto watched it in conjunction with the prince consort. Such progress, under the Almighty aid, and your own supervision, she considers as mainly depending upon the intelligence and refinement of character and mind so remarkable in the king.

"Believe me, dear Lord Bishop, most sincerely yours,

"JEROLD WELLESLY,

"*Dean of Windsor, Resident Chaplain, &c.*"

I may say here, that while I deprecated the sending of a bishop to the Hawaiian Islands, at the present stage of their religious development, I believed it was desirable to send to Honolulu an evangelical presbyter of the Episcopal Church, such as the king requested. A year or more before the date of the letters of Dr. Armstrong and Secretary Wyllie to Mr. Ellis, I advised a bishop of the American branch of that Church to procure the sending of an evangelical presbyter to the metropolis of those Islands. I believed there was then a demand for one near the court, and that the right man would strengthen the influence of religion. As the Islands had been Christianized, I went even farther. Meeting a bishop of the Methodist Episcopal Church, at a somewhat earlier date, whom I had long known and esteemed, I suggested that it might prove a useful stimulus to the religious spirit on those Islands, were his Church to send a good man to Honolulu. This was done, but the enterprise did not prove successful.

Bishop Staley arrived at Honolulu on the 11th of October, 1862, accompanied by two presbyters, the Rev. G. Mason and Rev. E. Ibbotson; and another, Mr. Scott, arrived soon after. They could not have had a more cordial reception than was given them by the king and queen.

It is to be regretted that, in a land so lately recovered from a barbarous paganism, the members of this mission should have felt themselves rigidly bound by the conventionalities of the High Church. The Protestant clergy of Honolulu (missionaries and others), took an early opportunity to invite one of the newly-arrived brethren to attend a union monthly meeting for prayer, and he, after consulting his bishop, made the following reply: —

"He [the bishop] strengthened my own opinion, viz., that it would be inconsistent in a clergyman of our Church to attend a prayer-meeting in a place of worship belonging to a denomination of Christians who do not regard episcopacy of divine appointment."

There was no collision. The common civilities of Christian life were reciprocated. But that was all. Theoretically, practically, the office and work of the American brethren as Christian ministers, as well as their churches and native ministry, were ignored by the Reformed Catholics, as much as they ever had been by the Roman Catholics. If they met their American brethren at all, it was never as divinely authorized Christian missionaries; and this was beginning to be understood by the natives. Holding to baptismal regeneration, they thought it right, perhaps a duty, to baptize infants who had not been baptized, wherever they could do it, without regard to the Protestant churches to which the parents belonged, or to the relations sustained by the parents to the missionary pastors.[1]

It was the expectation of the bishop and his company, that they would have the privilege of baptizing the young Prince of Hawaii, heir to the throne, on reaching the Islands. But, to the great grief both of his parents and of the nation, the child sickened unto death, and Mr. Clark, pastor of the first church in Honolulu and one of the older missionaries, was summoned to the palace to administer the ordinance.

The following lines, quoted from a Honolulu newspaper, with the signature "G. M.," and the caption "The English Missionary's Approach to the Sandwich Islands, October, 1862," are understood to have been composed by one of the English presbyters before he reached the Islands: —

[1] This declaration is made on the strength of concurrent testimony at the Islands.

"E'en now expectant stands Hawaii's king,
As a kind nursing father, to embrace
The glorious system of restoring grace.
His royal spouse, with all a mother's joy,
Leads to the holy font their princely boy,
Where England's bishop, sent with power to bless,
Robes the young chief with Christ's own righteousness."

It may be that the difference in doctrinal and practical religious views between the two classes of missionaries is too wide to admit of much personal intimacy. Indeed, the difference must be regarded as very great; and the evidence of this is furnished by the bishop himself, in a public statement made soon after his arrival at the Islands.

Dr. Staley has printed two sermons at the Islands — one preached in London, the other at Honolulu. The following declarations in the sermon first preached, are enough to have fully justified the hope of a different result from the one above stated.

"Nothing," he says, "would shake all religious belief in the Islands more effectually than for us to assume an attitude of hostility to those forms of Christianity, with which they [the people] are now familiar." Again: "We must make it clear, that we do not go forth to ignore and override what has been done by others." And again: "The great object of the mission is the salvation of the souls and bodies of those among whom we are going to labor, and not the numbers we can count as members of our communion."

Some of the leading features of the religion, which the bishop proposed setting forth for the acceptance and salvation of the Islanders, are indicated in the second sermon.

Their worship was to be guided "by Holy Scripture, as interpreted by the ancient fathers, implying by that term those chiefly of the first five centuries — the purest ages of the Church." They were to be taught that their infants were, by baptism, "made members of Christ, children of God, and inheritors of the kingdom of heaven." And when the baptized children arrived at "years of discretion," they were to be encouraged to believe that they would "be strengthened by a new gift of the Holy Spirit, imparted to them by the imposition of hands," in "the holy rite of confirmation." Being thus "initiated into full communion with the Church," they were to be deemed fitted to "approach the Blessed Sacrament of Christ's Body and Blood." The baptized were also to be taught that they were not to wait till they were "converted by some sudden, irresistible impulse," but to regard themselves "as already, by baptism, grafted into Christ's church," and not only bound, but "able to crucify the old man, with his evil deeds, by the strength already imparted from above." If their consciences were "burdened with sin," they were to be encouraged "to come to the minister, and open their grief," and "receive the benefit of absolution." The Islanders, under the instruction of the missionaries, are wont to call one day in seven the *Sabbath*, but "most falsely and mischievously," in the opinion of Bishop Staley; "for the Church provides an order of prayer to be said *daily* throughout the year." "Such," he adds, "are some of the leading features in that church system we come to establish among the people of these Islands."

The reader is left to judge how very far these "forms of Christianity," which the bishop and his associates propose to establish among the people of the Hawaiian Islands, differ from those that have been already established, and how great must be their tendency "to shake all religious belief on the Islands."[1]

It was found hard to interest the people in this new form of religion. Excepting on a few extraordinary occasions, the audiences were everywhere small.

[1] In the Appendix the foregoing extracts are printed in their connections, that there may be no unfairness to their author. Should it be thought that the bishop honestly regarded himself as sustained by the standards of his Church, that might be admitted. Nevertheless it is true, that very few missionaries do actually go forth from that Church into the heathen world to promulgate those doctrines; and it is none the less true that they could not be "established among the people of those Islands" without a complete and dangerous revolution in their religious opinions and habits.

It was even so within the precincts of the Court. The worship was evidently too showy for the religious taste of the people; too like the Roman Catholic; — with surplice and stole; with alb, and cope, and crosier; with rochet, and mitre, and pastoral staff; with Episcopal ring and banner; with pictures, altar-candles, robings, intonations, processions, and attitudes.[1] The mitre was worn at the confirmation of the king and queen, but is said to be very seldom worn by a bishop in England. We have it from one present at the late king's funeral in the "temporary cathedral," that "more than one hundred and fifty candles were burning in that small church at noonday; while the bishop's back was most of the time towards the audience, with his altar, and pictures, and candles before him."

In the semi-official account of the funeral of Kamehameha IV., in The Pacific Commercial Advertiser, was this statement: —

> "Following the servants of the late king, came the clergy of the various denominations; but of the American clergy (the most numerous here) we observed but one representative, and understood that the reason of their non-appearance was the sneering way in which they were thought to be referred to in the programme."

[1] I find these all mentioned in the different accounts I have seen of the public occasions on which the bishop and his associates have had professional duties to perform. I cannot of course vouch for the entire accuracy of the statement.

That part of the programme was as follows: —

"Ministers of Religion of the several Denominations.
The Clergy of the Roman Catholic Church.
His Lordship Louis, the Rt. Rev. Bishop of Arathea,
and Vicar Apostolic of the Hawaiian
Islands.
Choir of the Hawaiian Cathedral.
Officiating Clergy.
His Lordship the Rt. Reverend Bishop of Honolulu."

The least that can be said in respect to this indecorum of denying to the American clerical body the title and standing of clergymen, which they have always had in the Christian Church of the Islands, as well as in their own country, is, that it must be numbered among the unfortunate consequences of this mission. The only Protestant clergyman present at the funeral solemnities — one who had been called to the palace, not long before, to baptize the dying young prince, the heir apparent to the throne, and to officiate at his funeral — gave public expression to his own feelings and those of his brethren.

"We do not object," he says, "that a section of the Christian Church — if it sees fit in its bigoted wisdom — should deny the Protestant clergy a standing in the Christian Church. But to thrust this bigotry into a public document of the government, which has been brought into being and taken a standing among the Christian nations of the earth mainly in consequence of the labors of these same Protestant clergymen, is what we do not approve. There was no necessity for the government, on so solemn an occasion, to treat with discourtesy any of its subjects, especially its best friends and truest benefactors."

The letter from the queen's chaplain at Windsor was virtually a letter of commendation from Queen Victoria to the king and queen of the Hawaiian Islands, and was made public immediately on the arrival of the mission at Honolulu. And the bishop was most cordially received by the late king, whose youthful devotion to his interests soon became manifest to the people. Of course it was proper for the king to connect himself with whatever branch of the visible church he might choose.

Considering his zeal, we cannot but feel surprise that so few of the people were moved by his example. But it has not been without influence among the higher officers of the government. At the present time, the Minister of Foreign Affairs, the Minister of the Interior, a Justice of the Supreme Court, the Attorney General, and perhaps one or two native gentlemen in office, are connected with the Reformed Catholic Church.[1] The only other cabinet minister — the one having charge of the finances — is a French gentleman and a Roman Catholic. The present king retains Bishop Staley as

[1] The present king, his venerable father, and his sister Victoria, have not connected themselves with that church.

his chaplain, and, though remaining at the head of his mission, has made him a member of his Privy Council.

Meanwhile there have been indications of unrest in the public mind. Soon after the formation of the new ministry, an earnest controversy arose in the newspapers, based on a credited report that the bishop was to be made President of the Board of Education, and so have control of the public schools. Mr. Wyllie, writing me on the 1st of May, 1864, mentions also a report as being then current, "that the king intended so to reform the constitution as to make the Episcopal religion the established religion of his kingdom, to tax his people for its support, and to place Bishop Staley in high political office." This report Mr. Wyllie pronounces, in strong language, to be without foundation. It grew out of the calling of a convention, by the king, for revising the constitution of Kamehameha III.

With the struggles for mere political ascendency in this little kingdom (if such there are), whether by France, England, or the United States, I have at present nothing to do. The two governments first named have pledged themselves never, in any form, to take possession of the Islands;[1] and the one last named, while I am confident it would not consent to

[1] Chapter XIII.

their coming under a foreign power, will do all it can to maintain their national independence.

But the American Board of Commissioners for Foreign Missions, as a missionary body, and the numerous and intelligent Christian churches which sustain its operations, cannot possibly be indifferent to the safety, on those Islands, of the glorious results which have cost them so much labor during the past forty years, and an outlay considerably exceeding a million of dollars.

As the case now stands, the Reformed Catholic mission on the Hawaiian Islands will seem like a breach of that courtesy, which is due from one Christian body to another, and which is so important in the work of missions. In the hour of victory, after a long and arduous conflict and a great expenditure, just when we were taking measures to secure our conquest for the Lord of the Church, a body of professed allies comes upon us from the land of our fathers, with the evident intent, if it be possible, of taking possession of the field! The principle involved in this proceeding should receive the serious consideration of our English brethren, and of all who are desirous of the future success of missions among the heathen.

Lately a movement occurred within the Church of England to send a mission, consisting of a bishop and six presbyters, to the capital of Madagascar. It was similar, in its nature and intent, to the one under consideration in this chapter, and it had a similar, though somewhat more imposing, origin. Such a mission would interfere vitally with missionary operations long carried on in that field by the London Missionary Society. A public meeting was therefore held in London in behalf of that Society, in February, 1863, at which the Earl of Shaftesbury presided. Some remarks then made by the noble and excellent Earl are applicable to the movement at the Sandwich Islands, and will be a suitable close to this narrative.

"I am certain," he says, "that there are persons whose names are on that list, who, if they were acquainted with the state of things in Madagascar, with what has been done, what is doing, and what is in preparation, would no more think of disturbing the operations of this noble body, than they would think of upsetting the Church of England, and spreading disorder in all parishes of this country."

And he continues, —

"I am afraid that it will introduce a new principle, that may be subversive of all harmony, and act most injuriously upon missionary operations in general. There has been hitherto recognized among all missionaries in the Protestant denomination a kind of courtesy, that they should not interfere one with another, unless it could be proved that a field was shamefully ill-worked, or that there were heretical doctrines taught, or that mischief was being done, instead of good. As to interfering one with another, thrusting yourself into another man's vineyard, not attending to your own, but ever spying out what your neighbor is doing,—that is contrary to the received principle of missionary operations. It is contrary to acknowledged courtesies, and if it be allowed to gain head, it will lead to a civil war among missionaries ten times more distressing in its consequences than even the civil war in America. I do hope that all parties will very seriously consider before they allow themselves to go one step farther. I should most deeply lament to see that the Church of England, which has been so true and so energetic, which has exhibited so deep and solemn an appreciation of the work of its brother Protestants and brother Christians in foreign lands, should now be coming forward in a spirit of selfishness and mean aggrandizement, for the purpose of tearing from the hands of others the work that they have so nobly and so signally performed."

CHAPTER XXI.

ROMAN CATHOLIC MISSION.—THE MORMONS.

Origin of the Roman Catholic Mission. — Claim made by the Government. — The First Missionaries sent away. — The American Missionaries not accessory to this. — Why they were sent away. — Protestant Missionaries opposed to Persecution. — British Consul and Irish Priest. — Violence of a French Naval Officer. — Oppressive Exactions. — Their Effect. — Present State of the Mission. — Defective Statistics. — Scantiness of Materials for a History of Romish Missions. — This true of their Mission on the Hawaiian Islands. — The Success and Comparative Power of Romish Missions over-estimated. — Dr. Venn's Work on the Life of Xavier a Corrective. — The Mormons.

The origin of the Roman Catholic mission was described in the second chapter. It came to the Islands in the year 1827. The Hawaiian government then claimed the same right in respect to the Romish missionaries, that it had claimed in 1820 in respect to the Protestant missionaries; namely, of deciding whether to allow them to remain. Regarding the papal missionaries as having come to teach a religion which resembled in its worship the old idolatry, the government refused them permission to stay, and ordered them to leave the Islands. And when they refused to go, it sent them away at its own expense, landing them safely in California, which was then under Mexican dominion.

The American missionaries have been accused of procuring the banishment of the Roman Catholic priests. This is not true. The charge has always been denied by them, and also by the Hawaiian government.

The priests "were sent away because they landed without permission from the government, and staid in contempt of its orders to depart; because they taught a religion so like the old idolatry of the Islands; because intelligent Englishmen told of the blood that Rome had shed in Europe, predicted like carnage here, and advised their expulsion; because they opposed the efforts of the government to teach the people to read; because they identified themselves with the party of Boki, of Liliha, of the family of Peliolani, of the British and American consuls, and of dissolute foreigners generally — a party which attempted to depose the regent and principal chiefs, and raise themselves to supreme power by civil war; and because they were believed, if not known, to have been active laborers in the cause of that party, by inducing men to join it." [1]

[1] Mr. Tracy adds in his History, — "The most important documents on this subject are, 1. The Missionary Herald, and Annual Reports of the American Board; 2. The Roman Catholic Annals of the Propagation of the Faith, especially volumes six and ten; 3. Letter of the king of the Sandwich Islands to the king of England, written in 1837, a copy of which is preserved in the archives of the Board; 4. The king's letter to the American consul, of October 28, 1839, which may be found in the Appendix to the Annual Report for 1841; 5. An account of the visit of the French frigate L'Artémise to the Sandwich Islands, by S. N. Castle, — first published in the Hawaiian Spectator in 1839, and republished in a pamphlet by sixteen offi-

The spirit of the Protestant missionaries is evinced in the following quotation from Mr. Tracy's comprehensive and very accurate History of the American Board: —

After the departure of the Romish priests for California, "some of their adherents were then called up, and required to renounce their seditious religion, and on their refusal were sentenced to imprisonment and hard labor. On learning this fact, Mr. Bingham immediately remonstrated with Kaahumanu, telling her, 'You have no law that will apply.' She answered, 'The law respecting idolatry; for their worship is like that which we have forsaken,' — referring to the order for the suppression of idolatry in 1819. Mr. Bingham, however, persevered in his remonstrances; and Mr. Clark, Mr. Chamberlain, Dr. Judd, Mr. Bishop, Mr. Richards, and probably others, urged to discontinue these punishments. There is no evidence, nor any reason to believe, that any of the missionaries ever gave different advice. Foreign visitors sometimes remonstrated, but with as little effect as the missionaries. As late as September, 1838, Kinau, in reply to a letter from Captain Elliot, of the British navy, asked him if he would advise the natives to return to their 'ancient mode of worship and bloodshed.' At last better counsels prevailed, and on the 17th of June, 1839, the king issued orders that no more punishments should be inflicted on account of reli-

cers of the U. S. East India squadron; 6. Supplement to the Sandwich Islands Mirror, — being a review of Mr. Castle's article, ascribed to Mr. John C. Jones, formerly American consul at Honolulu. A brief view of the leading authorities may be found in the Appendix to the Annual Report of the Board for 1841."—*Tracy's History*, p. 260.

gion, and that, if any were in confinement or at labor on that account, they should be set at liberty. On the 24th, however, two females were arrested and confined in the fort; but Mr. Bingham, being informed of the fact, immediately made it known to the governor, Kekuanaoa, who ordered them to be released, 'for their confinement was not by order of the chiefs.'"[1]

In 1835 the Romish missionaries in California received a brief from the Pope, exhorting them to persevere in their attempts to establish a mission on the Islands. Mr. Charlton, the British consul, was in correspondence with them; and in the following year an Irish priest, educated in Paris, arrived at Hono-

[1] Tracy's History, p. 406.

"By information obtained from those best informed on the subject, I was satisfied that the accounts of the persecutions undergone by Catholic converts, and of the cruelties said to have been endured by them, were much exaggerated. Nor were these in any case to be imputed directly to the missionaries, who had in many instances endeavored to prevent the infliction of punishment for religious reasons. Of cruel treatment for this cause I could learn no authenticated instance, nor did I meet with any one who could adduce facts from his own knowledge, although I sought information from those inimical to the missionaries, as well as from those who favor them. That the missionaries and their proselytes entertain apprehensions of evil from the propagation of Romanism, is true; but I found less illiberality on the subject of religious forms existing in the Hawaiian Islands, than in any place I visited on the cruise — less than is entertained by opposing sects in our country, and far less than exists in Catholic countries against those who hold the Protestant faith." — *Commodore Wilkes in U. S. Exploring Expedition*, vol. iv. p. 11.

lulu, and the consul insisted that he, as a British subject, should be allowed to remain.

It is not my purpose to go into a description of the acts of deceit, diplomacy, and violence, on the part of various agents, by means of which the firmness of the Hawaiian government was at length overcome. But I must not pass over one case, the most deplorable of all, for which the French government in the days of Louis Philippe is responsible.

"On the 9th of July, 1839, the French frigate L'Artémise, Captain Laplace, arrived at Honolulu. Captain Laplace issued his manifesto, declaring that he had come, by command of the king of the French, to put an end to the ill treatment which the French had suffered at the Sandwich Islands. He accused the government of violating treaties, alluding, probably, to the case of M. Maigret, who was not permitted to land there. He asserted, 'that to persecute the Catholic religion, to tarnish it with the name of idolatry, and to expel, under this absurd pretext, the French from this archipelago, was to offer an insult to France and to its sovereign.' With singular ignorance or disregard of truth, he asserted, that, among civilized nations, 'there is not even one which does not permit in its territory the free toleration of all religions; and yet, at the Sandwich Islands, the French are not allowed publicly the exercise of theirs.' He demanded,—

"'1. That the Catholic worship be declared free throughout all the dominions subject to the king of the Sandwich Islands; that the members of this religious faith shall enjoy in them all the privileges granted to Protestants.

"'2. That a site for a Catholic church be given by the government at Honolulu, a port frequented by the French, and that this church be ministered to by priests of their nation.

"'3. That all Catholics imprisoned on account of their religion since the last persecutions extended to the French missionaries be immediately set at liberty.

"'4. That the king of the Sandwich Islands deposit in the hands of the captain of L'Artémise the sum of twenty thousand dollars, as a guarantee of his future conduct towards France; which sum the French government will restore to him when it shall consider that the accompanying treaty will be faithfully complied with.

"'5. That the treaty signed by the king of the Sandwich Islands, as well as the sum above mentioned, be conveyed on board the frigate L'Artémise by one of the principal chiefs of the country; and also that the batteries of Honolulu do salute the French flag with twenty-one guns, which will be returned by the frigate.'

"In case of refusal, he stated, war would immediately commence. At the same time he addressed notes to the English and American consuls, announcing his intention, if his demands were refused, to commence hostilities on the 12th, at noon, and offering protection on board the frigate to such of their countrymen as should desire it. In his note to the American consul he added, —

"'I do not, however, include in this class the individuals who, although born, it is said, in the United States, make a part of the Protestant clergy of the Chief of this archipelago, direct his counsels, influence his conduct, and are the true authors of the insult given by him to France. For me they compose a part of the native population, and must undergo the unhappy consequences of a war which they shall have brought on this country.'

"The greater part of the pretexts for this aggression set forth by Captain Laplace were false. The treaty with Captain Dupetit Thouars was not intended to include Roman Catholic missionaries, and the exclusion of M. Maigret was no violation of it. French residents at the Sandwich Islands were not forbidden the public exercise of their religion. The American missionaries had not advised the government to adopt any of the measures of which he complained." [1]

The native government yielded to the violence of the French commander. The effect of the treaty then assented to was not only to give free course to the Romish missionaries, — which was not to be condemned, — but to set aside a law just made for the promotion of temperance, by which distilled spirits were excluded from the Islands, and a heavy duty imposed on the importation of wine.

The rule I have adopted, in writing concerning the present state of the Islands, allows me to say but little concerning the Roman Catholic mission. I saw nothing of the "Bishop of Arathea," the "Vicar Apostolic of the Hawaiian Islands," but heard him well spoken of; and the little I saw of two or three French papal priests gave me a favorable impression of their characters.

According to the report of the Bishop in 1862,

[1] Tracy's History, pp. 406-408.

the mission then contained eighteen European missionaries, twelve "catechist brothers," a convent of ten nuns, twenty-eight "decent chapels," thirty "chapels built of straw," eighty "religious pupils," a "college of forty pupils," fifty "schools," and 23,500 "Catholics." Both in 1860 and 1862 he states the baptisms at the round number of a thousand; and on both those occasions, although a Frenchman, he speaks of the tendency to introduce the English language, and to do away with the language of the country, with evident satisfaction. The number of "heretics" he places at 23,500. These are the members of the Protestant churches. The "infidels" he numbers at 23,300; but there are probably fewer among the Hawaiian people deserving of this appellation, than in any other country of Christendom. The term has a peculiar meaning in the Romish Church. As here used, the greater part of the persons to whom it is designed to be applicable, have more or less connection with the Protestant congregations, — as infants, young people, members of families, attendants on public worship, etc. It is believed there are as many as five thousand baptized children connected with Protestant congregations, who are not numbered among the church-members.

The Bishop uses the words *baptisms* and *conversions* as convertible terms; and the 23,500 "Catholics" must be understood as including all who had received baptism at the hands of Romish priests.

My inquiries while on the Islands led me to believe, that the number of adult members of the Romish Church is considerably less than this.

Whoever undertakes to write on the missions of the Romish Church, will be impressed with the scantiness of his materials. "Nothing," says Dr. Venn, in his recently published and valuable exposition of the Missionary Life and Labors of Francis Xavier, — "nothing is more striking, in reading missionary records, than the contrast between the scanty, vague, extravagant, and unsatisfactory notices of Romish missions, and the cautious, candid, and multitudinous records of Protestant evangelical missions." The Romish mission on the Hawaiian Islands will not be found an exception.

Writers not altogether in sympathy with the highly evangelical character of Protestant missions incline to over-estimate the successes of Romish missions, and their comparative power, in the same field with missions of the evangelical or puritan stamp, to make conquests among a barbarous or semi-barbarous people. The valuable work of Dr. Venn, already mentioned, will serve as an antidote to such erroneous estimates.[1] The strength of the Romish missions lies not so much in their doctrines and worship as in

[1] The Missionary Life and Labors of Francis Xavier, taken from his own Correspondence: with a Sketch of the General Results of

the influence they always seek, in some form, to wield in the state; and when they cannot secure that, they are not very much dreaded, in point of fact, by Protestant missionaries.

A few words will suffice in respect to the MORMONS. Their settlement, at least their principal settlement, is on Lanai, a small island opposite Lahaina, which I was unable to visit. I gained no reliable information as to their present number. In October, 1861, Captain Walter M. Gibson, at present their leading man on the island, writing to the Minister of Foreign Affairs, states the number of adults at 3580, to which he adds another thousand for unbaptized minors above seven years of age. He says the religious principles of the Mormons on the Islands differ from those in Utah only in not inculcating polygamy. He believes that this doctrine is never preached outside of Utah. The number of Mormons on the Islands is doubtless considerably over-estimated.

Roman Catholic Missions among the Heathen. By Henry Venn, B. D., Prebendary of St. Paul's, and Honorary Secretary of the Church Missionary Society.

VI.

THE PRESENT POSITION.

THE PRESENT POSITION.

CHAPTER XXII.

APPREHENDED DANGERS.

In Respect to the Missionaries. — Their Children. — The Native Ministry. — From the Complex Nature of the Protestant Community. — Of Decline in the Native Churches. — From Changes in the Industrial Pursuits. — From Invasions by Adverse Sects. — The Ground of Hope.

THIS volume should not be brought to a close without a more serious look at the shady side of the picture than has yet been taken. There has always been such a side at the Islands, but the shadows were perhaps never deeper than they are now, even while we are raising the cry of victory. I shall glance at a few of the apprehended dangers.

1. The first of the dangers I would specify arises from the age of the missionaries. Nearly all have seen fifty years, and some threescore. Soon it must therefore be said of the fathers, "Where are they?" The climate has been more favorable to their pro-

longed life and usefulness, than other climates have been to missionaries. There have not been the usual number of vacancies to be filled by young men, and hence the advanced age of the great body. What will be the consequence should they live beyond the activity and vigor of manhood, still retaining positions which perhaps would be better filled by men of the generation following? Will not the Romanists, the Reformed Catholics, the Mormons, take advantage of this? Will the aged men be able to retain their hold upon the young people? And what will become of the rising generation of the native population? Nay, will not their own children, who might take their places where that is desirable, — not finding openings to the ministry, — go into secular occupations, or leave the Islands? Yet there will long be a need of *patriarchal* influences in the Hawaiian churches, and we should therefore rejoice in the prospect, that there will be such an influence there for years to come.

2. The children of the missionaries are numerous, healthful, well educated, and to a great extent hopefully pious. For them the Hawaiian Islands have that mysterious charm which belongs to the place of one's nativity. The parents are there, and there most of them are likely to find their graves. The missionary sons, moreover, are beginning to settle on the Islands, as pastors of churches, as lawyers,

and in the different industrial occupations; and the missionary daughters are becoming the wives of these young men, and of others like them. There assembled on the college grounds at Punahou, on the 4th of July, 1863, for a public dinner, some hundreds of persons who rejoiced in their American birth or descent. A large proportion of them were young people. As has been remarked elsewhere, the population, capital, industry, and the purely national feeling at the Islands, — so far as it is not native, — are chiefly of American origin. The life of the Hawaiian nation seems to rest mainly on this body. Yet the general feeling, at the time of my visit, evidently was, that the late king and the leading spirit of his government were not in favor of it. The endeavor to supplant the native language in the schools by means of the English, whether so designed or not, tends to break down the influence that has been exerted by the American mission. So far as it succeeds, the Hawaiian Bible and Hawaiian books go out of use, without really substituting any other intelligent and effective reading, and evangelical ideas and the old national sentiments and feelings pass away.

The desirable thing — what the present king cannot fail to desire when he comes to understand fully the interests of his people, — what the native churches, pastors, and the whole Protestant people may be expected to desire — is, that this young community of native-born sons and daughters of American descent, may become thoroughly Hawaiian in all its instincts, feelings, and aims, and, against all hostile influences, go for the maintenance of that enlightened Christian government which was so nobly instituted by the Father of the Hawaiian People, Kamehameha III. They are citizens, and should claim the rights of citizens; — to speak freely to their fellow-citizens on all things affecting the public weal; to vote for such members of the national parliament as they deem most worthy of public confidence; and to sustain the king and his government against all foreign intervention whatsoever.

The danger is, that these native-born citizens of foreign descent will not come to the consciousness of their inherent privileges, rights, and duties soon enough to make their influence felt, for the counteraction of policies and schemes that jeopard the independence of the Islands.

Upon this subject, however, I had nothing to say during my visit. What I did then say to the children of the missionaries, respecting their duty of living for the life of religion on the Islands, may be seen in the Appendix, together with their hopeful response.[1] The greater part of these children are members of the church. They are enterprising, and are entering upon their appropriate work. A missionary son is the corresponding secretary and lead-

[1] See Address to the Children of the Missionaries, in the Appendix.

ing executive officer of the Hawaiian Board; four others are pastors of Hawaiian churches; one is a professor in the Oahu College; another is a teacher in the Lahainaluna College; still another is connected with the high school at Hilo; and others are settled as planters, traders, graziers, on all the larger islands. It should be added, that others are developing their public spirit elsewhere. One is serving the land of his fathers as a lieutenant-colonel in the army of the Potomac; another is a surgeon in the navy; and three, from one and the same family, are abroad as missionaries, — one of them in California, another in South America, another in Northern China. There being at least forty young men among the more than one hundred and fifty missionary children born on the Islands, who are able to speak the Hawaiian language, we may reasonably look with hopefulness upon their future influence. They will greatly need the prayers of God's people.

3. The native ministry has been, as yet, but partially tried on the Hawaiian Islands. Hawaiian missionaries have done well in the Marquesas Islands, and in Micronesia; yet it does not certainly follow that they will do as well amid the temptations and trials of their native Isles. So far as the experiment has been made there, they have acquitted themselves with credit. The guardian influence of their missionary fathers, and of their better educated brethren

from the missionary families, will be useful to them. But they will be exposed to the temptations of wealth, of ambition, and possibly to the paralyzing influence of a declining population. The native ministry is an indispensable element of success; and, if it does not succeed, the doom of the native churches, and of the nation as distinctively Hawaiian, is sealed.

4. Dangers grow out of the complex nature of the Protestant community, and from the impossibility of making the arrangements for it, in the absence of experience, with all the needful checks and balances. It would perhaps have been better, all things considered, had it been possible at the time, for the missionaries to have relinquished their support from the native churches gradually. As under the former system the missionary had a strong motive for not dividing his great church, and for not multiplying native pastors, so now the native Christians, though living in places remote from the centre, are tempted to decline having a native pastor, whom they must support, and to prefer remaining under the pastorate of the missionary, for whose support they pay nothing. Such is human nature. To meet the difficulty, further modification will be necessary, and it has been recommended.

5. Should the influence of the Holy Spirit not be

granted to the island community, as in times past, death will soon greatly reduce the number of church-members. At present they are more numerous in proportion to the whole population than they were some years since. The prayer of God's people should be, "O that thou wouldst rend the heavens, that thou wouldst come down, that the mountains might flow down at thy presence!" This, certainly, is a blessing to come in answer to prayer, and effectual prayer may be offered for it in all parts of the world.

6. There are dangers from the changes now in progress in the industrial pursuits of the Islands. I mention only the cultivation of the sugar-cane. The danger here is at least threefold: from the necessary absence of the laboring men from their homes; from the introduction of coolies from heathen countries; and from the transfer of the best lands to foreign owners. At certain seasons the planters need a large number of laborers; but they are not able, like the great manufacturing corporations in the United States, to establish and support families on or near their grounds. Hence there will be long separations of native men from their families, to the great detriment of their morals. And what will be the effect on the native population, and especially on the female portion of it, from the importation of hundreds of unmarried worshippers of Confucius, Boodh, or Brahma? Then there is the extensive alienation of

the lands. The plantations are generally owned by foreign capitalists, and the lands adapted to the growth of cane are rapidly passing into the hands of such.

7. The dangers apprehended from the invasion of adverse religious sects, have perhaps been sufficiently indicated in former chapters. So far as the extreme ritualists are concerned, whether Roman Catholic or Reformed Catholic, the chief danger arises, not so much from their direct labors among the people, as from the influence they may be able and disposed to exert through the government against whatever they regard as an obstacle to their success.

The hope for the Hawaiian Islands is in the providence and grace of Almighty God, who, amid greater dangers than all these combined, has heretofore so marvellously guarded and prospered the cause of evangelical religion on those Islands.

CHAPTER XXIII.

PRACTICAL LESSONS.

Supernatural Power involved in the Success of the Mission. — On Conflicting Testimonies concerning the Mission. — The Gospel precedes Civilization. — The Encouragement to be given to Native Effort. — Missions to be brought to a Seasonable Close. — The Native Pastorate. — Female Education. — The English Language.

SUPERNATURAL POWER INVOLVED IN THE SUCCESS OF THE MISSION.

No satisfactory account can be given of the religious changes on these Islands, without supposing a supernatural power to have been involved in them. There was both a providence and a spiritual influence. A directing providence is seen in the singular coincidence of time in the overthrow of idolatry and the embarkation of the mission. It is seen in the long delay, but most opportune arrival, of the vessel promised by Vancouver, bringing the English deputation, with Mr. Ellis, and the Tahitian chiefs. It is seen in the strange visit of Liholiho to England, throwing the government of the Islands, for a considerable time, into the hands of pious chiefs. It is seen in the qualities of mind given to the third Kamehameha, inclining him to listen to the disinterested friends of his people, and voluntarily to make extraordinary sacrifices of power for the elevation and happiness of his subjects.[1]

Still more apparent is the work of the Holy Spirit. We perceive it in the closing life of the venerated Keopuolani,[2] in the remarkable change of character in Kaahumanu,[3] and in the early conversion of so large a portion of the chief rulers of the Islands.[4] We perceive it in the all but national awakening to the concerns of the soul during the years following 1837, and in the large accessions then made to the Christian church, [5] and also in preventing the disastrous reaction which it was reasonable to expect might follow so great an excitement. We perceive it in the large annual additions to the churches in the years subsequent to the great awakening; causing the decrease in the number of church-members to be by no means proportionate to that of the population; and also in the vast change of manners, morals, and religious feelings and habits, visible among the people.[6] These results being once admitted, no candid mind, conversant with the relations of cause and effect, would attribute them to a merely human agency.

[1] Chapters I., II., XIII.
[2] Chapter X.
[3] Chapter II.
[4] Chapter II.
[5] Chapters III., IV.
[6] Chapter XVII.

ON CONFLICTING TESTIMONIES CONCERNING THE MISSION.

The testimonies concerning the results of this mission have been exceedingly various, and even conflicting.[1] To ascertain the truth, we need to consider both the character and opportunities of the respective witnesses.

1. There is a noisy, positive class of persons, who sometimes write works of fiction. Were these witnesses content with simply saying that they themselves *saw* nothing while on the Islands that deserved the Christian name, their statement might be received. But they were no more competent to give a correct account of religion on the Hawaiian Islands, than the man would be to describe the religion of Boston, who had no friendly relations, no familiar intercourse, with the religious people of that city.

2. There is another class of witnesses, not large, but respectable, who are reserved and somewhat doubtful as to the prevalence and power of the Christian religion on the Islands. These were suffi-

[1] The most elaborate statement adverse to the mission, and at the same time a remarkable specimen of recklessness in quoting authorities, is in a recently published Roman Catholic History of Christian Missions, their Agents, and their Results; by T. W. M. Marshall. The work is in two large octavo volumes, and is exceedingly unfair and unreliable, though a plausible comparison, or rather contrast, of the alleged results of Romish and Protestant missions.

ciently remarked upon in the chapter on the character of the Protestant churches.[1]

3. Witnesses of still another class are accurate as far as they go, but very properly keep within the range of their actual observations. The testimony of these persons accords substantially with that of the class next to be mentioned, and their facts imply the existence of that vital religion which the missionaries declare to exist among the people. Mr. Dana belongs to this class, and others might easily be named.[2]

4. The remaining class is composed of the missionaries. They testify as to what they have seen, or have known by unquestionable evidence on the ground. This is the class which is specially cognizant of the Protestant religion of the Islands; and we ought not to receive the testimony of others against their distinct affirmations, without conclusive reasons.

THE GOSPEL PRECEDES CIVILIZATION.

One of the most obvious facts in this history is, that on the Hawaiian Islands *the gospel preceded civilization*. At least, the progress of civilization was much slower than that of the gospel.

[1] Chap. XVII., p. 286.

[2] Chapter IV. To this class belongs Mr. James Jackson Jarvis in his excellent History of the Hawaiian Islands, the third edition of which was published at Honolulu in 1837.

The rulers were to a great extent Christianized as early as the year 1825. But not until ten years after this did they begin seriously to feel the need of carpenters, masons, shoemakers, tailors, paper-makers, type-founders, agriculturists, cloth-manufacturers, machine-makers, and instructors in the science of government. Application for these was then made to their religious patrons in the United States. The great mass of the people, at that time, were but slightly interested in the domestic arts that are in use among civilized nations. Their houses were small, with but a single apartment, and one low door of entrance — often an imperfect shelter from the rain, and with scarcely anything deserving the name of furniture. Most of the people wore only a cloth about their loins, and another thrown carelessly over the shoulders; perhaps even less than that.[1]

Yet even then spacious thatched houses of worship had been erected by the chiefs and people at the places of principal concourse, and orderly congregations assembled to hear the gospel. The Sabbath was professedly hallowed. Marriages were solemnized in a Christian manner, and sustained by law. The cause of temperance was promoted. The Holy Scriptures were anxiously desired, and received by the people as of divine authority.

[1] See p. 230.

But though civilization does not take the lead, it follows the gospel, and not far behind. A desire was gradually awakened among the natives to improve their houses, and to add to their social comforts. They learned the use of tools, and to make hats, bonnets, garments, and the more necessary articles of furniture. — So, according to the incomparable Williams, it was in the South Sea Islands.

"I am convinced," he says, "that the first step towards the promotion of a nation's temporal and social elevation is to plant amongst them the tree of life, when civilization and commerce will entwine their tendrils around its trunk, and derive support from its strength. Until the people are brought under the influence of religion, they have no desire for the arts and usages of civilized life; but that invariably creates it. The missionaries were at Tahiti many years, during which they built and furnished a house in European style. The natives saw this, but not an individual imitated their example. As soon, however, as they were brought under the influence of Christianity, the chiefs, and even the common people, began to build neat plastered cottages, and to manufacture bedsteads, seats, and other articles of furniture. The females had long observed the dress of the missionaries' wives, but while heathen they greatly preferred their own, and there was not a single attempt at imitation. No sooner, however, were they brought under the influence of religion, than all of them, even to the lowest, aspired to the possession of a gown, a bonnet, and a shawl, that they might appear like Christian women. I could proceed to enumerate many other changes of the same kind; but these will be sufficient to establish my assertion. While the natives are under the influence of their superstitions, they evince an inanity and torpor from which no stimulus has proved powerful enough to arouse them but the new ideas and the new principles imparted by Christianity. And if it be not already proved, the experience of a few more years will demonstrate the fact, that the missionary enterprise is incomparably the most effective machinery that has ever been brought to operate upon the social, the civil, and the commercial, as well as the moral and spiritual interests of mankind."[1]

The Encouragement to be given to Native Efforts.

The history of this mission teaches the importance of not only allowing, but encouraging and helping forward, the natives in their imperfect efforts to help themselves. The missionaries reared no model churches at the outset, beyond the native ideas and ability, but encouraged chiefs and people to erect grass houses of the rudest form for their worship. These preceded the coral and wooden church buildings, with pews, and tower, and bell, that came in the progress of civilization. The great, unsightly, thatched meeting-house suited far better the religious taste and wants of the people, five and twenty years ago, than its more imposing successors would have done. Far preferable was it for the people, and for the cause of religion among them, that

[1] Missionary Enterprises in the South Seas, p. 518.

they should then have only such meeting-houses as they were themselves able and disposed to build, and where half-naked or meanly-dressed people would feel at home, than that American Christians should have given them, at that early day, such church buildings even as they now possess. Expensive houses of worship at central stations have the effect to retard the church-building and the religious development in the surrounding rural districts. In a few cases this may have been the result at the Islands.[1]

So in regard to schools. Teachers were so far educated, at the central stations of the mission, as to be able to instruct in reading and writing; and then they went abroad to impart their new-made acquisitions to others, as they should find opportu-

[1] The Ceylon mission, after long use of the great stone churches originally built by the Dutch and Portuguese, came to the conclusion, in 1855, that, until the people desired something more costly, and built for themselves, the place of worship ought to be merely "an ola roof, supported by plain wooden posts, and walled in with mud half way from the floor to the eaves, or hung round with ola screens," — to cost only from five to fifteen pounds sterling. In the Madura mission, where are station churches, built many years ago, that cost thousands of rupees (the rupee being half a dollar), the mission decided, in the same year, that a station church ought not to cost more than five hundred rupees, and that the cost of village churches ought to range from twenty-five to one hundred rupees. In the Mahratta mission, it was voted, that suitable houses of worship could be erected for a sum varying from fifty to three hundred rupees. These were the results of experience.

nity, and at the expense of the people; the missionaries, meanwhile, giving themselves to the preaching of the word.

Yet it would seem that in one important line of policy, there must have been some mistake. The Islands were converted to Christianity as early as the year 1848. The leading object of the mission was then accomplished. In a retrospective view, it appears that *then* was the time for commencing in earnest what is *now* being done; namely, dividing, and so multiplying, the native churches, and constituting biblically-trained native pastors, as is now proposed; with the resolute purpose of devolving the responsibility of self-government upon the Christian community in ecclesiastical matters, and the earliest possible self-support. Had this been done soon after 1848, the Protestant community, having the benefit of so many subsequent years of oversight from the missionary fathers, might now have been able to dispense with much of this conservative influence. It would have been better (as it now appears) had this been done before the great body of the missionaries were past the meridian of life; before adverse sects had gained so much influence on the Islands; and while the government was better disposed than now to look with favor on the evangelical interests of the Islands.

MISSIONS SHOULD BE BROUGHT TO A SEASONABLE CLOSE.

The experience on the Hawaiian Islands shows, that missions should be prosecuted with the expectation, and upon the plan, of gradually giving place to a native ministry. It is quite possible to have too many missionaries in a district or country; it is possible that they may remain too long, and that they may trust too little to the influences of the Spirit in the hearts of the native converts, for sustaining those who are put into the gospel ministry. Making due allowance for differences in civilization (none need be made as to moral differences), it will be found that the gospel should be planted much as it was by the apostles and their associates; and it may now be done more rapidly and more permanently than then, because of the vastly more favorable state of the modern world, and the greater relative power of many of the Christian agencies now in operation.

It is not incumbent on us to prosecute missions anywhere, with American laborers, until the entire people is converted, nor until idolatry and superstition have been banished from every part of the community. The native churches will themselves *need* missionary ground to be left for them to operate upon, in order to the preservation and growth of their own religious life. The grand object of missions is *to plant the gospel institutions effectually*. The missionary's vocation, as a soldier of the cross, is to make conquests, and to go on, in the name of his divine Master, "conquering, and to conquer;" committing the maintenance and consolidation of his conquests to another class of men, created expressly for the purpose. The idea of *continued conquest* is vital to the spiritual efficiency of missions. It will doubtless be found, on inquiry, that missions among the heathen have ceased to be healthful, and to evince the true missionary energy, when they have ceased to be *aggressive* upon the kingdom of darkness. It is the business of the missionary to prepare churches and fields of labor for native pastors; and when they are thus prepared, and competent pastors are provided, he ought himself to move onward, — the pioneer of Christian institutions, and, in effect, of a Christian civilization, but in office, work, and spirit, an ambassador for Christ, to preach the gospel where it has not been preached.

The Native Pastorate.

While the extraordinary number of missionaries on these Islands in proportion to the population, had doubtless the effect to hasten the triumph of the gospel, it had also the effect to retard the introduction of a native pastorate, by diminishing the apparent necessity for it. Though most of the local churches were very large, the missionaries naturally felt (somewhat in forgetfulness of the not very distant future) that they could themselves discharge the pastoral duties for the whole, better than any native pastors. Along with this feeling, which was not without its strong reasons, and partly it may be in consequence of it, there was an apparent undervaluing of the native capabilities for the pastoral office. We should not wonder at this. Our brethren judged, felt, and acted just as most good men would have done in their circumstances. While, to meet an obvious exigency, they had boldly sent forth native missionaries to the Marquesas, to stand or fall among the most barbarous pagan savages to be found in all the world, with only the promise of an annual visit from one of their missionary fathers, and while they had sent others to live and labor, some of them alone, on the barbarous Islands of Micronesia; on their own Hawaiian Islands they had ventured to ordain only a very small number as pastors, and each of these was held in subordination to the missionary of the district. Not until the convocation at Honolulu in 1863, was there a movement for instituting a pastorate at the Islands, that should be independent of the missionaries in charge of the several districts.

But it was then found, that the experience at the Marquesas and in Micronesia had been satisfactory, and also that the natives who had received ordination as pastors at home, had served in their ministry without reproach. These facts had their proper influence, and it was resolved to enter at once upon measures for rearing a competent native ministry, to be placed on an official parity with the foreign pastors. This is now being done, and probably to the best advantage, in the way that was common in the United States before the institution of theological seminaries.

FEMALE EDUCATION.

The discontinuance of the female boarding school at Wailuku, on the Island of Maui, has been mentioned.[1] It was the great mistake in prosecuting the mission. In a country where females marry so young, a very few years suffice to develop the consequences of depriving them of such a training institution. My inquiries on the Islands brought no unmarried native female to my knowledge, who was deemed suitably educated for a native pastor's wife. The few who had received what is called an English education were not thereby fitted for the humble, self-denying position of wives of native pastors. There was but one opinion as to the importance of immediate arrangements for providing the means of suitably training native females, not only to act their parts well in their connection with the native ministry, but also as teachers of their own sex in the common schools. A boarding school was therefore resolved upon, and has since been commenced at

[1] Chapter X.

Waiohinu, in the south-eastern district of Hawaii, to be taught in the native language; and others will be opened in due time.

THE ENGLISH LANGUAGE.

The late king, and his brother, now on the throne, acquired a free use of the English language in their childhood, at the Chief's School. English was one of the studies in that school. And it became a natural though not logical inference, that if that language was good for the king and chiefs, it must be so for the people. While Dr. Armstrong was President of the Board of Education, the desire for acquiring English became extensive among the people, and he found it necessary to yield to the current, which he did reluctantly. Though English teaching has since considerably declined, what are called English schools seem to constitute a favorite department in the government system of instruction. In some instances, teachers are employed for these schools who even know nothing of the native language; and in such cases the English is necessarily the sole medium of instruction. The poor people appear to be satisfied with this. But it must needs be, that very few clear ideas, very little instruction, almost no mental discipline, can be imparted, and that the unfortunate pupils, while asking for bread, receive what is very little better to them than a stone. Happily the instruction in the common district schools is yet in the vernacular.

"If English is taught to any advantage," — says Mr. Andrews, the best judge on this subject upon the Islands, — "many years must be spent, much expense incurred, qualified teachers must be employed, the scholars must be kept learners, and there must be a watchful eye on the working of the whole system. This can be done only to a limited extent, even with all the school funds. But instruction ought to be urged forward as fast as possible everywhere. And instruction in their own language is the most natural, the easiest, the cheapest, the quickest, and hitherto it has been the most efficient. For the government to set up English schools, to the neglect of educating its own people in their own language, would, in my opinion, be a suicidal act."

CHAPTER XXIV.

CONCLUSION.

The Mission an Experiment in Foreign Missions. — Its Value enhanced by the Difficulties overcome. — Not dependent on Future Events. — Present Relations of the Hawaiian Protestant Community. — The Responsibilities. — What the Island Churches will most need. — Missionaries, as a body, not given to Exaggeration. — Why they are not. — No safer or more profitable Investment than in the Foreign Missionary Enterprise. — The Churches entreated never to forget this Portion of Christ's Kingdom.

THE Mission to the Hawaiian Islands may be regarded in the light of an experiment in foreign missions. It was avowedly such, as appears in the following passage from the Report of the American Board for 1837: —

"Do any ask why so many laborers are employed at the Sandwich Islands? The Committee would reply, that the work, which Providence, by signal interpositions, has made ready for our hands, may be done in the shortest possible time, and thus a glorious exemplification be afforded of what Christian missions, through the power of divine grace, may effect. In no other nation could the Board so well make the experiment as in that."

The missionaries were multiplied for the very reason that the nation was small, and conveniently situated, under one government, and easily accessible. The work was thus pressed onward to a speedy close that it might be seen and demonstrated what missions, by the blessing of God, might be expected to accomplish, if prosecuted in dependence on divine aid, and with a vigor corresponding to the nature and extent of the field.

It has been the aim of this volume to make a simple and true statement of the results thus far of this experiment, — to the glory of God, and of the gospel of his Son. Doubtless there are abatements to be made among the people of the Hawaiian Islands on the score of human depravity, as indeed there are in all other Christian nations. Much will be found that is unchristian along with much that is Christian. But it has become an imperishable truth, to be recorded and preserved on the pages of history, that the gospel achieved a glorious triumph on those Islands, through the labors of missionaries.

Some persons appear to think less of the value of this experiment, because, when the mission was instituted, the Hawaiian people were so low on the scale of civilization, so utterly depraved, so rapidly wasting away. But if our object was to show the remedial power of the gospel, then the value of the experiment is greatly enhanced by these extremely adverse circumstances. If the gospel took the people at the lowest point of social existence, — at death's door, — when beyond the reach of all mere human remedies, — with the causes of decline and destruction all in their most vigorous operation, and has made them a Christian people, checked the tide of depopulation, and raised the nation so on the scale of social life as to have gained for it an acknowledged place among the Christian nations of the earth; what more wonderful illustration can there be of its remedial power? Such is the Hawaiian nation. Our own government is now represented there by a Minister Resident, a rank only next to that of an Ambassador.

Nor does the decisive character of this gospel triumph depend on the perpetuity of the nation, nor even on that of the Protestant community. The simple memorial on the pages of this volume will be as truthful after the Hawaiian people shall have passed away, — should that be the will of God, — as it is now. However the facts may be ignored, denied, perverted, they have an immovable historic basis, and will never lose their credibility.

The direct and intimate relations of the Hawaiian Protestant churches are with the Congregational and Presbyterian bodies of the United States. From these went the men and women who were the means of planting and building up those island churches, and from them came the great outlay of funds.

These relations were simply modified by the proceedings recorded in the nineteenth chapter. They are now similar to those sustained by not a few of the churches in the West to the older churches in the Middle and Eastern States, to which they look for occasional pecuniary aid. The Hawaiian Protestant community is now self-governing. Whether it will be enduring, is a problem that cannot be solved at present. The future of that community, however, is no more really impenetrable at the present moment, than it has long been. For the past sixteen years at least, we have rarely seen farther in our progress than where to take the next step. But seeing that, and not hesitating to take the steps, we have been as effectually guided as if we had seen the end from the beginning.

The relation of the Congregational and Presbyterian churches of the United States to the Hawaiian churches, is the most interesting that can exist between religious bodies. As the great apostle said to the church at Corinth, so they might say to the churches on the Hawaiian Islands, "In Christ Jesus *we* have begotten you through the gospel." How often, in my tour through those islands, was this fact joyfully recognized by the island-people. This it was that everywhere secured for me such a welcome. I was received as a representative of the good people in America, to whom they owed their all. The relation belongs to the spiritual and everlasting kingdom of our Lord and Saviour Jesus Christ, and will be as enduring as that kingdom. Those churches in the far-off Isles constitute a part of his kingdom; and those who, from love to Christ, had an agency in planting them, may claim the same blessed relation to them, in its nature, that Paul did to the church in Corinth. This is as true of the widow with her "two mites" given for this object, as of the largest donor, or the most successful missionary with his life-long labors. Nor should we lightly esteem those churches because of their poverty and ignorance. Though we might say of them that "God hath chosen the foolish things of the world," and "the weak things of the world," and "base things of the world, and things which are despised," "yea, and things which are not," we should remember it is that "no flesh" might "glory in his presence;" and also that they, equally with ourselves, are of God in Christ Jesus, who is made unto them, as he is to us, "wisdom, and righteousness, and sanctification, and redemption."[1]

Many thousands have passed from the Hawaiian churches into the spirit-world; and, so far as they were in Christ, they have entered upon a heavenly inheritance. Many thousands more, belonging to the visible church, are still living; and, so far as they are in Christ, they are heirs, with us, to the same blessed inheritance. This volume will help the child

[1] 1 Cor. i. 27-30.

of God to judge how far we ought to recognize them as brethren in Christ Jesus.

The Protestant community on those Islands is responsible for *self-government* in all matters of the church, as well as in all matters of the state. It should be held to this. As the responsibility of self-government is devolved on a son, or a daughter, at the proper age, so should it now be devolved on the Protestant religious community of the Hawaiian Islands. We may aid them with our advice; we may annex conditions to our grants-in-aid; but no foreign nation, or ecclesiastical body, or missionary society should exercise authority in those Christianized Islands. They should be held responsible for a wise administration in all the departments of Christian charity and gospel effort. Composing that community are the older missionaries, their children, the native ministry, the native churches. Why should not that community be responsible, not only for a wise and efficient self-control, but also for the building up of Christ's kingdom within itself, and, somewhat, for its extension to the thousand islands in the far west of the Pacific Ocean? Why should it not be expected to find all the needed missionaries among the missionary children, among the children of the foreign Christian residents, and among the native Christians? Such a responsibility is just what the new community needs for its own healthful and vigorous intellectual, moral, and social development.

The island-community, in its present development, however, cannot support the missionaries that were once connected with the American Board, and at the same time its own native pastors. Those missionaries, continuing to reside on the Islands, should therefore look to the American churches for such aid as they will require towards their comfortable support. It will also be needful, for a time, to aid the Hawaiian Board in the education of native pastors and their wives, and in the publication of the Holy Scriptures, and other religious books, as well as in the support of their mission to Micronesia. Nor should we look on quietly, and see the churches, that have been planted at so much expense of money and labor, and with so many prayers and tears, fall a prey to invaders. A conquest that cost so much is worth a costly effort to sustain it; and who can doubt that, should there be a call for such an effort, it will be made?

But far more needful for the churches in those Islands than pecuniary aid will be the heartfelt interest, and fervent, constant prayers of the American churches. God has been their "refuge and strength," their "very present help in trouble;" and our prayer should be that he may continue to be their protection in time to come. Let it be said of the church in those Islands, "Though the waters roar and be troubled, though the mountains shake with the swelling thereof, God is in the midst of her; she shall not be moved: God shall help her, and that right early."

A feeling is more or less prevalent in a portion of our community, that missionaries are given to exaggeration when stating the results of their labors. To deny that there are cases of this sort would be claiming more for missionaries, than belongs to any other class of men. But that this can be affirmed of the missionaries of the American Board with whom I have been more especially connected, as the general result of their communications in any one year, or in any series of years, — or as they are found in any one volume of the Missionary Herald, or in its long series of volumes, — is what I am unable to believe. There is no more truthful history. In the prosecution of my official duty I have perhaps read more unabridged missionary letters than any other one now living. Yet such has been their influence on my mind, that my later visits to the missions under the care of the American Board, have been a source of grateful surprise at finding more than I had expected. This was especially true at the Hawaiian Islands.

Indeed, the missionary is more apt to undervalue his converts, churches, and the spiritual results of his labors, than are pastors at home to undervalue theirs. Going out young in life, with only a partial acquaintance with the imperfections of Christians and churches at home, his standard of Christian character is high, and his rule of judging the native Christian is too severe. And this is one reason why there has been so much backwardness among missionaries in putting forward the native churches and a native ministry. A visit home, after a dozen years, is, on this account, a great benefit to missionaries. When the venerable Levi Spaulding, of Ceylon, was about returning to his mission after a somewhat extended visit in the United States, I asked him what he then thought of the piety of his native churches. His reply was, that, making the proper allowances, he thought they gave as good evidence of piety as did the churches in his native land. My own conviction is the same as that which keeps the missionary so contentedly in his field, namely, that there is no safer, no better investment of time, labor, and money, than in the foreign missionary enterprise. Think of the investment made on the Hawaiian Islands. The outlay has been less than the cost of the Exploring Expedition to the Pacific Ocean under Commodore Wilkes, less than that of a first-class ship of war, or a moderate section of a railroad. Yet how vastly greater, how vastly more precious, are the results!

"Can a woman forget her sucking child?—Yea, they may forget, yet will I not forget thee." Such is the language which Jehovah addresses to every portion of his Church. And will not the churches of America, the churches of England, the churches of the whole Christian world, hold this youngest sister in the great Christian family in kind and prayerful remembrance? Doubtless He who came to seek and to save the lost rejoices to gather those sheep into his fold, and to carry those lambs in his bosom. They were embraced in his memorable prayer, "Neither pray I for these alone, but for them also which shall believe on me through their word; that they all may be one, as thou, Father, art in me, and I in thee, that they also may be one in us."[1] Ignorant, degraded they may be, and are to human view; but to the eye of faith they are exalted to a noble fellowship with us in Christ; they are one with him, and one in him. Therefore we will never forget them — the "heirs of God," and "joint heirs of Christ" "TO AN INHERITANCE INCORRUPTIBLE, AND UNDEFILED, AND THAT FADETH NOT AWAY."[2]

[1] John xvii. 20, 21. [2] 1 Peter i. 4.

APPENDICES.

NOTE.

[The Appendices are portions of the Introductory Address delivered at the Convocation in Honolulu; the Address to the Children of the Missionaries, with their Response; an account of the Organization of the Board of the Hawaiian Evangelical Association; the Address of the Association to the Foreign Secretary of the American Board; the Action of the Prudential Committee and of the Board on the Secretary's Report; and extracts from Bishop Staley's Sermons.]

APPENDICES.

APPENDIX I.

EXTRACTS FROM THE INTRODUCTORY ADDRESS AT THE CONVOCATION IN HONOLULU.

"It was stated in the printed document already placed in your hands, that after my visit to the Islands had been decided upon, there were consultations in the Prudential Committee, the results of which I was to communicate verbally to the Association. But I would first make a brief reference to my recent tour, with my wife and daughter, through the Islands.

"I have had, as you know, some experience of touring among missions, having once visited all our missions in India, and thrice our missions within and around the Mediterranean. Those visits were among the most agreeable religious and social experiences of my life; but I must say, that my late tour surpasses all the others, in the view it gives me of what God has wrought among the heathen, through the gospel of his Son. It is, at any rate, a fact that, after having read the reports and letters from these Islands for the space of forty years, my expectations have been exceeded. There has been no exaggeration, on the whole, in the result of these reports and letters upon one of their most constant and attentive readers. This may have been owing, in part, to the chastening effect of former observations in other missions. In passing through the Islands, I have thought it possible that my brethren who reside here are so familiar with the scenes around them, and withal have had so much experience of the unsanctified side of the native character, as to be scarcely able to appreciate the prodigious rise there has been in the native condition and character above the level of forty years ago. I am sure that, considering the time, there is nothing like it in the missions of this age or of any other. There is doubtless much under the surface to offset what we see; but it is so with the wonderful island we first travelled (Hawaii). I presume there is nowhere more evidence of raging fires beneath the surface, nowhere such burning eruptions, such tracts of barren lava. And yet, through the genial influence of sun and rain, there are fertile soils, and trees, and flowers, and grasses, and whatever tropical fruits men wish to cultivate. And so with this island-community. Whatever of volcanic fires there be beneath the surface of society, of burning eruptions and barren wastes, there are fertile surfaces, and trees and fruits of righteousness, visible even to the casual observer — a creation of grace, as the other is of nature, to the glory of God through Jesus Christ. As to the *national sin*, it may be said — as doubtless it might of the ancient church at Corinth — that it was so universal among the people in their heathen condition, and the manners, habits, language were so corrupted by it, that there has not yet been time to form a strong public sentiment, and create a sensitive conscience in respect to it, even in the church. We see something painfully analogous to this in relation to vices in the civilization of a commercial people, such as avarice, hoarding, hard bargains — vices at present quite beyond the reach of church discipline.

"I take great pleasure in expressing our lively gratitude to all our brethren and sisters for their unwearied kindness in our journey. Nothing was left undone that could promote our happiness, or the object of our visit. At every place, in every family, the feelings left in our minds towards our missionary fellow-laborers are what we shall love to cherish, and such as we shall hope to carry with us to enhance the joy of our reunion in the heavenly world.

"The brethren have everywhere freely let me into their temporal affairs; and I have been glad to find so many of them in circumstances favorable to comfort, and to the settlement of their children on these Islands. You are aware that, in common with our Committee, I have long deemed your continued residence here, with your children, an object of much importance. To this end the Prudential Committee transferred to you the property held by the Board on the Islands, and coöperated with the government in securing for you a right in fee-simple to the lands. To this end the same liberty was awarded you in the investment and acquisition of property which popular sentiment gives to pastors in our own country. To this end, also, the government of these Islands, some years since, gave you the privilege of purchasing land at a low rate. The result is, that you are now, as a class, believed to be in possession of more property than your brother ministers, as a body, in any one section of our own country; while, on the contrary, no one of you has been enriched, or has the prospect of becoming so. And I am free to declare, that your several missionary fields afford evidence of a laborious life, and of much self-denying labor; while I am fully persuaded that, as a body, you have gained in spirituality since the year 1848, when the change was made in your relations to property and to the Islands. While I hope that the fathers will not be anxious to increase their possessions, I shall not be backward to state my belief, on my return home, that, in a comprehensive and enlightened view of the subject, there is no more ground for regret or apprehension here, on the score of worldly possessions, than exists among the clergy in any one district at home, and that most of you will need more or less aid towards your support during the remainder of your lives."

"In entering upon the business of the meeting, it should constantly be borne in mind, that it is a new, as well as great, problem in the foreign missions, which we are providentially called upon to solve; and should we succeed in giving it a right solution, we do so not only for ourselves on these Islands, but ultimately for all missions. Not that there will be frequent opportunities, nor may there soon be another opportunity, as now and here, to apply it to a *nation;* but the principle will be easily applicable to particular districts in unevangelized countries. The question is, *How Missionary Societies and Missions should proceed in building up and establishing the Christian Institutions, after they have been introduced and have obtained a certain degree of ascendency.* This question was urged upon the Board, fifteen or sixteen years ago, by the remarkable progress of the work of God on these Islands. We now propose a practical solution, so far as these Islands are concerned, by the Board's retiring from the front, and taking a position in the rear, — acting as an auxiliary, rather than a leader. We shall throw the main responsibility upon the new Christian community, only aiding it by grants in the several departments of the work. And by the 'new Christian community' we mean the body of Christians made up of all the evangelical ministers and churches on the Islands, both native and foreign.

"Allow me to say, before going further, that we need to enter upon the discussions before us with the largest views, most disinterested feelings, and strongest faith and courage, we can possibly command; since there will be but little in our past experience to guide us, or in the recorded experience of the Christian church."

"It is the belief of the Prudential Committee, that the time has come for a change in the relations of the Board to this Island-community. And it is also their conviction, that the time has come for a corresponding change in your relations as missionaries to the same community; substituting the *ecclesiastical* for the *missionary*, and bringing yourselves, the native ministry and the people, all into one community. The community, thus organized, will of course need to make proper arrangements for doing the work; and the Board, acting for the churches at home, will then hasten to recognize the Hawaiian Christian community as fully competent to do the work within itself, — with the aid of such grants from the Board, from time to time, as there shall appear to be good reason for making. It may for a time — we know not how long — increase, rather than diminish, the outlay of the Board at these Islands. It cost our churches more than a million of dollars to evangelize this nation, and those churches will have no idea of seeing these evangelical institutions subverted, whatever be the cost of preventing such a disaster. But the course of measures we entered upon in 1848, and now propose extending somewhat further, we regard as the only one fitted to render this nation self-governing and self-supporting in its religious life, or to put the mission itself beyond the charge of having been a failure. Some such process, too, as we propose, is needful to reënlist the American churches vigorously in the effort necessary to finish the work they commenced in these Islands forty-three years ago.

"The work to be done by this community will, of course, be substantially the same as it is in our own country — ministerial labor and church-formation in destitute places, namely, Home Missions, in their several departments of Sabbath schools, colportage, etc.; also, the education of a Native Ministry, and of wives for the same, and perhaps of religious teachers; also, the cultivation of the Literature of the country, religious and moral; and Foreign Missions. The consideration of the work, under these several heads, and the instrumentalities for the same, will naturally occupy some time at the present meeting. For want of a vigorous prosecution of the three departments of labor first named, the foreign missions sent from these Islands have failed of exerting all that healthful reaction upon the Hawaiian churches which was the main object of the mission to Micronesia; and the foreign missions have proved, in some respects, exhaustive of the religious strength of the community. They needed a vigorous system of home missions, to open channels for their healthful reactionary influence to flow through these Island-churches."

"There needs to be, on these Islands, a process of Education for Native Pastors and Missionaries in some respects different from any heretofore existing, — having those ends avowedly in view, and so understood by the native churches and students; and also for educating native females in a manner fitting them to become teachers and the wives of native ministers. The questions involved in this important and necessary department will need to be carefully discussed at this meeting, with a view to immediate measures; and I will state the results of my inquiries when the discussion comes on. Probably no one plan for educating native pastors will meet the demands of all the Islands just now. I believe that suitable females may be found for training as teachers and the wives of ministers, though with more difficulty than the males."

"What is the amount of foreign ministerial labor needed at these Islands, and how it shall be obtained, is a subject requiring earnest consideration. We suppose that the four large islands, or at least that three of them, have each a centre that will require the residence of a minister of foreign origin or descent for years to come. How far this is a correct view, and whether there are more than three or four places requiring so long an occupation, will need our attention."

"It is an interesting question, whether the children of the mission will be disposed and able to exert the needful conservative influence in this new Christian community, when the missionary fathers are gone. It will perhaps be best not only to discuss this question among ourselves, but to carry it to the young people. The education received in the Oahu College is probably quite as valuable, on the whole, as that given at our American colleges in my early days. I hope an additional instructor may ere long be added, to carry the studies farther than they can be with the present force. It is worthy of consideration, whether the study of the language of these Islands should not be added, at least for those pupils who derive their college support from the funds of the American Board. That this has not been done already, I am informed, is owing to some aversion which the students have to learning the language. The evil is certainly not invincible; it is not one to be overcome by the trustees of the college, but by this body; and it seems a proper subject for our consideration. The young people need only to take a broader view of their future relations and duties. The fact will have good influence upon them, that a knowledge of the native language is found to be a valuable acquisition to those who possess it."

"The manner of prosecuting the mission in *Micronesia* has difficulties, which we hope this meeting will be able to remove. That mission, owing to causes I need not take time to mention, was commenced on too large a scale, territorially. It can meet only once a year, and then at great expense; and, in the mean while, there can be no intercommunication whatever between the stations. This is far from realizing our idea of a mission, and does not justify the expense of the annual meeting. At first it was thought we must relinquish altogether the two high islands farthest west; but this the number of hopeful conversions on Ponape and Kusaie has seemed to forbid. The latter island will be occupied by a native missionary, and the former by two American missionaries, with native aid, and will perhaps become a future base to the operations among the islands farther west. As to the Gilbert and Marshall Islands, we think them too low and unproductive, and too destitute of fresh water, to be the permanent residence of American families. I am informed, however, that the water is less brackish than that used by the natives in the southern districts of Hawaii. Our present impression is, that (excepting occasional residences for the sake of translating) the low islands should be occupied by Sandwich Islanders, to be visited by the missionaries once or twice a year; and the valuable experience gained at the Marquesas shows that this will suffice. Where the visiting missionaries should make their home is among the unsettled questions."

"The American Board will continue its interest — how could it do otherwise? — in the prosperity of the churches formed on the Hawaiian Islands. The channels for communicating with the American Christian public will continue open to the brethren, as heretofore. Indeed, the Board could not afford to make grants to the Islands, unless the brethren here do their share in cultivating the missionary spirit in the churches at home. The Hawaiian Islands will have a place in our Annual Reports, and at the Annual Meetings, so long as the Board continues to make grants. Indeed, the more completely these churches attend to their own affairs, and the less dependent they are on the parent churches, the more interesting will these islands be to our home community, as a monument of the efficacy of the missionary work."

"In conclusion, I may say, that after the American Board has transferred its responsibilities, in the manner proposed, to the newly-created evangelical community here, the Christian world will have a new and striking proof that the missionary work at these Islands is no failure. Men will then see, too, that a beginning, middle, and end should be aimed at in the missionary enterprise, as in every other progressive work. Thus there will be an accelerated progress in missions, because there will be more expectation of progress, and more direct effort to secure it, and to bring the work to a close."

[For the topics proposed in this Address for discussion in the Association, see Chapter XIX.]

APPENDIX II.

ADDRESS TO THE CHILDREN OF THE MISSIONARIES.

"My Young Friends: In the discussions of the Prudential Committee which led to my being sent to these Islands, it appeared that only four of the missionaries here are under fifty years of age, and that seven of them are more than threescore. In view of this fact, I was instructed to inquire into the expediency of sending three or four able young men from the United States to occupy the important centres, as they shall be left vacant by the fathers. This was virtually an inquiry whether there is that amount of intelligence and missionary spirit among the children of the missionaries which would render such a step unnecessary.

"The proposal made to the missionary fathers in the year 1848, that they all remain at the Islands with their families, and take the houses, lands, and herds then held by the Board, was based on the supposition, that, should they do so, it would not be necessary to send out new missionaries, because their children might be depended on for future exigencies. In the deliberations fourteen years later, a doubt was expressed whether it were not wiser for a portion of the parents to have gone home, with their families, and their places to have been filled with young missionaries from the United States. This doubt was founded mainly on two facts, well known to close observers of mankind — the backwardness of parents to realize that their sons of twenty-five years of age have attained to manhood; and the backwardness of sons practically to realize the same thing, in deliberative meetings where they are outnumbered by the fathers. It is proper to say, that I have myself had somewhat of this apprehension since coming to the Islands, and during the meeting now in progress. However, the fathers, on my raising the question, have promptly declared their belief, that their sons will be fully able and disposed to meet the demand for men of foreign origin, growing out of their own withdrawal from the field.

"I have come, with their cheerful concurrence, and in their presence, to ask whether you, their children, *will ratify their decision.*

"The question is one of great importance. It seems to me in no small degree to involve the results of your fathers' labors for the forty years past, and of very much that is precious in this young nation; and of much, too, that is needful to make these Islands a comfortable home for you and yours.

"It is no longer a question with me whether the American Board, under present circumstances, shall send additional missionaries to these Islands. We cannot well do that. The work is too far advanced for sending out men on the missionary principle. The nature of the field is changed. Young men will not be willing to come without knowing definitely what post they are to occupy; and the vacancies which occur cannot be kept open long enough for them to be enlisted, sent out, and become prepared in the native language. God therefore declares in His providence that the work to be done devolves on the sons and daughters of the missionaries.

"And it is a work, my young friends, that will soon be upon you in all its weight and magnitude. Your parents will not be able much longer to sustain the burden. Before the man of twenty years has attained the age of thirty, he will find himself in the midst of these grave responsibilities.

"You are sufficient in *numbers*. A tabular view, furnished me by one of you, is accurate enough for my purpose. According to this, the male and female children of missionaries now at the Islands, over eight years of age, are one hundred and fifty. The number on the Islands from eight to eighteen is fifty-seven. The young men speaking the Hawaiian language with some fluency, here and in the United States, are forty-two.

"Nor can there be any doubt as to the sufficiency of your *intelligence*. It is not even necessary that many of you should go to the United States, in order to supplement the education you may obtain here.

"I have had some apprehension in respect to the *missionary spirit* among you, — I mean in its application to the native population. I thought I saw, — as the result of the very natural anxiety and care of your parents, years ago, to prevent your learning the native language, even to keep you from hearing or speaking a word of it, lest your morals should suffer, — that you showed a sort of aversion to the people themselves, a shrinking from personal contact with them, a want of that sympathy with them which is essential to successful labors for their spiritual good. But my apprehensions on this score have been gradually subsiding, as I became acquainted with you, and I now expect a response from you that will assure my hopes.

"My young friends, I can hardly regard myself as otherwise than *God's messenger to you.* I come to ask whether you will sustain and carry forward the work that brought your fathers and mothers to these Islands. They came to bring the gospel to the *native race.* That was their work and they have done it. That race has been Christianized, but needs a large amount of labor before its Christian institutions can stand without foreign assistance. These Christianized people are now in a *transition* state, — passing over from a government by individual missionaries to a government by ecclesiastical bodies to which they themselves belong — to self-government. There is enough of revolution in such transitions to call for solicitude; and the fathers have wisely resolved to make a beginning now, while there is a prospect of their own presiding influence for some years to come. But there is not now time for *them* to complete the work, and the men who shall succeed them will be sure to find much of it on hand.

"Nor will it devolve alone on those of you who enter the sacred ministry. Those of you who are merchants at Honolulu, or planters and graziers in the interior, or lawyers, physicians, civilians, teachers, will all have a responsibility and agency. And it is desirable you should be found in all the lawful professions and occupations. You will be needed in every department. Should you not all find scope on these Islands, the same will be true of young men in New England. You will be under no greater uncertainty than they, and while they have the Great West for an ultimate resort, you will have the United States. But your *first* duty will be *here,* — to your native land, — that you may complete the great work begun and successfully prosecuted by your fathers. The wilderness of forty years has been traversed, the land of promise is before you, and the Lord calls upon you to go up and possess it.

"I have heard remarks as if the native population were fast passing away; as if foreigners were soon to occupy the land, and become the nation, displacing the Hawaiian language; and as if your chief concern would be with them, rather than with the Hawaiian people. I have given attention to this matter in my tour through the Islands, and doubt not that you and your generation of natives will both pass before such a result is reached. The argument proves too much. If *you* ought not to give yourselves to the natives, then ought your honored *parents* to have gone elsewhere. I will only say, that *you* will best subserve the religious future of this nation by laying deep the foundations of the gospel in the native mind and heart.

"This, then, my young friends, is my appeal to you — that you regard it as your great calling *to look after this Christianized native people.* I entreat you, —

"1. To realize that *your* calling of God is to complete the work which your fathers cannot expect to live long enough to finish.

"2. To cultivate a fellow-feeling with the native people. Do not look down upon them. Do not despise them. Do not take up evil reports against them, especially against the native ministry. The natives are prone to originate such reports; but believe none unless they are proved. The Hawaiian people are kind-hearted. I have found it easy to love them. Nowhere is there a more hearty expression than in their word *aloha.* It is their characteristic word. If they have not words to express some of the great ideas, they certainly have a word expressive of one of the sweetest, richest, strongest sentiments of the human heart, — that of *loving good will* — ALOHA! I have myself used it thousands of times, and have never tired with the repetition.

"3. Learn their language. It is the language of your native country; and you will find the power of using it idiomatically and fluently to be an invaluable acquisition. It will be your only medium to the hearts of this people. Instruct classes in the Sabbath schools; attend the native prayer-meetings; hold religious meetings; you will then come to an understanding with the people. Make the principles and construction of the language your study.

"4. Stand by the native pastors. They will need your countenance, encouragement, and it may be your protection, especially in rural districts. Let the people see that you respect their pastors. Let the pastors feel that you are their cordial friends.

"5. Sustain the Hawaiian Board, just formed. It is intended to prosecute both foreign and domestic missions, to educate a native ministry, and to enrich the literature of the country. It is the representative both of the native and foreign population — of the evangelical Protestant community on these Islands. It is a simple but comprehensive organization, and will need, deserve, and doubtless receive, your support in all its departments of labor.

"Finally, be united among yourselves, — one in feeling, one in measures. If divided, the enemy will prevail against you. United in a good cause, you have no reason for apprehension. You live under a good government, and should be loyal subjects. Stand together in supporting your king, your constitution, and your religious liberties.

"Should you assume the responsibilities I have described, I shall take pleasure in reporting the fact, on my return home, to the fathers and friends of this mission and these Islands, and they will hear it with joy, and will pray that the blessing of Almighty God may rest upon you."

THE RESPONSE.

After the Address, the following Resolutions, proposed by Mr. Henry A. P. Carter, were unanimously adopted: —

"*Resolved,* That we have heard with heartfelt pleasure and deep feeling the solemn truths so eloquently presented to our consideration by the Rev. Dr. Anderson.

"That we recognize a voice of authority to us in the utterances of a voice for so many years raised in behalf of Christian missions.

"That we earnestly commend these remarks to the prayerful consideration of this Society, and to those about us who with us feel an interest in the spread of Christ's kingdom.

"That, in response to this call, we do hereby pledge ourselves, so far as we are able, to carry forward the work devolving upon us."

APPENDIX III.

ORGANIZATION OF THE BOARD OF THE HAWAIIAN EVANGELICAL ASSOCIATION.

"ARTICLE VII. — This Association shall appoint an Executive Board, to be denominated, The Board of the Hawaiian Evangelical Association, which shall consist of a Corresponding Secretary and Treasurer, to be chosen annually by the Association, together with not less than eighteen members, one third of whom shall go out of office annually, eligible to reëlection. They shall be divided into three classes, not less than six in each class, to be numbered first, second, and third class; those of the first class to go out of office at the end of one year, those of the second class at the end of two years, and those of the third class at the end of three years.

"It shall be the duty of the Board to perform any agency requested of it by the Prudential Committee, in respect to former missionaries of the American Board of Commissioners for Foreign Missions at these Islands, and the education of their children at the Islands; and to take charge of Home Missions on these Hawaiian Islands; the education of a native ministry, and of females who may become teachers and pastors' wives; the preparation, publication, and circulation of useful books and tracts; and also of foreign missions, so far as the conduct of them from these Islands shall be found practicable and expedient; and shall take the charge of disbursing the funds contributed for these objects, from whatever source."

The following persons were elected members of the Board, in addition to the Corresponding Secretary and Treasurer, who are members of the Board *ex officiis,* — one third of them Hawaiians, according to a rule adopted, viz.: —

For Hawaii.

Rev. J. D. Paris, Rev. E. Bond,
Rev. T. Coan, S. Kipi,
G. W. Philipo.

For Maui and Molokai.

Rev. W. P. Alexander, Rev. J. F. Pogue,
L. Aholo.

For Oahu.

Rev. E. W. Clark,	Rev. L. Smith,
Dr. G. P. Judd,	Rev. S. C. Damon,
Rev. E. Corwin,	Rev. C. T. Mills,
Rev. B. W. Parker,	Hon. Ioane Ii,
S. N. Castle, Esq.,	S. Kumuhonua.

For Kauai.

Rev. J. W. Smith, G. W. Lilikalani.

The following are the Officers: —

Rev. TITUS COAN, President.	Rev. E. W. CLARK, Rec. Seo.
Dr. G. P. JUDD, V. President.	E. O. HALL, Esq., Treasurer.
Rev. L. H. GULICK, Cor. Sec.	I. BARTLETT, Esq., Auditor.

APPENDIX IV.

ADDRESS TO THE FOREIGN SECRETARY OF THE AMERICAN BOARD.

"THE Members of the HAWAIIAN EVANGELICAL ASSOCIATION to the Rev. R. ANDERSON, D. D., Foreign Secretary of the American Board of Commissioners for Foreign Missions.

"HONORED AND DEARLY-BELOVED BROTHER: With no ordinary pleasure, and with no vain compliment, we assure you of the profound satisfaction we have enjoyed in your visit to these shores.

"We had long desired such a visit, but had not expected to

realize it. God, in his wise counsels, prepared the way for you to come to us. He has kindly watched over you, and your excellent wife and daughter, while on your way hither, and during all your sojournings in these Isles. You have visited most of the islands and stations of our group, and we have joyfully welcomed you to our homes and our hearts. You have seen something of our fields and of our labors. You have addressed our churches and congregations, and mingled with the multitudes of our people. You have felt the warm grasp, and heard the heartfelt, expressive *aloha* of ten thousand Hawaiians; and they will ever remember you as a beloved and venerated father, and your most faithful companion as a precious mother in Israel. Your eyes have witnessed the marvellous work of God in this land, and your ears have heard the songs of ransomed Hawaiians.

"We have held endearing communion with you in consultations, in social intercourse, and at our domestic altars. And we have met you, from day to day, in our sessions, and have enjoyed your wise and timely counsels in our deliberations. Questions of a difficult and delicate character, involving great interests, have come before us, and your wisdom and experience have helped us to solve them; so that, in almost all things, we have, through the grace of God, come to harmonious conclusions. In the discussion of principles and of measures, and in the reorganization of our plans for the firmer establishment and the more perfect development of Christ's kingdom around us, your presence and suggestions have been of invaluable service to us.

"For all this we thank the Lord, and we feel assured that you were led to this vineyard at the right time, and by Infinite Wisdom and Love.

"And now, as you and yours are about to leave us, to return to your native land, there to resume your arduous and responsible labors, we bid you a heartfelt farewell. Our best and holiest sympathies are with you. Our prayers shall ever follow you. With our wives and children, and with all the friends of Zion in this land, we repeat our earnest ALOHA, and offer our ardent supplications that the God of Abraham may still guide you, that the wings of Emmanuel may cover you, and that your life may long be spared to labor in the great vineyard of our Lord.

"We may meet no more on earth. God grant that we may all meet on the heavenly hills, and from those heights of glory review the way in which He has led us, and with songs and joy survey the field of our toils and conflicts, ascribing thanksgiving, honor, and dominion to Him who gives us the victory through our Lord Jesus Christ.

"With our highest Christian esteem, and our warmest desires for the welfare of yourself and family, we again say *farewell.*

"On behalf of the Hawaiian Evangelical Association.

"T. COAN, *Committee.*

"Honolulu, July 1, 1863."

APPENDIX V.

ACTION OF THE PRUDENTIAL COMMITTEE.

AT a meeting of the Prudential Committee of the American Board of Commissioners for Foreign Missions, on the 29th of September, 1863, subsequently to the return of Dr. Anderson, the following Minute, reported by Messrs. Child and Aiken as a subcommittee, was adopted: —

"Dr. Anderson having recently returned from a visit to the Sandwich Islands, which he made at the special request of the Prudential Committee, accompanied by his wife and daughter (the two latter going at private expense), for the purpose of ascertaining, by personal intercourse with the missionaries, the members of their churches, and the people generally to whom they had ministered, more fully than could be done in any other way, the real condition of the people, the state of the churches, and the character of their members, and witnessing on the ground the results effected among the people of the Islands by the power and Spirit of God, through the labors of the missionaries; for the further purpose of freely conferring and advising with the missionaries, and with members of the Hawaiian churches, upon the present condition and further prospects of the missionary work there, and devising such plans of future action as should bring the native churches, as speedily as possible, in what is believed to be the natural order in such cases, (1.) to a condition of *self-government*, and (2.) by means of the greater activity and earnestness which would be developed by this self-government, to a condition of *complete self-support;* and also for the purpose of determining, by such free conference with the missionaries, what may best be their future relations to the Board and its work; and Dr. Anderson having, since his return, orally and in writing, made a Report to the Committee respecting his mission and its results; and having prepared, to be submitted to the Board, at its approaching meeting, a portion of his intended full Report, embracing the two following topics, to wit: (1.) *The Organization of the Civil Community*, and (2.) *The Organization of the Protestant Christian Community at the Islands*, — the Committee deem it expedient to place upon record their matured conviction in relation to said mission of the Secretary and its results, as expressed in the following resolutions: —

"1. *Resolved*, That the recent mission of Dr. Anderson to the Sandwich Islands was wise and seasonable; and that Mrs. Anderson rendered most important aid, by enabling him to obtain fuller knowledge of the real character and condition of the people than could have been procured without the information derived from her free and intimate intercourse with the female portion of the population.

"2. *Resolved*, That the course pursued by Dr. Anderson at the Islands, as reported by him, was eminently wise and successful; that his doings, and the plans adopted by the brethren at the Islands, acting with his counsel and advice, for the future prosecution of their work, are cordially approved and sanctioned; and that, for the wisdom and success granted to the Secretary and his fellow-laborers at the Islands, thanks should be rendered to our gracious Lord, who has promised to be always with his servants, when they go forth to teach the nations.

"3. *Resolved,* That while it does not appear, from the report of the plans and measures adopted, and the proceedings had during the late visit of the Secretary, that the Protestant Christian community of the Islands has attained to the position of *complete self-support,* as to its religious institutions, there is yet ample occasion for gratitude to God for his signal blessing upon this mission, since the Secretary is permitted to report, that it has attained to such a degree of capacity for *self-government* as to render it expedient that it should now assume, not only the management of its own ecclesiastical matters and its religious charities, but the responsibility of directing the future prosecution of the work for building up the Redeemer's kingdom at the Sandwich Islands, and extending it into Micronesia.

"4. *Resolved,* That the proposition made by the Protestant Christian community at the Sandwich Islands, who have organized a working Board, called 'The Board of the Hawaiian Evangelical Association,' to relieve the American Board of Commissioners for Foreign Missions, and the American churches, from the responsibility of future oversight and direction in the work referred to in the foregoing Resolution, — upon the condition that it may have the privilege of applying to the American Board for such grants-in-aid as it shall need in its several departments of labor, and as the Board shall be able and judge it wise to give, — is hereby accepted by this Committee upon the condition specified; it being understood that this plan, in respect to *Micronesia,* will not go into effect until the brethren now in those Islands, who have not been heard from on the subject, have the opportunity to communicate their views to the Prudential Committee. And this Committee joyfully commits to the Board of the Hawaiian Evangelical Association the future care and direction of this evangelizing work in those Islands, and hereby concedes to that Board the right of applying for grants-in-aid, as specified in said proposition.

"5. *Resolved*, That the Committee having proposed, in December last, to the former missionaries now at the Sandwich Islands, to afford them, from the funds of the American Board, such salaries as shall be needful, in addition to their several private incomes, for their comfortable support; thus relieving the native churches from any further contributions for this purpose, and removing a serious obstacle to increasing the number of native churches and pastors, and to obtaining a support for these pastors from the native community; and the missionaries having acceded to this proposition, and the amount of their respective salaries having been agreed upon by them, at the late meeting of the Hawaiian Evangelical Association, at which Dr. Anderson was present, — the Committee hereby assents to the several salaries, as thus agreed upon.

"6. *Resolved*, That while we would render devout thanks to our gracious Lord for what he has been pleased to do at the Sandwich Islands, and for the great success he has given to the labors of our missionaries among that once degraded people, we remember, and would remind the friends of missions, that much remains to be accomplished, and that there is now, and will long continue to be, great occasion for watchfulness and earnest prayer against impending evils; and we ask of the friends of Christ, everywhere, continued supplication for the divine blessing upon the labors of his servants in this interesting portion of the vineyard of the Lord.

"7. *Resolved*, That the proceedings of the Hawaiian Evangelical Association, at its recent meeting, at which the Secretary was present, together with the Reports made to that meeting for the use of its members, and the full Report by Dr. Anderson of his late visit to the Islands, and also this Minute, be printed for the use of the Board."

APPENDIX VI.

ACTION OF THE BOARD.

At the Annual Meeting of the Board in Rochester, N. Y., in October, 1863, besides a verbal statement of considerable length from Dr. Anderson, there were laid before the Board his written Report (in part), which had been submitted to the Prudential Committee, and the nine Reports made and adopted at the recent meeting of the Hawaiian Evangelical Association, embodying the results of deliberations at the Islands; and these were referred to the committee on the Sandwich Islands and Micronesia missions, consisting of Leonard Bacon, D. D., Hon. William Strong, Rev. David Greene, Miles P. Squier, D. D., John W. Loud, Esq., S. G. Boardman, D. D., and Rev. Edmund K. Alden. This Committee subsequently presented the following Resolutions, which were adopted: —

"1. *Resolved,* That the sending of Dr. Anderson, by the Prudential Committee, to the Sandwich Islands, for the purpose of personal intercourse with the missionaries and pastors there, and of observing the actual condition both of the churches that have been established in that lately heathen land, and of the nation that has been lifted up from the lowest barbarism to civilization, and for the purpose of aiding, by personal conference and consultation, in the arrangement of new relations between the Board and the missionaries and churches there, seems to have been necessary, and is hereby sanctioned and approved.

"2. *Resolved,* That the arrangement by which the support of native pastors and evangelists in the Sandwich Islands, and of the whole work of home evangelization there, is to devolve henceforth upon the Christian people of those Islands, while the support of the surviving missionaries, instead of being divided, as heretofore, between the churches to which they minister and the Board by which they were sent forth, is to devolve upon the Board, is hereby sanctioned and approved.

"3. *Resolved,* That the arrangement by which the Micronesia mission is transferred from the immediate superintendence of the Prudential Committee of this Board to that of the Board of the Hawaiian Evangelical Association, is hereby sanctioned and approved; and that the Prudential Committee are hereby authorized and instructed to aid the foreign missions of that Board by such grants of money as the exigencies of their work in Micronesia, or in Polynesia, may require, and the contributions to our treasury may justify; always requiring, from year to year, so long as such grants shall be continued, a full report of the manner in which they are expended, and of the condition and progress of those missions.

"4. *Resolved,* That, in taking this additional step towards the conclusion of our work in the Sandwich Islands, we record anew our grateful and adoring sense of the marvellous success which our missionaries there have been enabled to achieve, by the blessing of God, to whom be all the glory.

"5. *Resolved,* That while we rejoice, with all our surviving missionaries, in the results of which we and the world are witnesses, we offer our special congratulations to the two venerable fathers of the mission, the Rev. HIRAM BINGHAM, and the Rev. ASA THURSTON, who, having been consecrated and commended to the grace of God for that work by our predecessors, forty-four years ago, are still among the living, to praise God, with us and with all the saints, for this great victory of the gospel, and to say, 'Lord, now lettest thou thy servants depart in peace, according to thy word, for our eyes have seen thy salvation.'"

APPENDIX VII.

EXTRACTS FROM BISHOP STALEY'S SERMONS.

[See p. 352.]

1. *From the Sermon preached in London.*

"SUCH, Brethren, are the chief outlines of the task we are undertaking. I cannot hide the fact that its accomplishment seems beset with difficulties and perils. If the ground were wholly unoccupied, as it was when we were first invited to take possession of it in Christ's name, the case would be very different from what it actually is. It is hoped that the introduction of that pure and complete development of Divine truth it is our happiness as English Churchmen to enjoy, concentrating in its worship and teaching all that is good, and beautiful, and true, in the two extremes, without running into the excesses of either, may dispel some of those doubts which systems so antagonistic as those now at work there must have created in their minds. It may be so; but it may produce the contrary effect. And a vast responsibility devolves on those to whom is intrusted the direction of this sacred enterprise, to see that the former, and not the latter, be the result of their efforts. Nothing would shake all religious belief in the Islands more effectually than for us to assume an attitude of hostility to those forms of Christianity with which they are now familiar. We must show the people how beneath the defects and corruptions of this or that communion there lies a substratum of truth in the admission of the great historic facts of the Creeds, which may well increase their faith in those facts, and lead to greater charity and forbearance in our treatment of those Articles of the Faith which are called in question. We are to speak the truth, but it must be in love; and we are to give all who have been hitherto laboring with so much devotion and earnestness in their Master's cause, while we have been looking on with cold indifference, the credit they deserve. We must make it clear we do not go forth to ignore or override what has been done by others.

"And this suggests another danger — that of seeking to proselytize. It is an admitted fact that a large number of people are in active communion with none of the existing bodies, and among them we must seek to labor, not doubting that, as we thus exhibit and carry to them the Church's message, in all fidelity, and zeal, and love, she will attract many others, whom she would effectually repel were she to assume a posture of unfriendliness or aggression. If we keep before our eyes the fact, that the great object of the mission is the salvation of the souls and bodies of those among whom we are going to labor, and not the numbers we can count as members of our communion, we may hope, by God's blessing, to escape this danger."

2. *From the Sermon preached at Honolulu.*

"And we come in all love and good will to those who have been laboring here before us. However much we may conscientiously differ from them, we desire not to ignore the work which they have done to the best of their ability, nor withhold from them the credit they deserve. In turn, we claim from them the same consideration and forbearance. There is the more need to ask this because in many important points our Church differs from the sects professing Protestant Christianity no less than from the Roman Church; and consequently there will be parts in her worship and teaching which will seem strange to those who are only familiar with the former. At the Reformation she avoided the two extremes of a slavish adhesion to the existing order on the one hand, and of irreverence for Catholic antiquity and practice on the other. Accordingly, in her preface to the Book of Common Prayer it is expressly stated that its compilers sought to be guided by Holy Scripture, as '*interpreted by the ancient Fathers,*' implying by that term those, chiefly, of the first five centuries — the purest ages of the Church. The Liturgy was not composed for the first time at the Reformation. It contains the ancient Collects, Litanies, Hymns, and Communion Office which were in the Roman Breviary and Missal, translated into the vernacular, and cleansed of the errors which had crept into them during the middle ages. Yes! we utter the same venerable forms wherein Christians have breathed their aspirations to the Throne of Grace — probably since the times of the Apostles, certainly during fourteen centuries. She holds that the Sacraments are not bare symbols and figures of spiritual truths, but that they 'are outward and visible signs of inward and spiritual grace,' *by* and *in* them 'given to us,' when administered by the hands of Christ's duly appointed ministers. She teaches parents to bring their infants to be admitted into the Christian covenant by Holy Baptism, wherein they are declared to be 'made members of Christ, children of God, and inheritors of the Kingdom of Heaven.' But they are reminded that all this will be of no avail unless they are endeavoring to fulfil their parts of the covenant by renouncing the world, the flesh, and the Devil, believing the articles of the Christian Faith, and endeavoring to do their duty in that state of life to which they have been called. On arriving at years of discretion the baptized are invited to the Holy Rite of Confirmation, that they may not only 'ratify and confirm their Christian obligations,' but be strengthened by a new gift of the Holy Spirit, imparted to them 'by the imposition of hands.' This rite is designed to serve as an initiation into full communion with the Church — when the devout recipient may approach the Blessed Sacrament of Christ's Body and Blood, which, in the language of the Catechism, 'are verily and indeed taken and received by the faithful in the Lord's Supper.' She deems this the highest act of Christian worship, and, as an intimation that she would have it accompanied with externals to impress the senses as well as the heart, she directs in her 24th Canon that it be celebrated in every Cathedral with special vestments to be worn by the clergy.

"Through all the ever-varying scenes of this life, in trouble and in joy, she follows her children with her heavenly consolations, her prayers and benedictions, until that body which in this life she had taught them to regard as 'the Temple of the Holy Ghost' is committed to the earth, in hope of the resurrection to life eternal.

" In all this her principle is, do not wait till you are converted by some sudden, irresistible impulse, but regard yourself as already, by baptism, grafted into Christ's Church, and bound to crucify daily the old man, with his evil deeds, and able to do so by the strength already imparted to you from above. It is this gradual formation of Christian character at which she aims — a process going on from Baptism till Death. It enters into all her teachings and formularies. So with regard to Church discipline. All whose consciences are burdened with sin she requests, in her exhortation to the Communion, to come to the minister and open their grief, that they may 'receive the benefit of absolution, together with ghostly counsel and advice.'

" Regarding her children as having bodies as well as souls, senses to be exercised for good or evil, she sanctions the consecration of all that is beautiful in nature and art to the service of the sanctuary. Her old Cathedral worship has consequently been retained in all its splendor. The peal of the organ as it rebounds along the vaulted roof, the stained-glass window, the painted altar-piece, the furniture for the Holy Table, these have received her high approval, and are found not only in her Cathedrals but many of her other churches. Except as accessories and aids to devotion, or as offerings of love to Christ, — the ointment poured out, — we value them not. If we are to address our worship to them, if they shut out Christ from our eyes, away with them! I am persuaded there are some natures to whom a ritual is more acceptable, more necessary, than to others; and such I believe to be the case with the natives of these Islands. Let, then, such of you as lean to a more purely subjective and mental worship remember this, and be willing to sacrifice something of their own individual preferences for the good of the whole body.

" Regard in this light our humble attempts to adorn God's service and temple. We have as yet only a very poor building. But it is a Cathedral, for it is the seat of a Bishop of Christ's Holy Catholic Church.

"Once more. We do not regard religion as a system of frames and feelings, merely, separate from common life. It is to leaven and hallow all the instincts of our nature, not to override and crush them. It is therefore not a business of one day in seven,—Sunday,—often called, I think most falsely and mischievously, the Sabbath; for the Church provides 'an order of prayer to be said *daily* throughout the year.' She wishes the daily sacrifice to be offered. And she has appointed the observance of fast and festival each in its due course. On her Christmas, her Easter, her Ascension Tide, she would have all rejoice, not only in the temple, but in innocent mirth and healthful recreation. He who was present at the marriage of Cana in Galilee, and turned the water into wine, designs to unite with us—if we drive him not away by impurity and sin—in our social and festal gatherings no less than in our seasons of sorrow and bereavement. Surely Christianity is not all sourness, all *taboo!* God would have us use thankfully and in moderation all the gifts He has given us, not abstain from them altogether. This is true self-restraint, this real temperance.

"Such are some of the leading features in that Church system we come to establish among the people of these Islands. We come not unasked, and we come seconded by the prayers and alms of Christ's faithful people in the country we have left. O, pray that though we are 'sowing in tears'—in the first outburst of a nation's grief for the loss of the princely boy so untimely removed to the bright world above—we may yet 'reap in joy;' that they who go about 'weeping, and bearing good seed,' may 'come again with joy, bringing their sheaves with them'!"

INDEX.

INDEX.

THE END.

Valuable Works,

PUBLISHED BY

GOULD AND LINCOLN,

59 Washington Street, Boston.

GOD REVEALED IN NATURE AND IN CHRIST; including a Refutation of the Development Theory contained in the "Vestiges of the Natural History of Creation." By Rev. JAMES B. WALKER, author of "THE PHILOSOPHY OF THE PLAN OF SALVATION." 12mo, cloth, 1.50.

THE SUFFERING SAVIOUR; or, Meditations on the Last Days of Christ. By FRED. W. KRUMMACHER, D. D., author of "Elijah the Tishbite." 12mo, cloth, 1.75; cloth, gilt, 2.75; half calf, 3.50.

"The narrative is given with thrilling vividness and pathos and beauty. Marking, as we proceeded, several passages for quotation, we found them, in the end, so numerous that we must refer the reader to the work itself." — *News of the Churches (Scottish).*

THE TESTIMONY OF CHRIST TO CHRISTIANITY. By PETER BAYNE, M. A., author of "Christian Life," etc. 16mo, cloth, 90 cts.

☞ A work of great interest and power.

THE BENEFIT OF CHRIST'S DEATH; or, The Glorious Riches of God's Free Grace, which every True Believer receives by Jesus Christ and Him Crucified. Originally written in Italian by Aonio Paleario, and now Reprinted from an Ancient English Translation. With an Introduction by Rev. JOHN AYER, M. A. 16mo, cloth, 75 cts.

WREATH AROUND THE CROSS; or, Scripture Truths Illustrated. By the Rev. A. MORTON BROWN, D. D. Recommendatory Preface, by JOHN ANGELL JAMES. With a beautiful Frontispiece. 16mo, cloth, 1.00.

EXTENT OF THE ATONEMENT IN ITS RELATION TO GOD AND THE UNIVERSE. By Rev. THOMAS W. JENKYN, D. D., late President of Coward College, London. 12mo, cloth, 1.50

"We consider this volume as setting the long and fiercely agitated question, as to the extent of the Atonement, completely at rest. Posterity will thank the author, till the latest ages, for his illustrious argument." — *N. Y. Evangelist.*

CHRIST IN HISTORY. By ROBERT TURNBULL, D. D. A New and Enlarged Edition. 12mo, cloth, 1.75.

THE SCHOOL OF CHRIST; or, Christianity Viewed in its Leading Aspects. Ry the Rev. A. R. L. FOOTE, author of "Incidents in the Life of our Saviour," etc. 16mo, cloth, 75 cts.

PHILOSOPHY OF THE PLAN OF SALVATION; a book for the Times. By an AMERICAN CITIZEN. With an Introductory Essay by CALVIN E. STOWE, D. D. ☞ New improved and enlarged edition. 12mo, cloth, 1.25.

THE PERSON AND WORK OF CHRIST. By ERNEST SARTORIUS, D. D., Konigsberg, Prussia. Translated by Rev. OAKMAN S. STEARNS, D. D. 18mo, cloth, 60 cts.

THE GREAT DAY OF ATONEMENT; or, Meditations and Prayers on the Last Twenty-four Hours of the Sufferings and Death of our Lord and Saviour Jesus Christ. Translated from the German of CHARLOTTE ELIZABETH NEBELIN. Edited by Mrs. COLIN MACKENZIE. Elegantly printed and bound. 16mo, cloth, 1.25; cloth, gilt, 2.00; Turkey mor., gilt, 3.50.

THE HEADSHIP OF CHRIST, and the Rights of the Christian People; A Collection of Personal Portraitures, Historical and Descriptive Sketches and Essays, with the Author's celebrated Letter to Lord Brougham. By HUGH MILLER. Edited, with a Preface, by PETER BAYNE, A. M. 12mo, cloth, 1.75.

THE MISSION OF THE COMFORTER; with copious Notes. By JULIUS CHARLES HARE. With the NOTES translated for the AMERICAN EDITION. 12mo, cloth, 1.75.

THE IMITATION OF CHRIST. By THOMAS A KEMPIS. With an Introductory Essay by THOMAS CHALMERS, D. D. Edited by HOWARD MALCOM, D. D. A new edition, with a LIFE OF THOMAS A KEMPIS, by Dr. C. ULLMANN, author of "Reformers before the Reformation." 12mo, cloth, 1.25.

FINE EDITION, TINTED PAPER. Square 8vo, cloth, red edges, 2.25; cloth, gilt, 3.00; half calf, 4.00; full Turkey mor., 6.00.

The above may safely be pronounced the best Protestant editions extant of this celebrated work.

LESSONS AT THE CROSS; or, Spiritual Truths Familiarly Exhibited in their Relations to Christ. By SAMUEL HOPKINS, author of "The Puritans." With an Introduction by REV. GEORGE W. BLAGDEN, D. D. New edition. 16mo, cloth, 1.00.

THE BETTER LAND; or, The Believer's Journey and Future Home. By the Rev. A. C. THOMPSON. 12mo, cloth, 1.25; cloth, gilt, 1.75.

A most charming and instructive book for all now journeying to the "better land."

HEAVEN. By JAMES WILLIAM KIMBALL. With an elegant vignette title-page. 12mo, cloth, 1.25; cloth, gilt, 2.00; Turkey morocco, gilt, 3.25.

"The book is full of beautiful ideas, consoling hopes, and brilliant representations of human destiny, all presented in a chaste, pleasing, and very readable style." — *N. Y. Chronicle.*

THE STATE OF THE IMPENITENT DEAD. By ALVAH HOVEY, D. D., Prof. of Christian Theology in Newton Theol. Inst. 16mo, cloth, 75 cts.

SAINTS' EVERLASTING REST. By RICHARD BAXTER. 16mo, cloth, 75 cts.

HARVEST AND THE REAPERS. Home Work for All, and how to do it. By Rev. HARVEY NEWCOMB. 16mo, cloth, 90 cts.

Gould and Lincoln's Publications.

LIFE, TIMES, AND CORRESPONDENCE OF JAMES MANNING, AND THE EARLY HISTORY OF BROWN UNIVERSITY. By REUBEN ALDRIDGE GUILD. With Likenesses of President Manning and Nicholas Brown, Views of Brown University, The First Baptist Church, Providence, etc. Royal 12mo, cloth, 3.00.

A most important and interesting historical work.

MEMOIR OF GEORGE N. BRIGGS, LL. D., late Governor of Massachusetts. By JOHN TODD, D. D. With Illustrations. Royal 12mo. *In preparation.*

THE LIFE OF JOHN MILTON, narrated in connection with the POLITICAL, ECCLESIASTICAL, AND LITERARY HISTORY OF HIS TIME. By DAVID MASSON, M. A., Professor of English Literature, University College, London. Vol. I., embracing the period from 1608 to 1639. With Portraits and specimens of his handwriting at different periods. Royal octavo, cloth, 3.50.

LIFE AND CORRESPONDENCE OF REV. DANIEL WILSON, D. D., late Bishop of Calcutta. By Rev. JOSIAH BATEMAN, M. A., Rector of North Cray, Kent. With Portraits, Map, and numerous Illustrations. One volume royal octavo, cloth, 3.50.

☞ An interesting life of a great and good man.

THE LIFE AND TIMES OF JOHN HUSS; or, The Bohemian Reformation of the Fifteenth Century. By Rev. E. H. GILLETT. Two vols. royal octavo, 7.00.

"The author," says the *New York Observer*, "has achieved a great work, performed a valuable service for Protestantism and the world, made a name for himself among religious historians, and produced a book that will hold a prominent place in the esteem of every religious scholar."

The *New York Evangelist* speaks of it as "one of the most valuable contributions to ecclesiastical history yet made in this country."

MEMOIR OF THE CHRISTIAN LABORS, Pastoral and Philanthropic, of THOMAS CHALMERS, D. D. LL. D. By FRANCIS WAYLAND. 16mo, cloth, 1.00.

The moral and intellectual greatness of Chalmers is, we might say, overwhelming to the mind of the ordinary reader. Dr. Wayland draws the portraiture with a master hand.—*Method. Quart. Rev.*

LIFE OF JAMES MONTGOMERY. By Mrs. H. C. KNIGHT, author of "Lady Huntington and her Friends," etc. Likeness, and elegant Illustrated Title-Page on steel. 12mo, cloth, 1.50.

DIARY AND CORRESPONDENCE OF AMOS LAWRENCE. With a brief account of some Incidents in his Life. Edited by his son, WM. R. LAWRENCE, M. D. With elegant Portraits of Amos and Abbott Lawrence, an Engraving of their Birthplace, an Autograph page of Handwriting, and a copious Index. One large octavo volume, cloth, 2.50.

THE SAME WORK. Royal 12mo, cloth, 1.75.

DR. GRANT AND THE MOUNTAIN NESTORIANS. By Rev. THOMAS LAURIE, his surviving associate in that Mission. With a Likeness, Map of the Country, and numerous Illustrations. Third edition. Revised and improved. 12mo, cloth, 1.75. ☞ A most valuable memoir of a *remarkable man.*

THE CHRISTIAN LIFE, SOCIAL AND INDIVIDUAL. By PETER BAYNE, M. A. 12mo, cloth, 1.75; half calf, 3.50.

There is but one voice respecting this extraordinary book, — men of all denominations, in all quarters, agree in pronouncing it one of the most admirable works of the age.

THE CHRISTIAN'S DAILY TREASURY; a Religious Exercise for every Day in the Year. By Rev. E. TEMPLE. A new and improved edition. 12mo, cloth, 1.50.

☞ A work for every Christian. It is, indeed, a "Treasury" of good things.

THE CHURCH MEMBER'S GUIDE. By the Rev. JOHN A. JAMES. Edited by J. O. CHOULES, D. D. New Edition. With Introductory Essay, by Rev. HUBBARD WINSLOW. Cloth, 60 cts.

THE CHURCH IN EARNEST. By Rev. JOHN A. JAMES. 18mo, cloth, 75 cts.

CHRISTIAN PROGRESS. A Sequel to the Anxious Inquirer. By JOHN ANGELL JAMES. 18mo, cloth, 65 cts.

THE MEMORIAL HOUR; or, The Lord's Supper in its relation to Doctrine and Life. By JEREMIAH CHAPLIN, D. D., author of "Evening of Life," etc. 16mo, 1.25.

This is a precious volume, strictly devotional in its character, exhibiting the Lord's Supper in many aspects, presses home the lessons which it teaches, shows the feelings with which it should be regarded, and by its suggestions and admirable selections of hymns assists the communicant to prepare for this solemn service.

THE MEMORIAL NAME. Reply to BISHOP COLENSO. By ALEXANDER MACWHORTER. With an Introductory Letter by NATHANIEL W. TAYLOR, D. D., late Dwight Professor in Yale Theological Seminary. 16mo, 1.25.

THE MERCY SEAT; or, Thoughts on Prayer. By A. C. THOMPSON, D.D., Author of "Better Land," etc. 12mo, cloth, 1.50.

Fine Edition, Tinted Paper. 8vo, cloth, red edges, 2.50; cloth, gilt edges, 3.50.

THE STILL HOUR; or, Communion with God. By Prof. AUSTIN PHELPS, D. D., of Andover Theological Seminary. 16mo, cloth, 60 cts.

CHRISTIANITY AND STATESMANSHIP; with Kindred Topics. By WILLIAM HAGUE, D. D. A new, revised, enlarged, and much improved edition. 12mo, cloth, 1.75.

THE EVIDENCES OF CHRISTIANITY, as exhibited in the writings of its apologists, down to Augustine. By W. J. BOLTON, of Gonville and Caius College, Cambridge. 12mo, cloth, 1.50.

CHRISTIAN BROTHERHOOD. By BARON STOW, D. D., Pastor of Rowe-street Church, Boston. 16mo, cloth, 75 cts.

THE CHRISTIAN WORLD UNMASKED. By JOHN BERRIDGE, M., Vicar of Everton, Bedfordshire. With a Life of the Author, by Rev. THOMAS GUTHRIE, D. D., Minister of Free St. John's, Edinburgh. 16mo, cloth, 75 cts.

Gould and Lincoln's Publications.

THE PURITANS; or, The Court, Church, and Parliament of England, during the reigns of Edward VI. and Elizabeth. By SAMUEL HOPKINS, author of Lessons at the Cross," etc. In 3 vols. Octavo, cloth, per vol., 3.00; sheep, 4.00; half calf, 6.00.

It will be found the most interesting and reliable History of the Puritans yet published, narrating, in a dramatic style, many facts hitherto unknown.

THE PREACHER AND THE KING; or, Bourdaloue in the Court of Louis XIV.; being an Account of the Pulpit Eloquence of that distinguished era. Translated from the French of L. F. BUNGENER, Paris. Introduction by the Rev. GEORGE POTTS, D. D. *A new, improved edition*, with a fine Likeness and a BIOGRAPHICAL SKETCH OF THE AUTHOR. 12mo, cloth, 1.50.

THE PRIEST AND THE HUGUENOT; or, Persecution in the Age of Louis XV. From the French of L. F. BUNGENER. Two vols. 12mo, cloth, 3.00.

☞ This is not only a work of thrilling interest, — no fiction could exceed it, — but, as a Protestant work, it is a masterly production.

THE PULPIT OF THE AMERICAN REVOLUTION; or, The Political Sermons of the Period of 1776. With an Historical Introduction, Notes, Illustrations, etc. By JOHN WINGATE THORNTON, A. M. 12mo, cloth, 1.75.

THE LEADERS OF THE REFORMATION. LUTHER, CALVIN, LATIMER, and KNOX, the representative men of Germany, France, England, and Scotland. By J. TULLOCH, D. D., Author of "Theism," etc. 12mo, cloth, 1.50.

A portrait gallery of sturdy reformers, drawn by a keen eye and a strong hand. Dr. Tulloch discriminates clearly the personal qualities of each Reformer, and commends and criticises with equal frankness.

THE HAWAIIAN ISLANDS; their Progress and Condition under Missionary Labors. By RUFUS ANDERSON, D. D., Foreign Secretary of the American Board of Commissioners for Foreign Missions. With Maps, Illustrations, etc. Royal 12mo, cloth, 2.25.

WOMAN AND HER SAVIOUR in Persia. By a RETURNED MISSIONARY. With beautiful Illustrations and a Map of the Nestorian Country. 12mo, cloth, 1.25.

LIGHT IN DARKNESS; or, Christ Discerned in his True Character by a Unitarian. 16mo, cloth, 90 cts.

LIMITS OF RELIGIOUS THOUGHT EXAMINED, in Eight Lectures, delivered in the Oxford University Pulpit, in the year 1858, on the "Bampton Foundation." By Reu. H. LONGUEVILLE MANSEL, B. D., Reader in Moral and Metaphysical Philosophy at Magdalen College, Oxford, and Editor of Sir William Hamilton's Lectures. With Copious NOTES TRANSLATED for the American edition. 12mo, cloth, 1.50.

THE CRUCIBLE; or, Tests of a Regenerate State; designed to bring to light suppressed hopes, expose false ones, and confirm the true. By Rev. J. A. GOODHUE, A. M. With an introduction by Rev. E. N. KIRK, D. D. 12mo, cloth, 1.50.

SATAN'S DEVICES AND THE BELIEVER'S VICTORY. By Rev. WILLIAM L. PARSONS, D. D. 12mo, cloth, 1.50.

CRUDEN'S CONDENSED CONCORDANCE. A Complete Concordance to the Holy Scriptures. By ALEXANDER CRUDEN. Revised and re-edited by the Rev. DAVID KING, LL. D. Octavo, cloth arabesque, 1.75; sheep, 2.00.

The condensation of the quotations of Scripture, arranged under the most obvious heads, while it *diminishes the bulk* of the work, *greatly facilitates* the finding of any required passage.
"We have in this edition of Cruden the *best* made *better*." — *Puritan Recorder.*

EADIE'S ANALYTICAL CONCORDANCE OF THE HOLY SCRIPTURES; or, the Bible presented under Distinct and Classified Heads or Topics. By JOHN EADIE, D. D., LL. D., Author of "Biblical Cyclopædia," "Ecclesiastical Cyclopædia," "Dictionary of the Bible," etc. One volume, octavo, 840 pp., cloth, 4.00; sheep, 5.00; cloth, gilt, 5.50; half calf, 6.50.

The object of this Concordance is to present the SCRIPTURES ENTIRE, under certain classified and exhaustive heads. It differs from an ordinary Concordance, in that its arrangement depends not on WORDS, but on SUBJECTS, and the verses *are printed in full.*

KITTO'S POPULAR CYCLOPÆDIA OF BIBLICAL LITERATURE. Condensed from the larger work. By the Author, JOHN KITTO, D. D. Assisted by JAMES TAYLOR, D. D., of Glasgow. With over five hundred Illustrations. One volume, octavo, 812 pp., cloth, 4.00; sheep, 5.00; half calf, 7.00.

A DICTIONARY OF THE BIBLE. Serving also as a COMMENTARY, embodying the products of the best and most recent researches in biblical literature in which the scholars of Europe and America have been engaged.

KITTO'S HISTORY OF PALESTINE, from the Patriarchal Age to the Present Time; with Chapters on the Geography and Natural History of the Country, the Customs and Institutions of the Hebrews. By JOHN KITTO, D. D. With upwards of two hundred Illustrations. 12mo, cloth, 1.75.

☞ A work admirably adapted to the Family, the Sabbath School, and the week-day School Library

WESTCOTT'S INTRODUCTION TO THE STUDY OF THE GOSPELS. With HISTORICAL AND EXPLANATORY NOTES. By BROOKE FOSS WESTCOTT, M. A., late Fellow of Trinity College, Cambridge. With an Introduction by Prof. H. B. HACKETT, D. D. Royal 12mo, cloth, 2.00.

☞ A masterly work by a master mind.

ELLICOTT'S LIFE OF CHRIST HISTORICALLY CONSIDERED. The Hulsean Lectures for 1859, with Notes Critical, Historical, and Explanatory. By C. J. ELLICOTT, B. D Royal 12mo, cloth, 1.75.

☞ Admirable in spirit, and profound in argument.

RAWLINSON'S HISTORICAL EVIDENCES OF THE TRUTH OF THE SCRIPTURE RECORDS, STATED ANEW, with Special reference to the Doubts and Discoveries of Modern Times. In Eight Lectures, delivered in the Oxford University pulpit, at the Bampton Lecture for 1859. By GEO. RAWLINSON, M. A., Editor of the Histories of Herodotus. With the Copious NOTES TRANSLATED for the *American edition* by an accomplished scholar. 12mo, cloth, 1.75.

"The consummate learning, judgment, and general ability, displayed by Mr. Rawlinson in his edition of Herodotus, are exhibited in this work also." — *North-American.*

www.ingramcontent.com/pod-product-compliance
Lightning Source LLC
LaVergne TN
LVHW021122110826
845150LV00005B/917

* 9 7 8 1 4 2 5 5 5 1 0 8 7 *